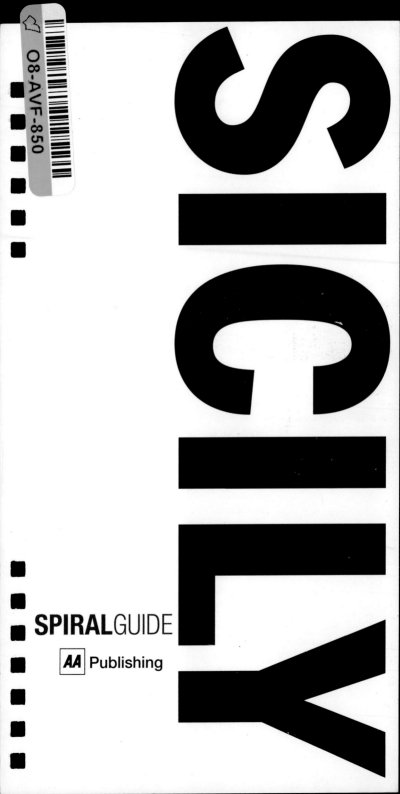

# SICILY

08-AVF-850

**SPIRAL**GUIDE

**AA** Publishing

# Contents

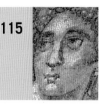

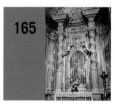

Original text by Sally Roy
Revised and updated by Adele Evans

Project editor Stephanie Smith
Project designer Carole Philp
Series editor Karen Rigden

Published by AA Publishing, a trading name of AA Media Limited,
whose registered office is Fanum House, Basing View, Basingstoke,
Hampshire, RG21 4EA. Registered number 06112600.

ISBN 978-0-7495-7170-2

All rights reserved. This book may be used for private and personal
use. This book or any part of it may not be reproduced or stored by
any means or in any form. Inquiries related to any uses of this book
should be directed to the Publisher.

The content of this book is believed to be accurate at the time
of printing. Due to its nature the content is likely to vary or
change and the publisher is not responsible for such change and
accordingly is not responsible for the consequences of any reliance
by the reader on information that has changed. Any rights that are
given to consumers under applicable law are not affected. Opinions
expressed are for guidance only and are those of the assessor
based on their experience at the time of review and may differ from
the reader's opinions based on their subsequent experience.

We have tried to ensure accuracy in this guide, but things do
change, so please let us know if you have any comments at
travelguides@theAA.com.

A CIP catalogue record for this book is available from the
British Library.

© AA Media Limited 2008, 2012
New edition 2012

Cover design and binding style by permission of AA Publishing
Colour separation by AA Digital Department
Printed and bound in China by Leo Paper Products

Find out more about AA Publishing and the wide range of services
the AA provides by visiting our website at theAA.com/shop

A04601
Mapping in this title produced from map data © New Holland
Publishing (South Africa) (Pty) Ltd. 2008

# The Magazine

A great holiday is more than just lying on a beach or shopping till you drop — to really get the most from your trip you need to know what makes the place tick. The Magazine provides an entertaining overview to some of the social, cultural and natural elements that make up the unique character of this engaging island.

# Island of FIRE

**Over three or four millennia, Sicily has been at the heart of the known world. When the vast mass of what became Christendom, and later Europe, was inhabited by barbarians, sailors and adventurers from the more Mediterranean lands and North Africa were using the island and its satellites as a crossroads. It wasn't just because of the location: Sicily's fire-god mountain, Etna, was a veritable beacon for them.**

Beautiful Sicily is the largest island in the Mediterranean, and, thanks to the smouldering presence of Mount Etna, provider of lava-rich soil, one of the most fruitful. Etna, Europe's largest and most active volcano, holds the world record for eruptions, and has been called the greatest pyrotechnic show on earth. Small wonder, therefore, that this fire-breathing dragon has been held in awe and respect by generations of Sicilians.

There is evidence of geological activity up to 6,000 years ago, but Etna's first known rumblings were around 1500BC when the original inhabitants of Sicily – the Sicels – worshipped Adranus the fire god under the volcano. Legend says Adranus was driven out by the Greek god Vulcan, who made it into his forge. Since then Vulcan's playing with fire has resulted in a ceaseless series of eruptions, some more notable than others.

The most violent was on 11 March 1669, during which lava flows destroyed villages around its base and submerged part of the town of Catania; more than 20,000 people were killed. In 1971, lava buried the 19th-century Etna Observatory, destroyed the first Etna cable-car and seriously threatened several small villages on Etna's east flank. Major eruptions again in 2001 and 2002–03 demonstrated that, even in the third millennium AD, Etna is still capable of great explosive activity.

For all its permanence, its landscape is inconstant, changing with every spew, belch and hiccup from the many mouths of Mount Etna. The newest of these, Bocca Nuova, came to life in November 2006, when cascades of lava engulfed the mountain. Then, at 3:10pm on 25 August 2010, a significant ash explosion occurred at the western crater of the Bocca Nuova. The explosive activity continued for about 30 minutes and produced an ash plume that rose 800m (2,620 feet) up into the air.

Because of the unpredictability of Etna, it is rarely possible to get up close to the source of its fireworks. Most visitors are quite happy to keep their distance, as are those who make the expedition to the see Sicily's other great pyrotechnic display on the Aeolian isle of Stromboli – little more than a vocanic peak peering out of the water – whose cascading, burning debris is best viewed safely from a boat at night.

## MOUNT ETNA AT A GLANCE

- Mount Etna is 3,329m (10,919 feet) high.
- The lower slopes hold many of Sicily's endemic species including Etna broom, Etna violet and Etna greenweed.
- The fertile volcanic ash has made it ideal for planting olive groves, orchards, nut plantations and luscious vineyards.

## ETNA'S TIMEBOMB

Among at least 20 significant eruptions, these are the most notable:

**1500BC** First recorded eruption.

**AD1669** Catania laid waste by Etna's most violent eruption. A new 9km (5.5-mile) fissure opened on the mountain in March and lava poured downhill, destroying the town of Nicolosi and two nearby villages on the first day. It reached Catania in April, killing more than 20,000 people in total. Less than 25 years after the eruption, Catania and its surrounds suffered a destructive earthquake and tsunami.

**1928** The most destructive eruption of the 20th century destroyed the entire town of Mascali.

**1971** Lava buried the 19th-century Etna Observatory and destroyed the first generation of the Etna cable-cars.

**2001–2003** Spectacular eruptions were visible from space and volcanic debris landed in Tunisia.

# The MELTING POT

**As you travel around Sicily you will be struck by sometimes bizarre racial, cultural and historical paradoxes. A quick look at the history of the island, one of the world's earliest melting pots, helps to explain how these came about.**

Explore the island and you'll soon see evidence of the intermingling of cultures, such as the coexisting architectural remnants of Ancient Greek temples, Byzantine mosaics, cathedrals that would be more at home in northern France – and the absence of Renaissance buildings in Sicily. It explains why Sicilians grow date palms and cotton, and why are they so addicted to sugary treats. It unravels the mystery of the contrasting racial mix of Sicilians with blue eyes and red hair and those with darker complexions. Even the cause of the island's deep-rooted and persistent poverty is explained by this cultural melting pot, which, since mass emigration in the late 18th and early 19th centuries, has spilled into the

**Above: The ancient Greek temple at Segesta. Above right: Monreale cathedral
Opposite: Mosaic floor in the Villa Romana del Casale, Piazza Armerina**

wider world. Track back across the centuries and all becomes clear;
history may be complicated but it certainly explains a lot.

## Classical Times

Emerging from the mists of history in the eighth century BC, Sicily was
colonized by the Greeks, seeking new lands and trade routes. A brilliant
culture emerged, with separate colonies at Catania, Syracuse, Agrigento
and Selinunte. Fabulous temples were built, rivalled by the cities of the
Phoenicians, who occupied the west of the island. The Greeks stayed until
290BC. Then came the Romans, who saw Sicily as nothing but a source
of wheat and slaves. Over the next 600 years they destroyed the Greek
and Phoenician civilisations and plundered the island, leaving little for the
invading Goths and Vandals who swept in during the fifth century.

## The Golden Years

These were replaced by the Byzantines from Constantinople, who lasted
for 300 years until the arrival of the Arabs in the late eighth century AD.
The Arabs brought revival to the island, making it a tempting target for
the Normans, who had first arrived in southern Italy around 900, hiring
themselves out as mercenaries to the local barons. They acquired lands,
and the 12 sons of the greatest of them, Tancred de Hauteville, pushed
into Sicily, where one became ruler, Roger I. The Normans ruled Sicily
for little more than a century but left an indelible mark in administration,
justice, religious tolerance and the arts.

### WHERE DID YOU GET THAT HAIR?

Once in Sicily, forget the stereotype of the short, dark southerner. Centuries of
invaders have left their mark, and a Sicilian is frequently a bit of a mongrel.
Straight, ash-blonde locks, blue and green eyes, fine straight noses and mops
of carrot-red spiky hair all distinguish some native Sicilians – the legacy of
strong Norman genes almost a thousand years down the line.

S Giovanni Eremiti, Palermo

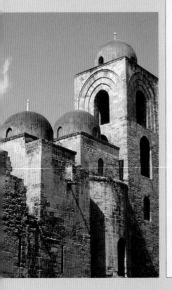

## MELTING POT TIMELINE

**735BC** First Greek settlers on the east coast followed by build up of Phoenician colonies on the west coast (650–580BC)

**397BC** Phoenicians expelled by Greeks

**AD264–261** Start of Roman occupation

**Fifth century** Goths and Vandals occupy Sicily

**535** Start of 300 years of Byzantine rule

**827** Muslim invasion and a new Golden Age

**1040** Normans move in against Muslims

**1091** Roger de Hauteville crowned Roger I, and the beginning of the Norman period

**1282** King Peter III of Aragon rules Sicily

**1291–1720** Systematic impoverishment under Spanish rule

**1860** Giuseppe Garibaldi lands in Marsala, takes Palermo; Sicily part of unified Italy

**1866–90** Emergence of the Mafia

**1890–1920** Quarter of the population emigrates

### From Neglect to Unity

By the 12th century, all was once more confusion, and the next centuries saw a bewildering procession of foreign rulers occupy and ruin the island. By the late 14th century Sicily was under Spanish control, where it remained for 400 years, a backwater, neglected, plundered and bypassed by the advances of the Renaissance. The 19th century finally saw the flickerings of something better for the by now impoverished island, and in 1860 Sicily became one of the first elements in the newly united Italy. At the time, the Piedmontese, helped by the French, were gradually uniting the north, but Giuseppe Garibaldi, hero of an earlier uprising in 1848, hatched a scheme to speed up the process by stirring up southern Italy. Accompanied by a somewhat motley thousand-strong crew, fetchingly clad in red shirts, he landed at Marsala in May and declared himself dictator of Sicily on behalf of the Piedmontese. He promptly defeated the ruling Neapolitans and marched triumphantly on Palermo. Thousands flocked to join him as he fought his way across the island, taking Messina in July before crossing the Straits and, in a final victory, getting rid of the Neapolitans forever.

Enthusiasm for the new unified Italy didn't last, however, because, yet again, the eternal problems of land reform and investment were ignored. The time was ripe for the emergence of the Mafia (➤ 22–23) and hundreds of thousands of Sicilians emigrated, mainly to the Americas. Throughout the 20th century Sicily's fortunes followed those of Italy, and the island today is very much part of Italy, though one that's still at a huge disadvantage compared with other areas.

## THE ARAB LEGACY

The Arabs set their sights on Sicily as early as 700, but it wasn't until 827 that a full invasion took place. By 965 the island was under Arab control and remained so for the next 200 years. Palermo was the brilliant and cosmopolitan capital, but it's not here that the Saracens left their longest lasting legacy. The Arabs understood agriculture: they resettled the land, extended the irrigation system, introduced new crops such as cotton, sugar cane, date palms and citrus trees. They introduced the newest ideas in science and philosophy, while their policy of religious tolerance made Sicily a centre for scholarship. They're still remembered in Sicilian place names – anywhere with the prefix "calta" (castle) reminds us of their occupation.

The main entrance to Palermo Cathedral, with its distinctive green-domed roof

## A HERO FOR HIS TIMES – KING ROGER II

The greatest Sicilian-Norman ruler, Roger II (1095–1154), transformed Sicily from an Arab outpost to a Christian kingdom. Succeeding his father and brother, he began his rule in 1105 as a mere count; by 1144 the Norman kingdom included Sicily itself and the entire southern mainland, a kingdom whose boundaries would remain unchanged for the next seven centuries. He instituted a strong central government, established Sicily as the Mediterranean's leading maritime power and made Palermo, his capital, one of Europe's most splendid and cultured cities. It was a golden age, with Arabs, Greeks and Normans coexisting and thriving together; its legacy is the wonderful churches and palaces, some of Sicily's great architectural glories.

# The Art of **THE BAROQUE**

**There's ebullient and ornate baroque architecture all over Europe, but nowhere is it better experienced first hand than in Sicily, where entire town centres are a glorious parade of design, gaiety and ostentation.**

Born in Rome in the late 16th century, full-blown baroque style reached Sicily some 50 years later, where it was transformed into something unique, a fusion of planning, architecture and ornamentation spiced up with its own particular brand of Sicilian enchantment.

Sicilian baroque was born out of catastrophe and tragedy. In 1693 the southeast of the island was hit by an earthquake that virtually destroyed Catania and completely flattened Noto, Ragusa and Modica. Architects seized their chance. Backed by aristocratic money, they built entirely new towns, where the emphasis was on the whole and the experience of walking through a cityscape was an essential part of the vision. Vistas, wide streets and visual effects are the trademarks of baroque towns, the decorated facades of the churches, palazzi and villas reflecting the wealth and status of their owners. Over-the-top decoration is another keynote. Exteriors flaunt sensuously curving staircases, graceful balconies, elaborate carving, swags of fruit and flowers and wildly gesticulating saints, while interiors are a riot of stucco decoration and richly polychrome inlaid marbles. It's still all there, crumbling in patches, but remaining the backdrop to everyday life.

**Elaborately carved balcony on the Palazzo Villadorata, Noto**

## Best Baroque Towns

**Noto** (► 100–102) the realization of the baroque ideal city, built completely from scratch after 1693.

**Ragusa** (► 103–104) the post-earthquake upper town is a perfect baroque grid-plan. Ragusa Ibla, the lower town, combines medieval layout with ebullient architecture.

**Grammichele** (► 109) post-1693 hexagonally planned town.

**Catania** (► 107–108) wide streets drawing the eye to Mount Etna, stage-set piazzas and facades designed for impact are hallmarks of the baroque.

**Palermo** (► 44–68) the facades and interiors of individual churches and palaces illustrate the best of baroque.

## Best Baroque Architects and Where to Find Their Work

**Giacomo Amato** (1643–1732) a monk who spent time in Rome. Dazzled by Roman baroque he came home to Palermo and designed churches. Sant'Ignazio all'Olivella and San Domenico (► 166) are his finest.

**Rosario Gagliardi** (1698–1762) responsible for much of the rebuilding of Noto (► 100–102); sophisticated facades marrying grandeur, flamboyance and rhythm are his hallmarks.

**Tommaso Napoli** (1659–1725) a monk who designed some of Sicily's most worldly aristocratic houses, the Villas Palagonia and Valguarnera at Bagheria outside Palermo.

**Andrea Palma** (1664–1730) Trapani-born designer of the ebullient cathedral at Siracusa (► 96–99).

**Giacomo Serpotta** (1656–1732) specialized in flamboyant stucco decoration and moulded plasterwork. His masterpiece is the oratory in Santa Zita in Palermo.

**Vincenzo Sinatra** (c.1720–c.1765) married Gagliardi's niece and worked on the rebuilding of Noto.

**Giovanni Battista Vaccarini** (1702–68) – responsible for the design and rebuilding of Catania after the 1693 earthquake.

Top: San Giorgio, Ragusa
Middle: San Giorgio, Modica
Bottom: San Nicolò, Noto

# FOOD : AND DRINK :

Seasonal, local and fresh, the food alone makes the journey to Sicily worthwhile. Intensely robust flavours, vivid colours, texture and balance are the keynotes, while the island's history makes itself known in food combinations that are unique. Greeks, Romans, Arabs, Normans and Spanish have all left their mark on ingredients and recipes alike, producing a cuisine that is the essence of what good eating should be.

## A Taste of the East

It's the Arabic legacy that makes Sicilian food different. It's there in the food combinations, in the love of aubergines, citrus fruit, couscous and almonds, in the subtlety of spices such as saffron and the fire of *peperoncini* (chilli), in the elaborate *pasticceria* (pastries) and sweetmeats. Sample it in *pasta con le sarde*, pasta with a sauce of sardines, anchovies, wild fennel, pine nuts, raisins and saffron, or one of the fish and couscous dishes you'll find in the

Top: Marzipan fruit. Middle: An *arancino*, a fried rice and meat ball. Bottom: Sticky cakes in the Pasticceria di Maria Grammatico, Erice

western Sicily. Seek out *caponata*, a preserved, cooked salad with celery, finely chopped and fried aubergine, raisins, olives and pungent capers, or try *sarde a beccafico*, sardines with pine nuts and currants. Sicily also has its own fast food, exemplified by dishes such as Arab-inspired *arancini*, deep-fried rice balls with a nugget of filling.

## Pasta and Fish

Pasta has been around in Sicily for some 2,000 years and you'll probably eat it every day – with fish and seafood, with vegetables, with herbs, nuts and breadcrumbs. Try *spaghetti alle vongole*, pasta with tiny clams and a touch of chilli, *pasta alla Norma* with aubergines, tomato, basil and salted fresh ricotta cheese, a dish said to have been inspired by Bellini's opera heroine, or one of the *timbali*, a type of elaborate pasta-based savoury pie. Eat it, like the locals do, with bread – Sicilian bread is possibly the finest in Italy. Fish and seafood dominate menus – you'll find clams, *fritto misto* (mixed fried fish), *dorata* (bream), *sogliola* (sole) and the humble but delicious sardine almost everywhere, along with the big boys, *tonno* (tuna) and the exquisite *pesce spada* (swordfish), usually served grilled with lemon and olive oil.

## A Spoonful of Sugar

Sicilian food artistry appears in sweets and desserts, found in *pasticcerie* (pastry shops). Most famous are *cannoli*, deep-fried pastry tubes filled with sweetened ricotta with candied fruit and chocolate; and cassata, another Arab legacy of ricotta, sponge cake, candied fruit and almond paste; both are tooth-rottingly rich. Almonds appear too, in *frutta alla Martorana*, the incredibly realistic marzipan fruits and vegetables in all shapes and sizes that were originally made by the nuns in the convent of the same name in Palermo. More refreshing are the wonderful *gelati* (ice creams), made from pure, fresh ingredients in every conceivable flavour.

### DRINKS WORTH TOASTING

Local wines, served by the jug, are fine, but for something a bit more special look out for:

**Santa Cecilia** modern-style wine made from Nero d'Avola grapes

**Corvo** dry fruity white and solid reds

**Alcamo** a fine dry white good with fish

**Etna** red and white wines from grapes grown on the volcano's slopes

**Cervasuolo** red and white from Vittoria

**Marsala** fortified wines from Marsala

**Moscato** dessert wine from Pantelleria

**Vino alla mandorla** almond wine from Taormina

**Averna** aromatic *digestivo* from Caltanissetta

# FESTIVALS & Fun

**There are few treats on a trip to any of the Mediterranean's Christian regions that rival the happenstance of a major festival coinciding with your visit. Sicily has more than its fair share of colourfully spectacular festivals, and, happily, by no means all of them fall around Easter, as is so often the case elsewhere. Some of them are rated the best in Italy – or even the world.**

Two weeks of parties, music, parades, and fireworks herald the *Festival of Santa Rosalia* in Palermo's – and Sicily's – biggest traditional *festa*, known in Sicilian dialect as *U Fistinu*. It is held during the first fortnight of February in honour of the city's patron saint, Rosalia, a hermit whose miracle rid Palermo of The Plague in 1624–25. The celebrations' nightly

focus is a 9pm re-enactment of the miracle, performed by a huge cast of actors, singers and musicians. It culminates in a procession and torchlit pilgrimage to Rosalia's sanctuary on Monte Pellegrino.

**Festival mask**

### Knights and Almond Blossom

In the second week of August, the town of Piazza Armerina to the southeast of Enna erupts into a major medieval *festa*, known as *Palio dei Normanni*, celebrating the arrival of Roger I (1031–1101), the island's first Norman ruler. There are musical parades and displays of splendid horsemanship – all leading up to the *Palio* when "knights" joust in spectacular and fierce competition.

The residents of Enna have kept alive the tradition of confraternities, passed down to them by the Aragonese who ruled from the 15th to 17th centuries. Enna now has 15 confraternities (officially recognized groups of lay people committed to promoting Christian works) with different traditional costumes, each of which is attached to a different church. The most important event is the week-long festival of the *Processione della Settimana Santa*, beginning on Palm Sunday and culminating on Easter Sunday in a spectacular celebration of the resurrected Christ.

In Agrigento and the Valley of the Temples the almond blossom signals the arrival of spring and a great celebration called *Sagra del Mandorlo*

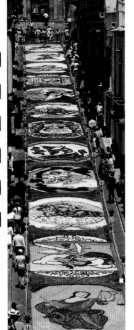

**Via Corrado Nicolaci in Noto during the Flower Festival**

*in Fiore* (first week of February). As well as an international folklore festival with performances, there are also parades, singing, music, puppet shows and feasting.

A little later in Noto, on the third Sunday of May, the *Infiorata* (Flower Festival) celebrates the arrival of spring by decorating the streets and floats with flower petals in a week-long festival, which also includes dances and parades.

### King of Couscous

The ancient fishing village of San Vito lo Capo hosts an annual Couscous Festival each September (usually the third week), when chefs from Israel, Morocco, Egypt, France, Algeria, Tunisia and Italy participate to determine who is the *capo* of couscous (the best chef) in the Mediterranean. The festival also includes six evenings of music, featuring free performances by Sicilian and African artists in the Piazza Santuario in the heart of the ancient town.

## SOME OF THE OTHERS

- *Misteri di Trapani* is one of Sicily's most famous Easter processions, with enormous floats topped with scenes from the Passion of Christ passing through the streets of Trapani on Good Friday and Holy Saturday.
- The pre-Lenten carnival at Sciacca, known as *Carnevale*, is especially famous for its elaborately adorned allegorical floats, music and fireworks, and is rated as one of the best in Sicily.
- The Feast of Santa Agata in Catania (3–5 February) features a spectacular procession of huge wooden floats, tableaux and fireworks following the silver reliquary of the martyred patron saint of Catania through the streets, witnessed by around a million people.
- *Carnevale* ("farewell to meat") is celebrated in Acireale, Trapani, Taormina, Sciacca and Caltanissetta during the week before Ash Wednesday with parades, floats and street parties.
- *Aballu de li Diavoli* (Dance of the Devils) held on Easter Sunday in Prizzi, features "devils" in grotesque masks rampaging through the town.
- The Feast of the Assumption – three-day processions with gigantic puppet shows, floats and general fun – takes place at Messina, Trapani, Petralia Sottana and Randazzo, starting Friday on the second weekend of August.
- In Siracusa the silver statue of Siracusa's patron saint, Santa Lucia, is paraded round the city, with fireworks and music, in mid-December.

# THE SICILIAN
# *Way of Death*

**Perhaps it's the almost tangible sense of the past. Perhaps it's fervent religious conviction or a legacy from the classical past. One thing is certain: death and its rites and customs are marked more strongly in Sicily – especially in smaller towns and villages – than anywhere else in Italy.**

**Top: Death notices posted in the street**
**Bottom: Heading to the cemetery, Ragusa**

As you walk the streets of any town, you'll probably see black-bordered posters, sometimes with a photo, always with a name and dates. These are notices announcing death and giving details of funeral arrangements, which will take place only a couple of days later. During that time the family maintains a vigil. If the person did not die at home, the body is brought home and displayed in an open coffin.

## Our Way

Unlike mainland Italian custom, the front door of the family home will be left open day and night for people to come and pay their respects and sit with the bereaved family, ensuring they are never left alone. Friends, family and acquaintances talk easily about the dead person, about their own feelings, their grief and sorrow. Some families leave a window open, so the soul can depart easily, and no one would ever take advantage of the open door to commit a crime. Death, the great leveller, is too sacred for

On All Souls' Day (2 November), Sicilians will visit the family tombs and light candles

that. Close friends of the family will bring *il conzu*, prepared meals unique to the island, ensuring the mourners are properly fed, as it's considered disrespectful to cook at this time.

## The Rites of Death
Churches are packed for the full requiem mass at the funeral, and one of the enormous number of huge floral tributes will be placed outside the church door to alert passers-by. The coffin is then closed and, after the service, a procession leaves for the cemetery. People cross themselves as the cortege passes, and the body is committed to the ground with more prayers. In Sicily, as elsewhere in Italy, bodies do not stay buried forever, but after some months they are interred in tiers of niches in the cemetery walls, each tomb illuminated at night by a flickering nightlight. Ever practical, families expect to be billed annually for the cost of electricity.

Following the death of a close relative, people in Sicily wear black for up to a year or, in the case of the widow, even longer and sometimes for life. You'll still see many elderly ladies wearing nothing else, and right up to the 1970s or later women could expect to wear black permanently from their 30s on, as the older generation gradually died off.

## The Flip Side
Birth, like death, is a community event. Keep your eyes open for huge ribbon bows on front doors, balcony railings and windows. They come in pink and blue, proudly announcing to all the world the safe arrival of either *un bel maschio* or *una bellissima femmina*, a male or female, the words used for a beautiful newborn boy or girl.

# The Magician from

# PALERMO

**Sicily is rife with superstition, its folklore packed with tales of magic, sorcery and necromancy. Talismans, amulets, potions, curses, spells and magic prayers have abounded for thousands of years, ancient beliefs sitting easily alongside Christian teaching. Down the centuries a procession of colourful figures has entranced both Sicilians and the wider world – and none more so than self-styled Count Alessandro Cagliostro, the Magician from Palermo.**

### Fame and Fortune

Charlatan, imposter, conman and alchemist, Cagliostro was born Giuseppe Balsamo in Palermo in 1743. A bright little urchin with a gift for chemistry, he studied the rudiments of medicine with the good monks at Caltagirone before embarking on a spree of forgery and theft back in Palermo. He fled the city one step ahead of the law, eventually, via Greece, Egypt and Malta, landing up in Rome, where he met the ravishing young beauty Lorenza

> "Faith-healing, alchemy and necromancy kept him busy"

Feliciani. Her ambition matched his and, when married, the couple embarked on a career of magic, their alchemy and mysticism gulling the thrill-seeking aristocracy all over Europe. They became purveyors of the elixir of eternal youth, founded Egyptian Rite Masonic Lodges, sold pills and potions, forecast lottery numbers and generally pulled the wool over the eyes of enchanted punters from St Petersburg to London.

Never remaining anywhere long enough to be unmasked, by 1771 Giuseppe had assumed the title of Count Cagliostro and was claiming an orphaned past, noble parentage and an education in magic and the Kabala under an alchemist called Salaahim. London loved him, but Paris loved him more and by 1778 he was happily installed in the household of Cardinal Rohan, a close relative of Louis XIV. Faith-healing, alchemy and necromancy kept him busy, with a reputation that was to inspire Goethe's

Faust and the character of Sarastro in Mozart's *The Magic Flute*. He was, seemingly, made for life.

## The Charlatan Unmasked

This was the Age of Enlightenment, however, and, gradually healthy scepticism took hold among Cagliostro's fan club. A scandal over a diamond necklace saw him expelled from France in 1785, the London gutter press exposed his humble origins and he was forced back to Italy. Here, Lorenza betrayed him to the Inquisition to save her own skin, and in 1789 he was sentenced to death. The old skills hadn't entirely left him and the Pope was persuaded to commute the sentence to life imprisonment in the Castel Sant'Angelo. He blew his chances by attempting to escape and was banished to a rat-infested hellhole in the forbidding castle at Rocca di San Leo in the Apennines. Here, quite insane, he died in 1795.

Palermo never forgot him; in 1869 the city council named a dark and squalid alley deep in the slums of the Albergharia the Vicolo Conte Cagliostro. It's still there: a decaying street preserving the name of a tarnished legend.

**Count Cagliostro learning the secrets of the occult from his master, Althotas**

# Our thing
# THE MAFIA

**The beautiful island of Sicily is still blighted by the influence of organized crime. Although the tourist is unlikely to notice the far-reaching effects of the Mafia, *la cosa nostra* (our thing) is part of the lives of Sicilians.**

Forget the glamourized images of films and literature. The reality of the world's most enduring criminal organization is one of political corruption, bribery, theft and murder.

Need a job? You need to know the right people for the vital *raccomandazione* (recommendation). Running a business? Pay your *pizzo* (protection money) or risk the consequences. Trying to complete a contract? Everything has its price and the price is fixed by the Mafia. It controls the economic sector and is behind the sale of public appointments. It diverts funds destined for Sicily's development, appoints politicians, launders money, and kills judges who pass sentence on its members.

> "Everything has a price and the price is fixed by the Mafia"

### The Past and the Present

The term "Mafia" is based on an Arab word (*mu'afah*, loosely meaning protection and safety), and some scholars believe the organization dates to the 12th century. Others claim it goes back to the rise of the *gabelloti*, rent collectors or mediators between feudal landlords and peasantry, who became a separate class with their own codes. They were joined by other peoples' representatives – the *amici* (friends) and *uomini d'onore* (men of honour) – and by the 20th century were transformed into the Mafia we know. Mussolini was its enemy and might have eliminated it if the Allies hadn't needed Mafia intelligence to facilitate the 1943 invasion of Italy. Post-World War II the Mafia transferred its operations to the cities, getting into construction, real estate, banking and narcotics.

The Italian government responded by establishing the anti-Mafia Commission, which, from 1963, provoked a vicious Mafia reign of terror

**Above: Wanted: Matteo Messina Denaro**
**Right: Pope Benedict XVI praying at a**
**memorial to Giovanni Falcone in 2010**

that continues today. Journalists, lawyers, judges, priests and politicians have all been targeted. The killing of police chief Prefect Dalla Chiesa, who was investigating corruption in top-level political circles in 1982, led to the *maxiprocessi* (super-trials), which saw various *pentiti* turning state's evidence. Throughout the trials, bloodshed continued, culminating in the assassination of two judges, Giovanni Falcone and Paolo Borsellino, in 1992. Public outrage led to the arrest of Salvatore Riina, the *capo dei capi* (chief of chiefs) and since then arrests and murders have proceeded in equal measure. More recently, in March 2010, an anti-Mafia police swoop in Trapani arrested Salvatore Messina Denaro – brother of Mafia big boss Matteo Messina Denaro – among 19 men accused of fraud, extortion and helping Matteo avoid arrest. Official sources say that this operation increases the chance of finally catching Italy's currently most wanted man.

An organization as all-pervasive and all-powerful as the Mafia may never entirely disappear, but perhaps the myth of its impregnability is gradually being eroded.

## La Verità – the Truth

"The Mafia is oppression, arrogance, greed, self-enrichment, power and hegemony above and against all others … It is a criminal organization regulated by unwritten but iron and inexorable rules … The myth of a courageous and generous 'man of honour' must be destroyed, because a mafioso is just the opposite." These blunt words were written by Judge Cesare Terranova shortly before his murder in 1979 and summarize the stark reality of life under the Mafia.

# The
# **OFFSHORE** Islands

North, west and south of Sicily lie its islands, tiny archipelagos that pull in the crowds seeking sun, sea and natural beauty. Tourism's important, but so, too, is fishing – the waters around these islands are among the most abundant in the Mediterranean. Throw in some impressive natural phenomena with a couple of live volcanoes, some history and archaeological treasures, and the islands become a destination unto themselves.

### The Aeolian Islands

Volcanic in origin, the seven compelling Aeolians lie off the northeast coast of Sicily. Lipari is the biggest of the group, and its main settlement, Lipari Town, complete with picture-book port, chic hotels and good restaurants, is one of Sicily's most popular resorts. Visitors come for the great beaches, clear sea, and the spectacular scenery, long slopes of bleached pumice, streams of obsidian and extinct craters. For the real live thing, head for still-active Stromboli, with its nightly performance of red sparks, volcanic rumblings and spews of molten debris. You can climb this, the world's most active volcano, to catch the nightly pyrotechnics, or take a boat trip to watch the hellish scene from the sea. Vulcano is equally dramatic, with acrid fumaroles, sulphurous fumes and stinking, regenerative mud. The other islands – Salina, Panarea, Filucudi and Alicudi – are less touched by tourism, and locals make their living mostly from fishing, wine-making and exporting capers.

## The Egadi Islands

Favignana, Levanzo and Marettimo make up the Egadi Islands, just a hop from Trápani on Sicily's west coast. Tourists flock to Favignana (► 171–173), the largest and most populated, for its tufa landscape, its beaches and sea, but the island is also famed for its history as a tuna fishing centre, whose annual spring catch once produced over 150,000 tonnes. Today, Favignana holds the last ritual *mattanza*, the tuna slaughter, annually, when tuna are guided through funnel-shaped nets to the killing waters, which turn red as the fish are harpooned. There are more fishermen on Marettimo, a self-contained and mountainous island that keeps itself to itself and makes few concessions to the tourists that come to see its rock formations and sea grottoes. Levanzo, too, has grottoes, including the Grotta del Genovese, whose shadowy interior contains 10,000-year-old rock carvings and paintings.

**Left: Lipari. Centre: Panarea, in the Aeolian Islands. Right: Traditional roofs, Pantelleria**

## Ustica, Pantelleria and the Pelagie

Some 56.5km (35 miles) north of Palermo, the black island of Ustica, surrounded by one of the Mediterranean's richest marine environments, is a mecca for divers. The island itself, beautiful and verdant, has wonderful walking. Far to the south, Pantelleria juggles tourism with its traditional way of life, dependent on agriculture and fishing. The farmers still live in traditional *dammusi*, square-domed houses built to withstand the heat. Further south still, and nearer to Tunisia than Sicily, are the Pelagie – Lampedusa, Linosa and uninhabited Lampione, remote outposts set in clean, turquoise waters.

# SCENES OF SICILY:
## from papyrus to film

**Long before Mario Puzo put pen to paper to write *The Godfather* – the Mafia epic with its roots in Sicily that generated *The Godfather* movie series – the island and its satellites had been well celebrated in print, on parchment and on papyrus over thousands of years.**

The Greeks had a fascination for Sicily that focused on the mystique of Mount Etna; the fifth-century BC philosopher Empedocles is even said to have committed suicide by hurling himself into the mouth of the volcano. Similarly Sicily features strongly in Homer's works, the *Iliad* and the *Odyssey*.

There are, more recently, some dozen or so works of fiction set in Sicily at various times. They include *Little Novels of Sicily* by Giovanni Verga, a series of evocative short stories written in the 19th century; they were translated into English in the 20th century by English writer D H Lawrence.

*The Leopard*, by Giuseppe Tomasi Di Lampedusa, which was published posthumously in 1957, became the all-time Italian bestseller and was made into a 1963 film with Burt Lancaster and Claudia Cardinale. It is set at the time of the start of Garibaldi's campaign to unite Italy in the mid-19th century and deals with the social upheavals that resulted.

There are at least half-a-dozen major films and TV dramas about or featuring Sicily. The most obvious are *The Godfather* films, which used Sicilian locations, including the massacre at Palermo at the end of *The Godfather Part III*. There's also *Cinema Paradiso* (1989), *Il Postino* (1994,

**Left:** *Cinema Paradiso* (1989), starring
Philippe Noiret and Salvatore Cascio
**Above:** *The Leopard* (1963)

> ## SUICIDE OF EMPEDOCLES
>
> '*And thou, fiery world,*
> *That sapp'st the vitals of this*
> *terrible mount*
> *Upon whose charr'd and*
> *quaking crust I stand—*
> *Thou, too, brimmest with*
> *life!—the sea of cloud,*
> *That heaves its white and*
> *billowy vapours up*
> *To moat this isle of ashes*
> *from the world,*
> *Lives...*'
> From *Empedocles on Etna*,
> an interpretation of the
> philosopher's last moments
> by Matthew Arnold (1852)

filmed largely on Salina, one of the Aeolian Islands) and *Stromboli: Terra di
Dio* (1949, starring Ingrid Bergman).

Recently there has been a very popular TV series (in Italy and Germany)
called *Il Commissario Montalbano*, about a fictional, fractious Sicilian
detective called Montalbano, adapted from the novels by Andrea Camilleri.
Marina di Ragusa is one of the locations and the series is mainly shot in
the province of Ragusa.

## SOME FICTION ABOUT SICILY

*Conversations in Sicily*, by Elio Vittorini, is a hard-hitting political story set in
the 1930s, which also paints a picture of the features and customs of the
islands, some of which – like the sound of shepherd pipers celebrating the
nativity in the hills – still exist today.

*Don Giovanni in Sicily*, by Vitaliano Brancati (translated by Corrada Biazzo
Curry), highlights the Sicilian response to the Fascist regime with a mixture of
passive resistance and indifference. It was made into a sexy Italian language
film in 1967.

*Behind Closed Doors: Her Father's House and Other Stories of Sicily*, by Maria Messina,
covers the period of mass migration from Sicily and the position of women in
society at that time.

*Sicily Enough* by Claire Rabe. A fairly modern tale of a single woman with three
children who makes her home in Sicily.

*Six Days in Sicily: The Holiday with John* by Philip W Lupton and Hanzal Stephan,
about an elderly Englishman who, with his wife, reluctantly accepts an
invitation from a friend to join him on holiday in Sicily.

# **WILD** Sicily

**Once covered entirely by oak forests, Sicily remains incredibly fertile, with olive and citrus groves, almonds, vineyards and palm trees along the coast, and vast swathes of wheatlands in the hills. So forget the culture and beach for a couple of days, and get out there on the wild side.**

The island, which covers an area of 24,807sq km (9,675sq miles), has more than 200 plant species unique to the island. Poverty and the demands of the big landowners may have wreaked their worst, but Sicily has survived as a garden, packed with wild delights and superb landscapes, and encircled by a magical coast.

## Hiking

Italy generally has been laggard in discovering the joys of walking through unspoiled countryside, but slowly, things are improving, even in deepest Sicily, and nowadays you'll find hikes and trails, often waymarked, to suit all tastes. Routes range from strenuous mountain treks high on the slopes of Etna and through the Nebrodi and Madonie (► 176–179) mountains, to coastal strolls among dunes and saltflats rich in birdlife. One of the top favourites is the Zingaro (► 156), a 7km (4-mile) stretch of untouched coast in the far northwest, where tiny coves offer glorious bathing in crystal waters. Good paths run beside the sea and in the hills, and spring brings huge numbers of birds and astonishing spreads of brilliant wild flowers.

There are parts of wild Sicily that you mustn't miss, if only because of the views they provide. The great landmark, La Rocca, is an intimidating crag, 278m (912 feet) high, which hangs menacingly over the lovely north-coast town of Cefalù, to the east of Palermo. You'll find it quite a challenging climb. For spectacular views, take the steps from Piazza Garibaldi, signposted "Accesso alla Rocca" up to the vast rock. The whole ascent takes about an hour and you'll pass the ruins of the fifth-century BC Tempio di Diana (Temple of Diana) To get to the top, count on another 45 minutes of huffing and puffing before you are greeted by the

### BE LED BY THE HAND

- First step to discovering the richness of Sicily's wild places has to be online at www.parks.it, Italy's national parks portal.
- Pick up information on pony trekking opportunities at regional park information offices and local tourist bureaux, or contact Agrigento's Centro Ippico Concordia, which organizes riding outings, training and social events (tel: 388 185 3064 or 328 272 8654).
- If you're interested in joining an organized walking holiday, check out www.atg-oxford.co.uk, www.inntravel.co.uk and www.headwater.com.
- For organized diving holidays, try www.marenostrumdiving.it.
- For bird-watching tours, check out www.naturetrek.co.uk.

#### Pick of the Parks

- Parco Regionale dell'Etna (► 77–79) – landscape ranging from high volcanic lava to woodlands and upland meadows.
- Parco Regionale dei Nebrodi – most important and largest wooded area in Sicily, with beech, oak, ilex and wide range of mammals and invertebrates.
- Parco Naturale Regionale delle Madonie (► 176–179) – mountain park most noted for its superb spring limestone flora, which includes 150 of Sicily's 200 endemic species.
- Riserva Naturale dello Zingaro (► 156) – unspoiled coastal park featuring inlets, ravines and coves, noted for superb limestone flora.

ancient fortifications and absolutely stupendous views – stretching across from Palermo in the west to Capo d'Orlando in the east.

### Natural History

Botanists head for the Madonie mountains, which rise to 1,970m (6,462 feet) and whose limestone flora is among the richest in Italy. In spring the hills are carpeted by flowers, and there's a wide range of orchids and other rare species. You can find these, too, on the lower slopes of Mount Etna (► 77–79) and in the Nebrodi, where the thick woodland harbours a whole different flora. Woodlands are also good for animals: Sicily has plenty of foxes, and even wild boar, which you're just as likely to see ambling across a quiet mountain road.

Twitchers will find delights everywhere, from raptors in the mountainous interior to huge colonies of seabirds and waders along the coasts. Sicily is on an important migratory route, so keep your eyes open for exotics like bee-eaters and the beguiling hoopoe, with its butterfly-like flight.

**Capo Zafferano, seen from Solunto archaeological site**

## The Big Blue

Then there's the sea. Bathe in it, swim in it, snorkel and dive in it. Go sailing or take a boat trip. Sicily's coast and islands have no fewer than eight important protected marine environments, rich in fish and underwater life. There are coves, cliffs, caves and grottoes to explore, shallow lagoons for bird-spotting and deep waters for diving.

## Ride 'em, Cowboys

Pony trekking is a popular out-and-about option and is widely available throughout the island. Riders can follow in the hoof-steps of the Sicilian cowboys of old, who used to herd their cattle to and from winter pasture. Check with tourist offices at Madonie, Nebrodi, Etna and Alcàntara for details of local treks. There's also a horse-riding school at Agrigento's Centro Ippico Concordia, which organizes outings, training and social events.

---

## FLORA AND FAUNA

### Where to Go for the Rarest Flowers

■ Madonie mountains – very rich limestone flora with many rare species of orchid, peonies, lilies, fritillaries as well as huge spreads of more common species.

■ Zingaro – coastal and inland limestone flora, *macchia mediterranea* and many orchids.

### Great Places for Birdwatchers

■ Saline di Trapani (Trapani) – salt flats attracting a wide variety of resident and wintering shorebirds and waterfowl, including flamingos (► 158).

■ Lago di Lentini (Siracusa) – one of Italy's most important wetland areas and an over-wintering ground for rare gulls, ferruginous ducks, spoonbills and storks.

■ Vendicari (Siracusa) – very diverse habitats, including rocky coast, dunes, marshland and *macchia*, many rare gulls, grey shrike, golden plovers, stone curlew (► 108).

■ Oasi del Simeto (Agrigento) – river mouth with sand dunes that attracts migratory and wintering seabirds and waders.

■ Foce del Fiume Platani (Agrigento) – first stopping point for myriad migratory birds en route to and from Africa; best in late autumn and spring.

■ Zingaro (Trapani) – excellent for coastal birds (► 156).

# Finding Your Feet

# First Two Hours

## Arriving by Air

International air passengers flying direct to Sicily will arrive at either Palermo or Catania.

### Aeroporto Falcone Borsellino (Palermo)

Palermo's airport (tel: 800 541 880/091 702 0111, airport information 091 702 0273; www.gesap.it) handles international and domestic flights.

■ There are flights **direct** to Palermo from London Stansted and London Gatwick. Alitalia flies from London Heathrow to Palermo via Rome or Milan.

■ Passengers **from the US** will have to route through Rome or Milan.

■ Falcone Borsellino is at Punta Raisa, 31km (19 miles) west of Palermo, and is **connected with the city** by buses, trains and taxis. Buses and taxis leave from outside the arrivals building; trains leave from the departures terminal, a five-minute walk from arrivals. Before exiting the terminal you can pick up information at the English-speaking tourist office (tel: 091 591 698, Mon–Fri 8am–midnight, Sat–Sun 8–8), change money at the *cambio*, or use the cash machines.

■ **Taxis** (tel: 091 225 5455 or 091 513 311) are the fastest and most expensive way of reaching downtown Palermo; expect to pay around €40 for up to four people with an additional charge for extra-large pieces of luggage. They operate between 6am and midnight with a journey time varying between 35 and 50 minutes. Make certain the meter is registering zero at the start of the journey.

■ **Trains** (Trinacria Express, tel: 892 021; ticket office: 199 166 177; airport ticket office: 091 704 4007; www.trenitalia.it) run into Palermo roughly hourly 5:40am–11:40pm. Tickets cost €5.80 and the journey time is one hour.

■ **Buses** (Autolinee Prestia e Comandè, tel: 091 580 457; www.prestia-comande.it) run half-hourly from 6:30am to midnight to Palermo's Stazione Centrale. Tickets cost €5.80 and there are several stops en route to the city centre. Autolinee Segesta (tel: 091 616 7919; www.segesta.it) has a service from the airport to Trapani at 11am, 3pm and 8pm (tickets cost €9) and Autolinee Sal (tel: 0922 401 360; www.autolineesal.it) operates between the airport and Agrigento twice daily (tickets €11.50) from Monday to Saturday.

■ **To leave the airport by car** take the link motorway to connect to the E90/A19 *autostrada*.

### Aeroporto Fontanarossa (Catania)

Catania's airport (tel: 800 565 660, flight information: 095 340 505; www.aeroporto.catania.it) handles international and domestic flights.

■ There are flights **direct** to Catania from London Gatwick.

■ Passengers **from the US** will have to route through Rome or Milan.

■ Fontanarossa is 5km (3 miles) south of Catania, and is **connected with the city** by buses and taxis, both of which leave from outside the terminal buildings. The airport tourist information desk (095 730 6266/77/88; Mon–Sat 8am–9pm, Sun 8–2) has maps, timetables and accommodation lists and you can change money at the *cambio*.

■ **Taxis** (tel: 095 330 966/095 386 794) are the fastest and most expensive way to reach central Catania; four people will pay around €25, with an additional charge for extra luggage. Make sure the meter is registering zero at the start of the journey.

■ **Alibus** (tel: 800 018 696) services run every 20 minutes from 5am to midnight between the airport and the Stazione Centrale in Catania, with tickets costing €1.

■ **Other bus companies** connect with towns all over Sicily:
**AST** (tel: 095 746 1096; www.aziendasicilianatrasporti.it) to Caltagirone, Piazza Armerina, Etna and Acireale
**Etna Trasporti** (tel: 095 532 2716; www.etnatrasporti.it) to Giardini-Naxos, Taormina
**Giuntabus** (tel: 090 675 749; www.giuntabus.com) to Milazzo for ferries to the Aeolian Islands (Apr–Sep)
**Interbus** (tel: 095 532 2716; www.interbus.it) to Siracusa, Taormina, Trapani, Noto and Palermo
**SAIS Trasporti** (tel: 095 536 6168; www.saistrasporti.it) to Agrigento and Caltanissetta
**SAIS Autolinee** (tel: 0935 524 111; www.siasautolinee.it) to Enna, Messina, Gela and Palermo

■ **When leaving the airport by car** take the A19 motorway to head west or the A18 to head north.

## Arriving by Train

Passengers arriving by train from mainland Italy (► 185) and the rest of Europe may arrive either at Catania (Stazione Centrale, Piazza Giovanni XXIII, tel: 091 892 021) or Palermo (Stazione Centrale, Piazza Giulio Césare, tel: 091 603 1111); there are more services to Catania. Taxi ranks are outside both stations, and, for onward travel by bus, many of the Sicilian bus companies depart from Via Balsamo and Via Gregorio, both close to the station in Palermo.

## Arriving by Road

■ If you are driving to Sicily, all routes run through Italy. The distance from the France–Italy border is around 1,500km (930 miles) so you should allow two days driving. You can cut the driving time by catching a ferry at Genova, Livorno or Naples (► 185). If you drive the whole way south, you can cross the Straits of Messina either by ferry from Villa San Giovanni or by hydrofoil or ferry from Réggio di Calabria at the end of the motorway; follow the signs "TRAGHETTI". Ferries leave once or twice an hour, depending on the operating company, and there is no need to book. Drivers should buy their tickets from the kiosk on the dockside.

■ If you arrive by the car ferry from the north of Italy, you will dock at the Stazione Maríttima in Palermo.

## Car Rental

If you want to rent a car while in Sicily, all the major international firms have outlets at both Catania and Palermo airports and in the cities, though it may be less expensive to arrange a deal before you leave home. Note that the car rental desks at Catania are in a separate building opposite Arrivals. To contact a car rental firm:

**Avis** tel: 0870 606 0100; Palermo airport tel: 091 591 684; www.avis.com
**Budget** tel: 01442 276 266; www.budget.com
**Europcar** tel: 0870 607 5000; www.europcar.co.uk
**Hertz** tel: 0800 317 540; Catania airport tel: 095 341 595; www.hertz.com
**Holiday Autos** tel: 0870 400 0099; www.holidayautos.co.uk
**Maggiore** tel: 848 867 067; Catania airport tel: 095 536 927; www.maggiore.it
**National** tel: 0870 536 5365; www.nationalcar.co.uk

## Tourist Information Offices

There are tourist information desks at Palermo and Catania airports (► 32) and each city has a large, city-centre office. In addition, each of Sicily's nine provinces has a main office in the provincial capital and branches throughout the province. Many towns also have their own offices operated by the *comune* (town council). Details of all of these are given in the text.
**Palermo:** Piazza Castelnuovo 34, tel: 091 605 8351; www.palermotourism.com, Mon–Fri 8.30–2, 2:30–6:30
**Catania:** Via D Cimarosa 10, tel: 095 730 6211/095 730 6233; www.apt.catania.it, Mon–Fri 9–8, Sat–Sun 9–2

---

**Admission Charges**
The cost of admission for museums and places of interest mentioned in the text is indicated by the following price categories.
**Inexpensive** under €3    **Moderate** €3–€5    **Expensive** more than €5

---

# Getting Around

**Public transport in Sicily is good value, and generally buses cover a wider network than trains, which can be slow. However, while buses often go where trains do not, they do not run on Sundays and, depending on the destination, can have limited schedules linked to market or school times. A car gives the greatest flexibility and, in general, roads are good. However, Sicilians are fast and aggressive drivers, so it helps to have nerves of steel.**

## Driving

### Roads and Driving

■ Sicily is crisscrossed by excellent *autostrade* (motorways), spectacular feats of civil engineering. They link Messina–Catania (A18), Catania–Palermo (A19), Palermo–Trapani/Mazaro del Vallo (A29), Siracusa–Gela and Messina–Palermo (A20). The Messina–Catania and the Messina–Palermo *autostrade* are toll roads; take a ticket as you come on and pay on exit.

■ Other roads vary considerably. Mountain roads in particular can be tortuously slow, and signposting can be very poor.

■ Driving in Palermo and Catania is traumatic for foreigners unused to Sicilian driving and best avoided.

■ Sicilian towns generally are not designed for drivers, with narrow streets and labyrinthine one-way systems. The best time to negotiate towns is during the siesta time when the streets are at their quietest.

■ Drivers must be over 18 and need a valid EU or international driving permit and green insurance card if you're bringing your own car. You must carry both car documents and your passport with you and you are required to present them if you are stopped by the police, a far from uncommon event. You must also have a portable triangular warning triangle in case of breakdown – these are provided with rental cars.

■ Drive on the right.

■ Give precedence at junctions and roundabouts to vehicles from the right.

■ Observe the speed limits (50kph/31mph in built up areas, 110kph/68mph on country roads, 130kph/80mph on *autostrade*).

■ Dipped headlights are mandatory at all times outside built-up areas.

■ Seat belts are compulsory.

- The drink-drive limit is below 0.05 per cent alcohol in the bloodstream.
- If you break down, turn on the hazard lights and place the warning triangle 50m (165 feet) behind the vehicle. Contact the ACI (Automobile Club d'Italia, tel: 116); they will arrange help and a tow if necessary, though this is not a free service.
- For the latest information and further advice, visit www.theaa.com/motoring_advice/overseas.

## Driving Standards and Safety

Driving in Sicily requires a fair amount of nerve and verve; Sicilian driving habits are unique.

- Constant attention and concentration is vital.
- Keep moving at all times; drivers will make way for you only if you show what could be construed as aggression back home.
- Be prepared for tailgating and move over promptly.
- Flashing lights and horns are frequently used.
- In cities, head for a car park or parking space and do not attempt to negotiate badly marked road systems.
- Never leave anything of value in the car. Pay for garaging if you are going to leave a vehicle overnight in Palermo or Catania.
- Retract the aerial and tuck in the wing mirrors when you park in a town, where streets are often narrow.

## Buses

Sicilian buses (*autobus* or *pullman*) cover everywhere you'll want to go and are reliable, comfortable and often air conditioned. They are an excellent way of seeing the countryside and getting to smaller towns and villages. There are three main companies and numerous smaller regional operators. Bear in mind that services are drastically reduced, or even non-existent, on Sunday and that timetables on some out-of-the-way routes are geared to the school day or local markets, making departure times horribly early.

- Bus terminals (*autostazione*) can be found all over the bigger towns; in smaller places buses stop in a main piazza or outside the railway station.
- Timetables are available online, from company offices, bus stations or on the bus.
- Buy tickets on board or in advance from company offices.
- City buses are cheap and frequent; buy tickets at *tabacchi* or from kiosks before you board and validate them in the machine on the bus.

### Main Bus Operators

**AST** (tel: 095 746 1096; www.aziendasicilianatrasporti.it)
**Cuffaro T** (tel: 091 616 1510; www.cuffaro.info)
**Giuntabus** (tel: 090 673 782; www.giuntabus.com)
**Interbus** (tel: 095 532 2716; www.interbus.it)
**SAIS Trasporti** (tel: 095 536 6168; www.saistrasporti.it)

## Trains

Ferrovie dello Stato (Italian State Railways), marketed as Trenitalia (www.trenitalia.it), connects all the major Sicilian towns, while the privately run Ferrovia Circumetnea (www.circumetnea.it) traces a 114km (70-mile) circular route round the lower slopes of Mount Etna, a beautiful line that provides one of the best ways of viewing the iconic volcano. The east of the island is better served by the rail system than the west, and the deep interior has just one line, running from Catania via Enna to Palermo. As elsewhere in Italy, some stations are a good distance from the town they serve (Enna and Taormina are prime examples) and services do not run on

Sundays or holidays. There are five types of train: Intercity, Diretto, Espresso, Interregionale and Regionale.

- **Intercity** travel requires a 30 per cent supplement on the normal ticket price and reservations are obligatory.
- *Diretto*, *Espresso* and *Interegionale* trains are long-distance expresses, stopping only at major stations.
- *Regionale* are inordinately slow local trains, stopping at every station.
- You can make **reservations** (*prenotazione*) on the main routes, worth considering in summer; it's mandatory on some services.
- Stations have **information boards** displaying arrivals (*arrivi*) and departures (*partenze*) and timetables on boards on each platform (*binario*). You can also pick up a copy of *In Treno Sicilia*, published twice yearly by the FS. Make sure you read the timetable notes referring to seasonal changes and Sunday services.
- You must **validate** your ticket by stamping it in one of the yellow boxes at the station before boarding the train.
- **Fares** are low; children aged 4–12 receive a 50 per cent discount, under-fours travel free.

# Accommodation

**Sicily has an excellent range of accommodation, with prices, on the whole, marginally lower than the equivalent on the mainland. Options range from the sybaritic luxury of the grand hotels in Palermo, Catania and resorts such as Taormina to family-run, simple *pensione* and private rooms on farms. All accommodation is officially graded and the tariff fixed by law. In practice, pricing is more fluid, with mysterious extras hoisting up the price in high season and lower rates available off-season with a little negotiation. On the whole, rooms are abundant in the main towns and tourist areas, but it pays to book ahead in summer or if you're heading inland, where some towns may have very little accommodation.**

## Types of Accommodation

- **Hotels and *pensione*** Hotels (*alberghi*) are graded on a 1–5 star scale. These refer to the facilities provided – air conditioning, lift, swimming pool and so forth – rather than the character and comfort. On the whole, 5- and 4-star hotels should provide a high level of comfort and excellent service and facilities, and many are housed in historic, beautifully converted buildings where antique charm goes hand in hand with 21st-century luxury. Three-star establishments are more idiosyncratic, while 1- and 2-star *alberghi* are relatively inexpensive, clean and safe. There's little difference between a simple hotel and a pension. If you want to enjoy staying in a top-class hotel it may be worth booking a package holiday; operators are able to negotiate far lower room rates than individual travellers.
- **B&Bs and private rooms** Bed and breakfast accommodation is growing in Sicily and is usually simple, clean and well maintained, though increasingly smarter B&Bs, with pools and other facilities, are beginning to appear. Many of these are run by foreigners living in Sicily, who cater specifically to the expectations of non-Italian visitors. Local tourist offices have further listings.
- ***Agriturismo*** Agriturismo, country accommodation on working farms and estates, is a growing trend in Sicily. Most *agriturismi* are off the beaten track so you'll need a car, and few owners speak English. Some expect

guests to stay for a minimum of three nights, so check ahead. You can get more information from Agriturist, Via A di Giovanni 14, 90144 Palermo, tel: 091 346 046; www.agriturist.it, or check www.farm-holidays.it and www.agriturismo-sicilia.it.

- **Self-catering** Self-catering options include some *agriturismi* (see above), holiday flats in seaside resorts or often sumptuous villas, usually booked through a specialist UK-based operator. Private lets are also available through www.holiday-rentals.co.uk and upmarket villas specialist www.thinksicily.com.
- **Camping** Sicily has more than 90 officially graded, well-equipped campsites dotted around the coast – there are very few inland. During July and August they are packed and advance booking is highly recommended. Many are closed out of season. Further information is available from local tourist offices, on-line at www.camping.it or in the camping guide published by Touring Club Italiano (Corso Italia 10, Milano, tel: 02 85 26 245; www.touringclub.it).
- **Rifugi** On Mount Etna and in the Madonie and Nebrodi mountains it's possible to stay in staffed mountain huts (*rifugi*). Accommodation is simple, but the settings are superb and most have restaurants.Tourist offices have details or check the website of the Club Alpino Italiano (www.cai.it), who operate the *rifugi*.

## Finding a Room

- If you haven't booked ahead, visit the local tourist office, which will have listings of local accommodation, or head for the main piazza or *centro storico*.
- Aim to start looking for a room in the afternoon; there will be more rooms available and you can negotiate towns during the quieter siesta hours.
- It's perfectly acceptable to ask to see the room before you check in.
- You will be asked to leave your passport at reception for registration; don't forget it when you leave.
- Check-out time is normally noon. If you plan to leave very early, ask to pay the bill the night before as there may be no one around when you leave.
- If you're touring, an affiliation of privately owned hotels throughout Sicily markets itself as Hotels Catena del Sole (www.sicily-hotels.net); they will book ahead for you and there are considerable reductions if you stay in more than one of the group.

## Pricing

- Rates for high and low season (*alta e bassa stagione*) are posted on the back of the bedroom door (or in the wardrobe). Some hotels charge the same rate year round.
- Agree a price before you make the reservation; prices are per room. Hotels often show you the most expensive rooms, so ask if they have anything that costs less. Most hotels will put another bed in the room for an extra 35 per cent.
- In simpler hotels you may be charged extra for air conditioning; breakfast may be unavailable or not included in the room price.
- Some *pensione* and bed and breakfasts do not accept credit cards, so check when you book in.

---

**Prices**
Expect to pay per double room, per night:
€ under €130          €€ €130–€230                    €€€ over €230

# Food and Drink

Sicilian cooking (► 14–15) reflects the island's history, with culinary influences from its waves of Greek, Arab, and Norman invaders. As throughout Italy, it's an distinctly regional cuisine, with the emphasis on seasonal, fresh produce of the highest quality. Flavours are intense, the long-lasting Arabic legacy seen in every type of dish, making Sicilian food spicier, hotter and sweeter than anywhere else in Italy. The staples are bread, pasta, fish and vegetables, the embellishments an astounding array of sweets and *pasticceria*.

## When and How to Eat

- **Breakfast** (*colazione*) Many hotels serve a buffet-type breakfast from 8am until around 10, where you can help yourself to a wide array of the usual juices, cereals, yoghurts, breads, jams and cold meat and cheese. More Sicilian by far is a bar breakfast, taken at the counter, and consisting of a cappuccino and a freshly baked pastry (*briosc* or *cornetto*). In summer, a sweet roll filled with ice cream is a truly Sicilian breakfast speciality. Locals enjoy this any time from around 7:30 or 8 until 11 or so, after which the cappuccino gives way to a *caffè*, a shot of potent black coffee.
- **Lunch** (*pranzo*) Lunch is served from noon until around 3pm, and traditionally consists of *antipasti* (appetizer), the *primo* (first course), normally soup or some sort of pasta, rice or couscous, and the *secondo* (main course), meat or fish, served with a *contorno* (side dish) of vegetables or a salad (*insalata*). Dessert (*dolce*) is normally fruit (*frutta*), ice cream (*gelato*) or a simple flan (*crostata*); Sicilians patronize *pasticcerie* (pastry shops) for more elaborate confections.
- **Dinner** (*cena*) In restaurants, dinner, served from 7:30 until 10 or 11, follows the same pattern as lunch, though many Sicilians will cut down on the courses, as this is normally a lighter meal.
- **Opening times do vary**. The opening times for individual restaurants in this book are correct at the time of writing, but smaller places in particular can close early without notice.

## Where to Eat

There is often confusion about the names of Italian eating places, but all restaurants display the menu and prices outside so you can get some idea of what to expect. It's perfectly acceptable to order just a couple of courses, rather than wade through the entire menu. In tourist areas, avoid restaurants offering fixed-price set tourist menus, which are often poor value. As everywhere in Italy, pick places patronized by locals.

- **Ristoranti** are straightforward restaurants offering a full menu for both lunch and dinner. They range from very expensive and extremely chic to cheerful, family-run affairs. In Sicily, many restaurants offer an *antipasto* buffet, a huge selection of fish, meat and vegetable hors d'oeuvres dishes; diners help themselves to whatever they want.
- **Trattorie** are quintessential Italian family-run eating places, where the day's specialities may be conveyed by the waiter. The line separating *trattorie* from *ristoranti* is increasingly blurred, and the term *trattoria* may be used to denote a rustic, but sophisticated, style of cooking, with prices to match.
- **Rosticceria, tavola calda** and **gastronomia** are the names given to a type of establishment that has counters of freshly prepared hot and cold food; choose what looks good, eat, pay and go. Many will package the food to take away. If you want a light lunch, these are the answer.

■ **Pizzerie** Most *pizzerie* are open only in the evenings, though you will find take-out *pizzerie*, where huge pizzas are cut into slices and priced *a taglio* (by the slice), open in larger towns at lunchtime. Make certain you choose a pizzeria with a wood-burning oven.

■ **Markets** Markets are good places to eat in Sicily, with many stalls serving hot snacks and food to take away. It's a chance to sample specialities that rarely appear on restaurant menus and ideal for putting together a picnic.

■ Note that **smoking** is banned in all Sicilian (and Italian) bars and restaurants, though it is permitted at outdoor tables.

## Bars, Pasticcerie, Gelaterie and Fast Food

■ **Bars** sell coffee, other hot and cold drinks, beer, wine, spirits and snacks, and are open from early morning until late. The wonderfully strong Sicilian coffee comes as a *caffè* (espresso), cappuccino (made with frothy milk), *caffè latte* (milky coffee) or *macchiato* (small strong coffee with a dash of milk). If you want a long, weak coffee, ask for an *americano*. You can either stand at the bar or sit for waiter service; the latter adds around a third on to the price. By law, you should keep your *scontrino* (receipt) until you have left the bar. Some Sicilian bars also offer a selection of hot dishes at lunchtime; these are served between noon and 2pm. All bars, by law, have to have a publicly accessible lavatory; you may have to ask at the counter for the key.

■ **Pasticcerie** are confectioners where you can buy the wonderful pastries, sweets and cakes that are a Sicilian speciality (▶ 15). They will box up a selection to take away or you can choose something and eat it on the spot. Many also serve coffee and other drinks.

■ **Gelaterie** serve ice cream, one of Sicily's finest products. Look for one that features *produzione propria* (our own production); such establishments will have a large range of both creamy ices and granita, a water ice made with lemon, orange, coffee or seasonal fruit, very refreshing in summer.

■ **Fast Food** For a quick snack, bars and *rosticcerie* are a good bet. Don't fail to sample specialities such as *arancini*, literally oranges, but actually deep-fried breaded rice balls with a savoury middle; *tramezzini*, succulent, white-bread finger sandwiches; *sfincone*, a thick pizza with onions and anchovies; and *panelle*, fried chick-pea patties.

## Paying and Tipping

■ The waiter will bring the **bill** (*il conto*) when you are ready to leave.

■ **Service** is obligatory and is normally added as a percentage of the bill at the end, though it's customary to leave a few euros on the table.

■ You should receive a **receipt** in the form of a *ricevuta fiscale*; bills scribbled on scraps of paper are illegal.

■ **Prices vary** considerably in Sicily; restaurants in tourist areas can be very expensive, while simple eating places in remoter parts can offer superb food and local specialities at low prices.

## What to Drink

■ Sicilians drink **wine and water** with meals. Mineral water comes both still (*naturale* or *liscia*) and fizzy (*gassata* or *frizzante*) and wine can be ordered both bottled and by the carafe (*sfuso* or *vino locale*).

■ **Sicilian wines** are on the up and up, with local grape varieties such as Nero d'Avolo, Grecanico and Pignatello used to create modern wines of great quality. Names to look out for include Corvo, Alcamo, Regaleali, Cervasuolo, Etna and Mamertino, all producing both reds and whites.

■ Marsala is Sicily's own **fortified wine**, ranging from super sweet to almost dry; Moscato and Passito from Noto and Siracusa are dessert muscats

worth trying, and Pantelleria, from the eponymous island, is a deliciously scented dessert wine redolent of honey, melons, oranges and roses.
Amaro is a classic Italian post-prandial *digestivo*, a herby, bitter but delicious liqueur served straight or on ice. Sicilian Averna Amaro is made in Caltanissetta and is one of the most famous bitters. Other concoctions to try are Averna's Limoni (made with Sicilian lemons) and Mandarini (mandarins), which have a fresh taste and intense citrus flavours, but are also very potent.

- Sicilians have their own **beer**, Messina, and all the usual international brands of spirits, beers and soft drinks.
- In summer, look out for **iced tea** (*tè freddo*), flavoured with mint, lemon or peach, iced coffee (*caffè freddo*) and *latte di mandorla*, a refreshing cold drink made with almond paste dissolved in water.
- **Coffee** is superb, but there's little hope of a perfect cup of tea (*tè*) – the concept of using boiling water is virtually unknown. In cold weather, thick hot chocolate (*cioccolata*) is a better bet.
- Away from larger towns and resorts **milk** is usually UHT.

---

**Prices**
Expect to pay per person for a meal, including wine and service
€ up to €20          €€ €20–€35          €€€ more than €35

---

# Shopping

For most visitors, shopping is an integral part of the pleasure of holiday-making, and Sicily, although not on a par with mainland Italy, has plenty of temptations, ranging from the normal Italian delights of *alta moda* (high fashion), leather and shoes to its own particular products, many of then food and drink related. There are plenty of standard souvenirs on offer, often at hefty prices, but delve deeper and you'll find wonderful artisan and handmade objects, with a history going back centuries. The best places for shopping in Sicily for visitors are the capital, Palermo, where the range and quality of shops equals that of mainland Italy, upmarket and chic Taormina, and Cefalù on the north coast. If food shopping is your passion, you'll find that every Sicilian town of any size has its own local specialities.

## What to Buy

Most Sicilian shops are small and individually owned. You'll find a range of Italian high street and international designer names in Palermo and Catania, and upmarket shops aplenty in Taormina, but bear in mind that Italy has few department chain stores and, this far south, shopping malls are unknown and the range of goods more limited. Domenico Dolce, co-founder of Dolce e Gabbana, was born near Palermo and studied fashion design while working in his family's small clothing factory. Other famous native fashion designers include Marella Ferrera and Roberta Lojacono, while Marilu Fernandez creates beautiful coral jewellery from her gallery in Palermo. Once you're away from the bigger towns and tourist centres, however, you'll find little, except local food products, that's particularly tempting.

**Carpets** Erice is the centre for colourful rustic carpets called *frazzata*.

**Jewellery** Gold and silver jewellery can be beautiful or overly ornate; coral brooches and necklaces, the coral nowadays imported from the Bay of Naples, are still a speciality of Trapani.

**Lace and embroidery** Arab silk workers introduced lace and embroidery, which is still made today; look for exquisite underwear, nightwear and table linen.

**Pottery and ceramics** The pottery tradition dates back to the Arabs and, while you'll find ceramics all over Sicily, three towns, Sciacca, Caltagirone and Santo Stefano di Camastra, remain the main centres. Many producers can arrange shipment if you want to buy in quantity.

**Sicilian food** *Frutta alla martorana*, marzipan fruit and vegetables, are irresistible take-home souvenirs, as are handmade pasta, salted capers, *bottarga* (salt-cured tuna roe), pine nuts or a fine bottle of Marsala. You could also invest in good olive oil, among the world's most fragrant and appetizing due to Sicily's particularly fertile soil.

**Wooden puppets** Inexpensive replicas and beautiful hand-made puppets can still be tracked down in specialist shops.

**Wrought iron** bedheads and other smaller objects are still handmade in Giardini-Naxos. Big pieces can be shipped.

## Food Markets

Every town has its daily food market and even small villages will have a weekly market day, when itinerant traders drive in to sell everything from fruit and vegetables to pottery, household goods and clothes. The best food markets are in Palermo, Catania, Siracusa and many of the coastal towns, when the fish comes straight off the boats. Fruit and vegetables are sold by weight (*un chilo* = 1kg/2.2 lb, *un'etto* = 100g/3.5oz) or piece (*un pezzo*); most markets open from 7am to 1pm.

Markets are also good places to buy kitchen pots, pans and implements, shoes and cheap clothes. Stall holders will normally let you try things on by scrambling into the back of their vans – just don't expect market purchases to last forever and don't be tempted by cut-price DVDs, which are often pirated. The markets in big towns also sell wonderful, freshly prepared street food, giving you the chance to try a whole range of local flavours unheard of in restaurants. In inland Sicily, you'll often see goods, particularly fruit, vegetables and local produce, being sold from vans at the side of the road.

## Tax-Free Shopping and Shipping

Residents of non-EU states can claim back IVA (value-added tax) for goods purchased at shops that are part of the tax-free scheme. Such stores will have a sticker displayed in the window. Claims are made by filling in a form available at the tax-free counter at the departure airport. Many stores will pack and ship overseas but costs can be high.

## Opening Hours

- Small shops open around 9:30–10 (food shops at 8), close between 12:30 and 4pm, then reopen until around 7:30 or 8.
- Many non-food shops are closed on Monday morning.
- Markets are generally open 7am–1pm; the main markets in Palermo are open all day.
- Chemists operate a rota system for prescriptions and somewhere will be open 24 hours a day; the addresses and rota times are posted on pharmacy windows.

# Entertainment

There's no shortage of entertainment in Sicily, ranging from opera and classical theatre to street parades and food festivals. Many of Sicily's traditional festivals date back hundreds of years, and give a real insight into the joys and preoccupations of Sicilians. Try and fit in one of these religious celebrations – it will add a whole new dimension to your stay.

## Festivals

Nearly all traditional festivals are religion based and coincide with the great feasts of the church – Holy Week, Easter, Pentecost, the feast of the Virgin and Christmas – or local saints' days. All involve parades and processions, music, feasting, drinking and often dancing and fireworks. Throughout the summer, festivals include pilgrimages, fishermen's and harvest festivals, and jousting and dancing festivals whose roots lie in the Middle Ages, as do those of Sicily's own dramatic genre, the puppet theatre. *Sagre* (food festivals) devoted to local specialities are a feature of the island. Many villages and small towns celebrate the fruits of their labours with feasting and parades at different times of the year, such as pistachios in Bronte, capers in Salina and strawberries at Maletto near Etna. Almond treats feature in the Sagra del Mandorlo in Agrigento (► 16–17), while San Vito lo Capo hosts a couscous festival (► 17). Ask at local tourist offices for up-to-date information, and keep an eye open for posters advertising forthcoming celebrations.

## Culture

Palermo and Catania have a year-round vibrant cultural scene, with theatre, opera and dance all on offer. Sicily's chief cultural delights are the summer festivals, however, when live music spills outdoors, and you can even hear a classical Greek play performed in a Greek theatre. The main festivals run from June to August and include an international ballet festival at Siracusa, music, dance and theatre at Taormina, outdoor concerts at Trapani, opera outdoors in Enna, Pirandello plays at Agrigento and medieval and Renaissance music at Erice. Local tourist offices will have full details and can help with booking.

## Nightlife

Sicily's best nightlife is found in larger towns and holiday resorts, but it has to be said it's fairly low key compared with the scene in other Mediterranean destinations. Clubbing is distinctly provincial and big name rock bands rarely make it further south than Naples, though local groups do perform at summer events. The best bet for summer clubbing is Taormina; otherwise, find a late bar that offers live music or hunt out one of the weekend-only clubs in smaller places – tourist offices will help – or check the listings in *Tuttocittà* or the *Giornale di Sicilia*.

## Sports and Outdoor Activities

If you're staying on the coast you'll find swimming pools and tennis courts in many hotels and resorts, and the pleasures of Sicily's crystal clear, warm seas are myriad. Watersports, windsurfing, kitesurfing, sailing and diving are all on offer; tourist offices will have details. Inland, hikers should head for the slopes of Etna and the Madonie mountains, where marked trails are beginning to appear, or head for the protected coast between Scopello and Capo San Vito. In winter, there's skiing on Etna and in the Madonie range; the lower slopes of these ranges are also home to Sicily's two golf courses.

# Palermo and Around

# Getting Your Bearings

Embraced by two headlands and lying at the foot of Monte Pellegrino, Palermo has one of the most beautiful of all Mediterranean settings. Steeped in history, it's a city whose waves of rulers have left their mark in a parade of exquisite monuments. These explosions of creativity have left a melange of superb architecture, ranging from the serene austerity of the Norman buildings to the exuberance of the baroque churches. Palermo has pockets of immense wealth and areas of great poverty. It is noisy, dirty and decrepit, but supremely alive, and its edgy charms are truly seductive.

The cathedral clock tower

Old Palermo lies south of the Cattedrale, a Norman foundation within a few hundred metres of the other great early monuments, the Palazzo dei Normanni, home to the glittering Cappella Palatina, and the ancient churches of La Martorana and San Cataldo. In this same area you'll find some of the city's superb baroque structures – Quattro Canti, heart of the city, a clutch of churches and three fine museums, the Galleria Regionale Siciliana, the Museo Archeologico Regionale and the Museo delle Marionette, celebrating Palermo's own theatrical genre, the puppet theatre.

Behind the main streets lie warrens of alleyways, home to markets such as the Vucciria, while to the north, the grid-like streets of the 19th-century city stretch towards Monte Pellegrino and the beaches of Mondello. West from the centre lies the bizarre catacomb of the Cappuccini, while further out traffic-jammed streets lead away from the coast and up the hill to Monreale, a Norman cathedral whose sublime mosaics are among Sicily's greatest treasures.

### ★ Don't Miss

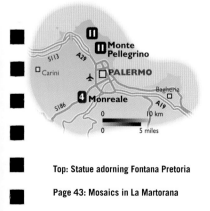

**Top:** Statue adorning Fontana Pretoria

**Page 43:** Mosaics in La Martorana

### At Your Leisure

# In Two Days

If you're not quite sure where to begin your travels, this itinerary recommends two practical and enjoyable days out in Palermo, taking in some of the best places to see using the Getting Your Bearings map on the previous page. For more information see the main entries.

## Day 1

### Morning

Much of what you'll want to see is confined to a comparatively small area. Start your first day in **Piazza Castelnuovo**, where you can pick up information from the **main tourist office** (Piazza Castelnuovo 34, tel: 091 605 8351; www.palermotourism.com). The piazza is also the starting point for the red tourist buses that follow two city routes, operating a hop-on, hop-off service – buy your ticket (valid for 24 hours) on board (www.palermo.city-sightseeing.it). From here, head for Corso Vittorio Emanuele to take in the **7 Vucciria market** (➤ 60) en route to the **2 Cattedrale** (right and opposite, ➤ 50); then stroll to the **3 Palazzo dei Normanni** (➤ 52), home to the Cappella Palatina (➤ 52).

### Afternoon

After lunch, walk down the Corso to the **9 Quattro Canti** (left, ➤ 61), walking through **Piazza Pretoria** (➤ 61) to visit the churches of **1 La Martorana** (➤ 48) and **San Cataldo** (➤ 48). From here, you could head east to take in a museum, either the **6 Galleria Regionale Siciliana** (➤ 59) or the **5 Museo delle Marionette Antonio Pasqualino** (➤ 59). Near here, too, you'll find the church of **San Francesco d'Assisi**.

## Evening

In the same area, head for a drink in **Piazza Marina**, a lovely square, lined with palazzi, with a wide choice of pavement cafés. Then head straight to dinner, or take a break at your hotel before setting out for the evening – perhaps to take in a performance at the Teatro Massimo (➤ 68).

# Day 2

## Morning

After breakfast, you might like to explore Palermo some more on foot (➤ 166) before visiting the **8 Museo Archeologico Regionale** (➤ 60). Then it's time to head out and experience the macabre underground cemetery at the **10 Catacombe dei Cappuccini** (➤ 62), before continuing to **4 Monreale** (➤ 55).

## Afternoon

You'll want to take your time visiting the cathedral to see the mosaics and the cloisters, and perhaps strolling round the little town. Aim to head back to Palermo in time to relax before an early start to the evening.

## Evening

Set off in time to take in the **Parco della Favorita** (➤ 63) before spending the evening at **11 Mondello** (below, ➤ 63), Palermo's favourite resort, where you can join the poseurs in the *passeggiata* before enjoying a wonderfully fresh fish dinner.

# Chiesa della Martorana and San Cataldo

Tucked against part of Palermo's old Roman wall and overlooking a pretty piazza lie the ancient churches of the Martorana and San Cataldo. Founded by Norman statesmen, they've survived the centuries, their contrasting interiors providing an insight into the religious fervour and aesthetic considerations of Palermo nearly a thousand years ago.

### Chiesa della Martorana (La Martorana)

Properly known as **Santa Maria dell'Ammiraglio** (Our Lady of the Admiral), La Martorana was founded c.1146 by George of Antioch, a Greek Orthodox admiral who served the Norman king Roger II. Nearly a century later, in 1233, the church was given to the nuns of a nearby convent founded by Eloise de Marturanu – hence its name. The nuns inherited one of the most beautiful Greek churches in Sicily, a Greek cross structure with a fine campanile (bell tower), whose interior was decorated with dazzling **mosaics**. These were executed by the same Greek craftsmen from Constantinople who worked in the Cappella Palatina (► 52) and at Cefalù (► 74).

Tragically, in the 1680s, the nuns destroyed many of the mosaics, and wrecked the Norman interior, when they demolished the atrium and narthex (entrance) and altered the interior in the baroque style. Ignore these alterations, and concentrate on the surviving 12th-century glories that decorate the dome, the apse, the side vaults and two panels at the back. These latter show George, the founder, and King Roger II, conveniently labelled Rogerius Rex in Greek, while the main mosaic scheme is devoted to Christ and his archangels, the four evangelists and scenes from the life of the Virgin. Hieratic but tender, these beautiful creations, glittering with gold, take us straight back into Palermo's golden age.

Intricate mosaics on the ceiling of La Martorana

## San Cataldo

After the riches of the Martorana, the extraordinary simplicity of San Cataldo evokes a deep sense of spirituality, heightened by the music that's often playing. Topped by three squat little red domes, the church was founded in 1154 by another key Norman helpmate, Maio of Bari, who was chancellor to William I, the second king of Sicily. Maio died in 1160, leaving the interior of the church without decoration. To modern eyes, it's this resulting simplicity that attracts, with nothing to detract from the simple harmony of the lines of the central nave and two aisles. These are covered with cross vaults and end in small apses; the plain altar is original,

as is the beautiful **mosaic pavement**, its swirling geometric design a sure sign of its construction by some of the Arab craftsmen who worked for the Christian rulers of Palermo. The church now belongs to the Knights of the Holy Sepulchre of Jerusalem.

Charming San Cataldo, with its three red domes, is relatively plain

### TAKING A BREAK

**Pizzeria Bellini** (€), right on the square, serves pizzas throughout the day Monday to Saturday – grab a table right beside the Martorana.

➕ 202 C1 ✉ Piazza Bellini 3 ☎ 091 616 1692 🕐 Mon–Sat 9:15–1, 3:30–7 🎟 Free 🚌 Tourist bus A, 101, 102, 103, 104

### San Cataldo

➕ 202 C1 ✉ Piazza Bellini 3 ☎ 091 637 5622 🕐 Tue–Fri 9:30–5, Sat–Sun 9–1 🎟 Inexpensive 🚌 Tourist bus A, 101, 102, 103, 104

### FRUTTI DI MARTORANA

Every self-respecting *pasticceria* in the city and province of Palermo displays hand-made *frutti di Martorana*, astonishingly realistic, highly coloured, marzipan fruits. The name comes from the church of the Martorana, whose nuns once raised a little hard cash by the sale of these sweetmeats. Strawberries, cherries, figs, peaches and apricots are favourites, and you'll often see more exotic creations in the form of seafood and fish, or even tiny cauliflowers. Made with the finest almonds, egg whites and sugar, the *frutti* are cloyingly sweet, a legacy of Sicily's Moorish past.

## CHIESA DELLA MARTORANA AND SAN CATALDO: INSIDE INFO

**Top Tips** Bear in mind that La Martorana is shut at lunchtime.
■ Concentrate on the mosaics in La Martorana; the baroque additions are second-class.

# ❷ La Cattedrale

Palermo's Cattedrale, dedicated to the Assumption of the Virgin, is among Palermo's largest Norman survivors. Its huge golden bulk rises to one side of the arrow-straight Corso Vittorio Emanuele. Time and man may have spoiled its original splendid lines, but it's still a potent symbol of the wealth and piety of old Palermo.

The Cattedrale was founded in 1185 and built on the site of an earlier Byzantine structure, which had served as a mosque during Arab times. It was the brainchild of an Englishman, Walter of the Mill, splendidly Italianized as Gualtiero Offamiglio, who was Archbishop of Palermo and tutor to the young William II. William founded Monreale (► 55), and Palermo's cathedral was Walter's answer, a symbol of the Archbishop's power and prestige. His work was thoroughly ruined by Ferdinando Fuga's 18th-century restorations, but the cathedral remains a much-loved religious powerhouse for the city.

## The Exterior

Walk round to the east end of the exterior to see the best of the Norman original, where three beautifully decorated apses are flanked by two towers, mirroring those at the west end. The main entrance, reached from the road through a spacious paved and planted piazza, is the superb Catalan-Gothic **three-arched porch**, finally finished in 1426. The stonework round the door shows Norman work, the serene Virgin above is older still and may have come from the earlier basilica, while the left-hand column has an Arabic inscription from the

Palermo's Cattedrale is a fine example of Sicily's Norman heritage

Koran, a survivor of the mosque. Above the arches you'll see a painted Tree of Life, dating from 1296 and decorated with lively birds, beasts, fruit and flowers. The ill-balanced dome was added in the 18th century by Fuga.

## The Interior and its Treasures

Fuga did his worst on the interior, removing much of the decoration and dismantling the wonderful high altar by Antonello Gagini – statues from it are scattered round the church. On the right as you face the high altar, you'll find the entrance to the **treasury** and **crypt**, burial place to Archbishop Walter – his tomb is bordered with some fine green, red and gold mosaic work. The treasury itself preserves the wonderful Norman crown worn by Constance of Aragon, first wife to Frederick II. Made in 1210, it's more a jewel-encrusted golden cap than a crown, a gossamer-fine filigree intricately worked and studded with gems.

## The Royal Tombs

At the back of the church in the south aisle are six royal tombs, the resting places of the Norman dynasty. Here lie buried Roger II (died 1154) and his daughter Constance (died 1198), Constance's husband, the Emperor Henry VI Hohenstaufen (died 1197) and their son, Frederick II (died 1250), a king so powerful he was known as Stupor Mundi, "the marvel of the world". Henry and Frederick lie in Roman sarcophagi, stolen by Frederick from Cefalù. These tombs are all set below *baldachini* supported by delicate columns decorated with bright strands of mosaic work. It's thought provoking to envisage the travels and lives of these rulers who came south from northern Europe and established one of the greatest of early medieval kingdoms.

### TAKING A BREAK

Walk a couple of blocks behind the cathedral to Piazza Papireto, where you can sit outside to eat superb fish and seafood at **Trattoria Mafone** (€–€€); for a snack try **Bar Marocco** (€; Corso Vittorio Emanuele 494) – *pasticceria*, ice cream, *arancini* and pizza.

---

➕ 202 B2 ✉ Corso Vittorio Emanuele ☎ 091 334 373;
www.cattedrale.palermo.it 🕐 For worship: daily 7–7; for visitors: daily 9–5:30
💶 Interior free; royal tombs and treasury inexpensive 🚌 Tourist bus A, 102, 103, 104

### LA CATTEDRALE: INSIDE INFO

**In More Depth** The opulent chapel, protected by ornate brass gates, to the right of the choir is dedicated to Santa Rosalia, the patron saint of Palermo; a silver reliquary holds her bones, while the marble eagle above the entrance is the symbol of the city. Each year on 15 July, in remembrance of Palermo's delivery from the plague at her intercession, the saint's relics are carried in procession to mark the end of the five days celebration in her honour – *u fistinu*, the feast.

# 3 Palazzo dei Normanni and the Cappella Palatina

Standing on the highest point of the old city, the Palazzo dei Normanni (Norman Palace) was home to the magnificent courts of the Norman kings, from which they oversaw huge kingdoms. Their living quarters were designed to impress, but it's Roger II's intimate and jewel-like Cappella Palatina (Palace Chapel) that is Palermo's greatest treasure. Entirely covered with mosaics, it illustrates the riches of the Norman kingdom, the skill of its artists and the deep faith and religious tolerance of the age.

The Phoenicians were the first to spot the advantages of this site at the top of the city and built a fort here, which was then rebuilt by both Romans and Arabs. Roger II chose it as his chief residence, enlarging the building and constructing the Cappella Palatina. Alterations continued over the centuries, the long front facade being added by the Spanish rulers in the 17th century. The palace became the seat of the Sicilian Regional Parliament in 1947, since when only limited parts have been open to the public.

**The Palazzo dei Normanni was home to the Norman royal court**

## The Royal Apartments

The former Royal Apartments, on the top floor of the palace, were largely decorated in the 19th century. These sumptuous, but pedestrian, apartments include the Sala dei Viceré, lined with portraits of Sicily's viceroys from 1754 to 1837 and culminate in the star of the show – the Norman Sala di Re Ruggero (King Roger's Room), built by Roger II's son William I and decorated in 1140. This intimate chamber is covered with **secular mosaics** showing wonderfully fierce leopards and peacocks strutting beneath palm and orange trees, while armed centaurs and stags mirror each other. The detail is charming, with birds and beasts beautifully portrayed – look out for the rabbit cowering between the talons of a bird of prey in the ceiling. The marble decoration on the lower part of the walls and the floor is contemporary.

## The Cappella Palatina

The Cappella Palatina lies right at the heart of the palace, hidden from outside view by later construction. It was built by Roger II between 1132 and 1143 as his private chapel, where he could pray for the diverse inhabitants of his kingdom. Tolerant in the extreme, Roger ensured that he would be surrounded by art that brought to mind the chief

religions of his kingdom, commissioning Normans, Greeks and Arabs to work on the building. The **exquisite ceiling** is the work of Arab wood carvers, the **mosaics** were laid by both Greeks and Italians, Normans worked on the intricate carving of the pulpit and huge paschal candlestick, while Romans were responsible for inlaid pavements in the Cosmati style – common enough in early Roman churches, but unique this far south. Roger consulted theologians to determine the iconology of the mosaics, and scholars agree the design was planned to celebrate his monarchy and the power of the Holy Spirit and its transforming light.

Stepping into this entrancing space is like entering a magical jewel casket, where every surface shimmers with reflected light. The chapel is divided by antique columns into a nave and two side aisles, whose floor, and the lower part of the walls, is paved with white marble inlaid with red, green and gold. At the east end is the **sanctuary**, comprising three apses, each decorated with mosaics by

**Shining mosaic saint in the Cappella Palatina**

Byzantine masters. The central figure is a Christ Pantocrator; on his left, a Madonna and Child, on his right, a Nativity. These are surrounded by scenes from the New Testament, stories that were familiar to Roger and his court. The mosaics in the nave, the last to be carried out, show scenes from the Old Testament, and you'll notice the *Creation* and the *Building of the Ark* – the ark looking remarkably like a vessel from the cold, northern waters off Normandy. St Peter and St Paul appear in the scenes in the aisles. At the back of the nave, the dais, backed by a mosaic of *Christ with Sts Peter and Paul*, was Roger's vantage point for services. Don't miss examining the **candlestick**, carved to hold the Easter candle with more than a hundred intricate animals.

## San Giovanni degli Eremiti

Down the street from the exit to the Palazzo you'll find another of Roger's churches, **San Giovanni degli Eremiti**, whose five red cupolas are a symbol of the city. Set amidst romantic gardens planted with palm trees and jasmine, this little building was built between 1132 and 1148, making it exactly contemporary with the Cappella Palatina. No mosaics here, but a simple and satisfying interior, a delicious courtyard, an older structure that was once a mosque and a charming cloister.

San Giovanni degli Eremiti, with its exotic garden

### TAKING A BREAK

Walk through a courtyard just across from the Palazzo dei Normanni to the **Trattoria ai Normanni** (€–€€) at Piazza Vittoria 25 (tel: 091 651 6011), a friendly restaurant with a wide menu.

➕ 202 A2/A1 ✉ Piazza Indipendenza 1 ☎ 091 626 2833; www.federicosecondo.org 🕐 Mon–Sat 8:30–12, 2–5, Sun 8:30–12:30 💰 Expensive 🚌 Tourist bus A, 104, 105, 108, 304, 309

San Giovanni degli Eremiti
✉ Via dei Benedettini ☎ 091 651 5019 🕐 Mon–Sat 9–1, 3–7, Sun 9–1 💰 Moderate 🚌 Tourist bus A, 104, 105, 108, 304, 309

### PALAZZO DEI NORMANNI: INSIDE INFO

**Top Tips** The entrance is round the back of the palace on the left hand side; buy your ticket at the kiosk before ascending the ramp.
- The light changes constantly in the Cappella Palatina – mid-morning and late afternoon are good times to visit in summer.
- It's best to visit the Royal Apartments first, concentrating on the Sala di Re Ruggero (King Roger's room).

**In More Depth** You'll approach the palace interior up a fine staircase (1735), which leads to a loggia overlooking a late 16th-century courtyard. Look out for the pillar set into the wall of the loggia, inscribed in Greek, Latin and Arabic. It relates to a water clock built for Roger II in 1142, when accurate time pieces were rare. The Arabs were noted for their inventions and the clock was probably made in Fez.

# 4 Monreale

Set in the hills 8km (5 miles) southwest of Palermo and overlooking the sweep of the Conca d'Oro, the "golden valley" south of the city, stands the little town of Monreale, home to the artistically greatest of all the Norman religious foundations. The Duomo di Monreale (Monreale Cathedral), founded in 1174 by William II, contains the world's second-largest mosaic-covered surface, a marvellous pageant of glittering Byzantine images that tell the Christian story from the Creation and Fall of Man to his salvation through Christ's sacrifice on the Cross.

The world's finest mosaicists created these glittering scenes

Monreale owes its existence to William II's deep dislike of his ex-tutor, the powerful English Archbishop of Palermo, Walter of the Mill (➤ 50). A new archbishopric would be a counter-balance to Walter's ambitions, so, in 1174, William embarked on the building of a great new cathedral, which was to be administered by the Cluniac Benedictines, whose abbot, with the blessing of Pope Alexander III, would become its archbishop. No expense was spared, the vast expenditure being justified by William's insistence that it was funded by treasure whose whereabouts had been revealed to him in a dream by no less than the Virgin Mary herself. Builders and craftsmen were brought in to work on Santa Maria la Nuova – the New St Mary's – including squads of the world's greatest mosaicists, the Greek experts from Constantinople. Unsurprisingly, Walter was furious, retaliating with his own scheme to rebuild the cathedral in Palermo (➤ 50).

## The Cathedral

Walk round to the main entrance of the cathedral to admire the 46 panels of the beautiful **bronze doors**, created by Bonnano da Pisa in 1186, before taking in the smaller pair in the colonnade on the north side, which are by Barisano da Trani and date from 1179. From here, you can make your way to the back (down Via del Arcivescovado) to see the best of the exterior, the **three magnificent apses** with the interlaced

ogival arches so typical of
Arab-Norman work. Inside,
the mosaics are instantly
striking, but make a point of
taking in the antique columns
of the nave, the wonderful
Cosmatesque flooring in the
presbytery, and the thrones
destined for the King and
his archbishop. A mosaic
above his royal throne shows
William receiving the crown
of Sicily from Christ. The
thrones are flanked by marble
screens decorated with
griffons and lions.

## The Mosaics

The mosaics tell the story
of the **Old and New
Testaments**, themes that
would have been totally
familiar to 12th-century
congregations, who might
not have been able to read
and write, but who had a
good knowledge of the Bible. The huge figures in the apse
were almost certainly the work of Byzantine Greek masters
and show Christ Pantocrator looming in benediction over
the Virgin and ranks of the saints. One of these is Thomas
à Becket, the English martyr who had been murdered by
William's own father-in-law, Henry II of England, just a
few years previously. More mosaics line the nave like some
celestial strip cartoon, graphically illustrating the Testaments.
Here are the scenes from the Creation, Adam and Eve expelled
from Paradise, the animals entering Noah's Ark, Abraham
about to sacrifice his only son and, in the transepts, the whole
story of the life of Jesus, from the Annunciation of his birth
to his death on the Cross. The arches of the side transepts
show the martyrdom of saints Peter and Paul – an inverse
crucifixion for Peter and a beheading for Paul. The mosaics
on the back wall are later (13th century) and stylistically
show similarities with those in St Mark's in Venice, leading to
the scholarly theory that workmen may have been sent from
Venice to work at Monreale. Don't miss the exquisite marble
and mosaic dado beneath the mosaics, and you might want
to see the opulent reliquaries in the **treasury** before climbing
the 180 steps to the terrace and roof – an effort rewarded with
superb views to Palermo and the sea.

**Above: Detail
of the beautiful
bronze doors**

**Opposite:
Dazzling
apse mosaic
of Christ
Pantocrator**

## The Cloister

To the right of the cathedral, and reached through a separate
entrance, is the 12th-century cloister that once served the
Benedictine monks. Its arcades run round a central garden
planted with bay trees and olives, and its 228 twin columns,
often decorated with flashing mosaic work, are all different.

The capitals, the work of French masters from Burgundy, show scenes from everyday life, animals, birds and foliage, biblical scenes, monsters and classical themes – superbly imaginative work, whose liveliness contrasts with the formality of the mosaic scheme in the cathedral. The covered fountain in one corner is in the form of a palm tree and was used by the monks to wash their hands before entering the refectory for meals.

Peaceful and shady, the 12th-century cloister

### TAKING A BREAK

There are several cafés in Piazza Duomo, some with outside tables – **Bar Mirto** (on the corner), **Bar del Sole** and **Bar Italia** (all €) are recommended.

✚ 193 E5

**Duomo (Cathedral)**
✉ Piazza Duomo ☎ 091 640 4413
🕓 Duomo daily 8–6; Treasury daily 8:30–12:30, 3:30–6 💶 Duomo free; treasury and terrace moderate 🚍 389 (from Piazza Indipendenza)

**Cloister**
✉ Piazza Guglielmo il Buono ☎ 091 640 4403 🕓 Mon–Sat 9–12, 5:30–7:30, Sun 9–1:30 💶 Moderate 🚍 389 (from Piazza Indipendenza)

## MONREALE: INSIDE INFO

**Top Tips** If you're driving, take the ring road (*tangenziale*) round Palermo and follow the signs to Monreale; you'll need to keep a good look out as they are few and far between. Heading from the east, remember you can't turn left so will have to branch right and come back across the *tangenziale* to head towards Monreale.
■ You can leave your car in one of the manned car parks on the way in to Monreale; this is highly recommended as there is no parking anywhere around the cathedral.
■ Nervous drivers should on no account drive anywhere in Palermo; leave the car and come by bus or taxi.
■ Bring plenty of €1 coins to illuminate the mosaics.

**In More Depth** The mosaics cover 6,370sq m (7,618 square yards).
■ The figure of Chris Pantocrator in the main vault is more than 6.6m (22 feet) high.
■ 2,200kg (4,840 lb) of pure gold were used in the mosaics.
■ The columns in the Duomo came from a pagan temple, those in the cloister possibly from the sunken Roman city of Baia, near Naples.
■ The Cathedral was built between 1174 and 1183, an astonishingly short construction period in the Middle Ages.
■ William II is buried in the transept to the right of the choir.

# At Your Leisure

## 5 Museo Internazionale delle Marionette Antonio Pasqualino

Puppet theatre is a traditional Sicilian entertainment, and this fascinating museum, founded in 1975, not only preserves more than 3,500 puppets, but also stages shows – a great place to take the kids.

The wonderfully crafted handmade puppets, 80cm (31.5in) tall, fully articulated and dressed in rich costumes, represent the finest collection of marionettes in the entire world. Many of them are centuries-old antiques and others come from as far afield as Indonesia, India and other Far Eastern countries – some of those from the Orient are distinctly exotic and, some might say, quite naughty. The puppets often depict figures in shining armour who act out historical episodes, for example from the times of Charlemagne, King William the Bad, or swashbuckling Saracens, and complicated stories based on chivalry and the exploits of saints and bandits. The hero is frequently a character called Orlando, who single-handedly dispatches or slays the enemy on a stage awash with blood. The puppets even tackle the tragedies of William Shakespeare with aplomb.

The museum also displays scenery, posters and puppets from all over the world, including good old English Punch and Judy.

✚ 202 E2 ✉ Piazzetta Niscemi 5 (Via Butera) ☎ 091 328 060; www.museomarionettepalermo.it 🕐 Mon–Sat 9–1, 2:30–6:30 💲 Visits: free; shows: expensive 🍴 An outdoor bar on Piazza Marina overlooking the Giardini Garibaldi 🚌 Tourist bus A, 103, 105, 139, 824

## 6 Galleria Regionale della Sicilia

Palazzo Abatellis (1488), an elegant Catalan-Gothic Renaissance mix by the architect Matteo Carnilevari, stands on the historic Kalsa district's most important street. It's home to the Galleria Regionale Siciliana, Sicily's finest art collection and among the greatest galleries in all of Italy, where two floors are crammed with the cream of the island's medieval sculpture and painting.

The ground floor is mainly devoted to sculpture, but one of the first rooms contains the remarkable 15th-century *Triumph of Death*, probably by a Flemish painter. Here you'll see a skeletal Death on his ghostly horse riding through trampled bodies as he approaches those as yet unaware of their fate. They hunt, play music and chat, and only the poor seem aware of his presence. Things are calmer in room 4, where Francesco Laurana's serene portrait *Bust of Eleonora d'Aragona* is displayed, a wonderfully natural image of this member of the ruling family.

Upstairs, there's a fine and representative collection of early Sicilian art, including 13th- and 14th-century works that clearly show a Byzantine influence. Pick of the bunch on this level is Antonello da Messina's superb *Annunciation* (1476), which shows the Virgin meditative and calm on hearing the news she is to be the Mother of God, her right hand raised in acknowledgment to

**Traditional Sicilian puppets**

the angel Gabriel, outside our range of vision. To see these heavenly messengers, move on to admire Flemish artist Mabuse's *Malvagna Triptych*, with the Virgin surrounded by angelic musicians.

🚩 202 E1  ✉ Via Alloro 4  ☎ 091 623 0011; www.regione.sicilia.it/beniculturali  🕐 Mon, Fri–Sun 9–1, Tue–Thu 9–1, 2:30–7  💰 Expensive  🍴 Trattoria Stella, Via Alloro 104 has tables in a courtyard  🚌 Tourist bus A, 103, 105, 139

## ❼ Mercato della Vucciria

Next to the church of San Antonio steps lead down to the Vucciria, Palermo's oldest and most ebullient market. Its very name is based on the local dialect word *vicciria*, which means "voices" or "hubbub" – and a hubbub it certainly is in the labyrinth of tight alleyways and side streets around the Piazza San Domenica. Daily there are dozens of stalls, where traders bellow their wares beneath strings of bare light bulbs. Crowds jostle to buy tuna and swordfish steaks carved from monster fish, live eels and shellfish, drippingly ripe fruit and super-fresh vegetables, sausages and eerily contorted brains, tripe and intestines. Vendors cram goods into baskets, split and fill *pannini* to eat as you go, all the while exchanging banter and insults in equal measure. Elsewhere you'll find a vast assortment of non-edibles – counterfeit designer bags, smuggled cigarettes, pirated DVDs and CDs, alarmingly vibrant sweaters and underwear and classic-design coffee makers and kitchen utensils. Come early to experience the full frenzy, or around lunch time when things quieten down and you can wander at leisure.

🚩 202 D2  🕐 Daily dawn–2  🍴 Bars and food stalls in market  🚌 Tourist bus A, 101, 102, 103, 104

## ❽ Museo Archeologico Regionale

An ex-convent houses Palermo's Museo Archeologico Regionale, one of the best in Italy and pretty much essential viewing if you're planning to visit the great archaeological sites in western Sicily. Most of the principal treasures are on the ground floor, and you'll access them via the cloisters, which now display finds from the seabed and Roman sculpture. Among the prize exhibits is the Pietra di Palermo (Palermo Stone), which is accorded the distinction of being referred to as the Rosetta Stone of Sicily. Discovered in Egypt in the 19th century and dating back to 2700BC, it is carved with hieroglyphics detailing

**A tempting array of fruits for sale at Vucciria market**

**Statues of naked nymphs decorate the huge Fontana Pretoria in Piazza Pretoria**

information about the Pharaohs –
and, like the Rosetta Stone, was a
means of breaking the Enigma-style
code to understanding the secrets of
Egypt's fascinating past.

Off the back cloister you'll find
superb Greek pieces, including a
massive Gorgon's head from Selinunte
(➤ 153) and 19 snarling lion's-head
waterspouts from Himera. Beyond
these is a magnificent collection of
*metopes* (stone reliefs set above a
Doric Greek temple) from Selinunte,
beautiful examples that range from
exuberant storytelling to the serenity
and idealized beauty of the classical
age (fifth century BC). These contrast
with the fine Etruscan collection,
full of life – look out for the alabaster
funerary urns, which show the
deceased enjoying a banquet in
the afterlife.

Upstairs, there's a dauntingly large
array of terracotta votive offerings
and some exceptional Hellenistic
pieces, including a bronze ram from
Siracusa (➤ 96) and fragments of
the Parthenon frieze. Upstairs again
are some superb Roman mosaics,
excavated in the heart of Palermo.

✚ 202 D3 ✉ Piazza all'Olivella 24
☎ 091 611 6805; www.regione.sicilia.it/
beniculturali/salinas ⏰ Tue–Fri 8:30–1:30,
3–6:30, Sat–Sun 8:30–1:30 💶 Moderate

🍴 Try one of the bars on Piazza Verdi
🚌 Tourist bus A, 101, 102, 103, 104

## 9 Quattro Canti and Piazza Pretoria

Right at the heart of Palermo, where
16th-century Via Maqueda intersects
the ancient line of Corso Vittorio
Emanuele, are the Quattro Canti, the
Four Corners, an iconic crossroads
decorated with three-storey facade
screens. These were commissioned in
1611 and are adorned with fountains,
allegories of the four seasons and the
patrons of the four city quarters that
meet here – the Kalsa, the Amalfitani,
the Sincaldo and the Albergheria.
It was a beautiful meeting place for
the citizens – today, you take your
life in your hands if you as much as
step off the pavement. But head east
a few steps and you'll come to Piazza
Pretoria, home to the Municipio (City
Hall), housed in the 15th-century
Palazzo Pretorio. In front looms the
Fontana Pretoria, an over-the-top
fountain that's locally known as
Fontana della Vergogna ("of shame").
The fountain –133m (436 feet) in
circumference and 12m (40 feet) high
– was the work of two Florentine
Mannerists, Francesco Camillani and
Angelo Vagherino in 1544–55. It
was originally designed for an estate

**The mummified bodies in the Catacombe dei Cappuccini are not to everyone's taste**

belonging to the viceroy, Don Pietra de Toldeo, but when he decided he didn't want it, Palermo city council stepped in to buy it for its present site. Examination of the flagrant nudity of its nymphs will be all the explanation you'll need for how it earned its sobriquet.

✚ 202 C2 ✉ Quattro Canti, Piazza Pretoria
🚍 Tourist bus A, 101, 102, 103, 104

## 🔟 Catacombe dei Cappuccini

The Capuchin monks have a long tradition of preserving and displaying the remains of their dead, either as bones artistically arranged, or by embalming the body. In the 16th century they used the catacombs beneath their church on the outskirts of Palermo to do just this, and it wasn't long before lay people were clamouring for the same process. You can see the result today – more than 8,000 bodies dating from the 16th to the early years of the 20th centuries. Bodies were preserved by a variety of chemical and drying processes and then, dressed in clothes chosen before death, allocated a niche or wall space in the underground corridors.

Bodies in the Catacombe are located according to the social standing of the deceased, but they are also divided into further groups by gender, age and profession, for example soldiers or priests. Many

were famous in their day, and it is said that they include the Spanish painter Diego Velazquez, although his body is not signposted.

The sight is macabre in the extreme, but there's poignancy too, in the sheer numbers of babies and young children who died in infancy. Saddest of all is two-year-old Rosalia Lombardo, perfectly preserved to look as though she is sleeping by a secret embalming process in 1920 – the doctor took the secret of the process with him to his own grave.

🔢 202 off A2 ✉ Via Cappuccini 1 ☎ 091 212 117 🕐 Daily 9–12, 3–5:30 💷 Inexpensive
🍴 Bars nearby on Via Cappuccini 🚌 327

## ⑪ Mondello and Monte Pellegrino

Escape the heat and noise of Palermo by heading the 11km (6.8 miles) round the looming bulk of Monte Pellegrino to the long, curving sandy beach of Mondello. Packed every weekend until late, Mondello has all the necessities for a lazy beach day – clean sand, clear sea and a plethora of beachside restaurants. Join the evening *passeggiata* – one of the liveliest in Sicily – before heading for one of the open-air discos. If you're driving, head back via the Santuario di Santa Rosalia, high on the slopes of Monte Pellegrino. Patron saint of Palermo, Rosalia (1132–66) was a niece of William II who renounced the world and fled to the mountain in 1159. Her relics were found in a cave in 1624 and promptly saw off a plague outbreak. The cave is now her shrine, complete with sacred waters and a statue of the saint. You can ramble further up Pellegrino to the huge statue of the saint on the cliff's edge – from where the views are stupendous.

🔢 193 E5 🚌 806, 833 (833 in summer only) to Mondello; 812 to Monte Pellegrino

### FOR KIDS

Palermo's pretty tough on small kids, but if you've got older children it's a fascinating place, probably unlike any other city they will have visited, and they'll enjoy watching the street life, browsing in the Vucciria and eating copious amounts of ice cream. On the culture front, the mosaics in the **Cappella Palatina** and at Monreale could be a hit, and the **Catacombe dei Cappuccini** are enthralling. If the city gets them down, head out for a beach day at **Mondello** or take them to let off steam for a few hours in the **Parco della Favorita**.

**View over the beautiful crescent bay of Mondello**

# Where to... Stay

## Prices

Expect to pay per double room per night

€ under €130   €€ €130–€230   €€€ over €230

## Centrale Palace €€€

The Palazzo Tarallo, right on the main Corso and a couple of minutes walk from the Cathedral, is home to one of Palermo's most luxurious hotels. Walk in and find yourself surrounded by frescoes, stucco work, thick carpets and deferential service – the bedrooms, by contrast, are far simpler and veer towards the streamlined. Bathrooms are sumptuous with deep tubs, there's WiFi access throughout the hotel and a wonderful roof garden for breakfast or a drink. The restaurant, though expensive, is well worth sampling for delicious food and service of the highest order.

🚇 202 B2 🖂 Corso Vittorio Emanuele 327
📞 091 336 666; www.centralepalacehotel.it

## Grand Hotel Piazza Borsa €€

This very stylish, well-placed hotel in the heart of Palermo has decor and quality of service that belies its four-star rating and reasonable price range. The hotel, opened in 2010, was created by the merger of three buildings. The central part of the structure was a 16th-century convent and the church of the Mercedarian Fathers, and the hotel lobby is bordered by the original cloisters.

🚇 202 D2 🖂 Via dei Cartari 18 📞 091 320 075; www.piazzaborsa.com

## Hilton Villa Igeia €€–€€€

If you want somewhere a little out of town, the beautiful Villa Igeia is the solution. This art nouveau building, set in lovely gardens on the sea, was originally built as a sanatorium and was converted into a luxury hotel by the famous Liberty architect Ernesto Basile in 1900. Today, it's part of the Hilton group, but manages to retain the elegance of its period, with superb public areas and wonderfully comfortable rooms and suites. The restaurant, the Belle Epoque, deserves its reputation for light Mediterranean-style cuisine with the accent on fish. You'll find a lovely pool and tennis court in the grounds. It's worth checking hotel booking websites for a reduced rate.

🚇 202 off E2 🖂 Salita Belmonte 43
📞 091 631 2111; www.hilton.com

## Hotel Gallery House €€

Just a few minutes walk from the Teatro Massimo, in the 19th-century area of town, this small, comfortable hotel has beautifully furnished rooms equipped with all mod cons, including satellite TV and WiFi. The decor throughout is warm, with reds and ochres predominating; nice touches include comfortable seating in the bedrooms, antique rugs and exceptional service. The junior suites have kitchenettes, and the hotel's own website is worth checking out for special offers.

🚇 202 C3 🖂 Via Mariano Stabile 136
📞 091 612 4758; www.hotelgalleryhouse.com

## Jolly Hotel del Foro Italico €–€€

Overlooking the sea and a stone's throw from the Botanic Gardens, this large hotel, part of one of Italy's most reliable chains, may be big and bland, but the position is great, and rooms are more than adequate and there's the bonus of a swimming pool in the heart of town. There's a good restaurant, and the friendly, English-speaking staff will rent you a bicycle. Recommended for its position, facilities and good value.

**➕ 202 E1** ✉ Foro Italico 22 ☎ 091 616 5090; www.jollyhotels.it

### Letizia €–€€

A pretty little hotel, set on a side street near the Piazza Marina, the Letizia has a wide range of comfortable rooms, some of which have balconies or a tiny courtyard. All the rooms have air conditioning, parquet flooring and good storage space, and the breakfast, aimed squarely at visiting foreigners, is served in a light and airy room, furnished, like the bar and sitting room, with antique pieces and attractive rugs.

**➕ 202 D1** ✉ Via Bottai 30 ☎ 091 589 110; www.hotelletizia.com

### Massimo Plaza €€€

A fine old Liberty building opposite the Teatro Massimo houses this small, comfortable hotel, renovated a few years ago as part of Palermo's ongoing drive to restore its historic buildings. The large, elegant rooms all have parquet flooring and excellent bathrooms and are soundproofed, a definite bonus in this busy area. The public rooms have plenty of comfortable seating to relax in and a pleasant bar. There is also off-site covered parking.

**➕ 202 C3** ✉ Via Maqueda 437 ☎ 091 325 657; www.massimoplazahotel.com

### Posta €

The Posta, set at the north end of Via Roma, opened its doors in 1921 and is still run by the same family today. It's always been popular with musicians and actors on tour, who appreciate its cosy public areas and cool, uncluttered rooms, not to mention the excellent value for money it represents. There is a private garage, which is useful if you are renting a car.

**➕ 202 D3** ✉ Via Gagini 77 ☎ 091 587 338; www.hotelpostapalermo.it

### Vecchio Borgo €€

This comfortable hotel is perfectly situated between historic and "new" Palermo, just off Piazza Politeama. It's light and airy, and the high-ceilinged rooms are plain and well-equipped, their style coming from the pretty fabrics used for the soft furnishings. Expect huge marble bathrooms with robes and fluffy towels, a good breakfast and convenient situation – all in all an excellent choice.

**➕ 202 off C3** ✉ Via Quintino Sella 1–7 ☎ 091 611 8330; www.hotelvecchioborgo.eu

### Carrubella Park €

Hotels in the Catena del Sole chain, a group of independently, family-run hotels, are always worth checking out, and the Carrubella is no exception. Just 1km (0.6 miles) from Monreale and 9km (5.5 miles) from central Palermo, it's set up in the hills with spectacular views towards the city and sea. Rooms are spacious, clean and comfortable, the breakfast buffet is generous if unexciting, and the friendliness of the staff a major bonus – excellent all-round value.

**➕ 193 E5** ✉ Via Umberto 233, Monreale ☎ 091 640 2187; www.carrubellaparkhotel.com

### Addaura €€

Don't be put off by the rather severe and bulky architecture of this waterfront hotel – it's a great find, with two pools, all manner of water sports, plenty of outdoor space and a garden and a fine restaurant. The tastefully furnished rooms nearly all have sea views and balconies and there's the option of the Residence, self-catering mini-apartments for two to six people. Book ahead if you are planning to stay between June and September.

**➕ 193 E5** ✉ Lungomare Cristoforo Colombo 4452, Mondello ☎ 091 684 2222; www.addaura.it

# Where to...
# Eat and Drink

## Prices

Expect to pay per person for a meal, including wine and service

€ under €20     €€ €20–€35     €€€ over €35

## PALERMO

### Al Cancelletto Verde €€

Typical Sicilian fare is on offer in a restaurant where the colourful surroundings are as authentically Sicilian as the diligently prepared food. Sicilian carts, hand-painted puppets and many other decorous touches complement the varied menu, which includes favourites such as the Palermitan classic *pasta alle sarde*, pasta with sardines, fennel, anchovies and pine nuts, and *penne alla Norma*. In summer you can dine outside under the delightful gazebo.

🚹 202 D3 (off map) 🖂 Via R Wagner 14
🕿 091 320 537; www.alcancellettoverde.it
🕘 Daily 12–3, 7–midnight

### Al Covo dei Beati Paoli €€

Piazza Marina is a lovely place to eat and this is a good choice – a restaurant, housed in a lofty 18th-century palazzo that overlooks the Giardini Garibaldi. Sit outside or in and take your time perusing the vast menu, where seafood and fish occupy pride of place – though there's plenty for carnivores as well.
🚹 202 D1 🖂 Piazza Marina 50 🕿 091 616
6634; www.alcovodeibeatipaoli.com 🕘 Daily
5pm–midnight

### Antica Foccaceria San Francesco €

Come to this long-established (1834) traditional eating place for the best pizzas and a great selection of traditional and tasty Palermitanan fast food – snacks such as *panelle* (chickpea fritters), *meusa* (grilled beef spleen) and *stigghiole* (stuffed intestines). More timid diners at the marble-topped tables can enjoy crisp pizza straight from the oven and other pastry-based snacks.
🚹 202 D1 🖂 Via Alessandro Paternostro 58
🕿 091 320 264; www.afst.it 🕘 Wed–Mon
11:30–3:30, 7:45–11

### Cappello €€

It takes a bit if tracking down, but this *pasticceria* near the Cathedral is considered to be Palermo's finest, with a vast range of superb pastries, cakes and sweetmeats made on the premises using the finest ingredients. Meringues, *cannoli*, *cassata*, profiteroles, rum Babas, traditional marzipan fruits and tarts are all here, and Cappello is particularly noted for its chocolate cakes and pastries.
🚹 202 A2 🖂 Via Colonna Rotta 68 🕿 091
489 601; www.pasticceriacappello.it 🕘 Tue–
Sun 8:30am–9pm

### Ilardo €

Palermo's most famous *gelateria* was founded in the 1880s and is still one of the top places to go – eat your *cono* (cone) or *coppa* (tub) while you walk through the gardens. There's a huge range of flavours of both true ice creams and water ices, and Ilardo is famous for its use of subtle flavourings, such as cinnamon, jasmine flowers and rose water – try at least three flavours.
🚹 202 E1 🖂 Foro Italico 11–12 🕿 091
616 4413 🕘 May–Sep daily 4–11pm
(earlier/later depending on trade)

### Le Tre Sorelle €€

The Three Sisters opened their restaurant in 1888, using produce from the nearby Capo market. The sisters are long dead, but the restaurant thrives and it's still one of the best places for true Palermo dishes, such as *pasta con le sarde* (pasta with sardines). Everything is still cooked with fresh ingredients from the market and the wine list is firmly Sicilian.

**+ 202 B3** ⊠ **Via Volturno 110**
☎ **091 585 960; www.ristorantisiciliani.it/letresorelle** ⏱ **Mon–Sat 12–2:30, 7:30–10**

## Osteria dei Vespri €€€

Once the coach house of the Palazzo Gangi, this elegant, laid-back restaurant sheds new light on what's happening to Sicilian cooking in the 21st century. All the old ingredients and combinations are here, but served up with a new twist – light and stylish plates of intensely flavoured ingredients. Try the varied tasting menu, combining it with a fine wine from the list, which includes more than 220 reds and 130 whites from all over the world.

**+ 202 D1** ⊠ **Piazza Croce dei Vespri 6**
☎ **091 617 1631; www.osteradeivespri.it**
⏱ **Mon–Sat 12–2:30, 7:30–10:30**

## Ristorante Ai Vecchietti di Minchiapitito €€

A great welcome awaits visitors to this taverna, and it's all the more fun if there's a special local celebration, such as a local saint's day. There are good, traditional Sicilian dishes on offer, including set-price menus accompanied by water, wine and coffee.

**+ 202 C3 (off map)** ⊠ **Piazza Sant'Oliva 10** ☎ **091 585 606; www.aivecchiettidiminchiapitito.com**
⏱ **Daily noon–midnight**

## Stella €€

The one-time Hotel Patria is now home to an immensely popular restaurant that is a wonderful place for alfresco dining. Sit in the crumbling courtyard, surrounded by the scent of jasmine, and enjoy good traditional Sicilian cooking. There is also a full range of *pizze* – and if you've had a surfeit of fish the grilled meat dishes are also excellent. Try the *sarde a beccafico*, sardines stuffed with spiced

breadcrumbs and rolled up to resemble a warbler bird (*beccafico*).

**+ 202 E1** ⊠ **Via Alloro 104** ☎ **091 616 1136** ⏱ **Jul–Sep Mon–Sat 12–2:30, 7:30–1:30, Sun 12–2:30; Oct–Jun Tue–Sun 12–2:30, 7:30–10:30, Mon 12–2:30**

## MONREALE

## Taverna del Pavone €€

The Pupellas started their restaurant in 1969 and today's owners are the second generation to follow the family maxim of genuine, no-frills cooking, excellent service and a warm welcome. Sit inside in the cool, vaulted dining room, or out, and choose from a range of classic Sicilian and well-crafted specialities, with *primi* such as *caponata*, *sarde a beccafico* and *pasta alla Norma* and *secondi* that include meat and fish dishes. Take your time perusing the very full Sicilian wine list.

**+ 193 E5** ⊠ **Vicolo Pensato 18** ☎ **091 640 6209; www.tavernadelpavone.it**
⏱ **Tue–Sun daily 12–2:30, 7:30–10. Closed 2 weeks in Aug**

## MONDELLO

## Charleston €€€

Right in the middle of the *lungomare* at Mondello, an extraordinary art nouveau fairytale palace, adorned with mythical sea creatures, juts out over the sea. This is home to the Charleston, one of Sicily's most famous restaurants, where the accent is naturally enough on fish. Chef Angelo Ingrao is the latest in a line of masters, dating back to 1913, who have made their mark here – expect subtle pasta dishes, the freshest of fish, a fine cheese selection from all over Sicily and desserts to die for; the *cassata* and almond *semifreddo* are deservedly famous. The restaurant offers a tasting menu and has an exceptional wine list. Book well in advance.

**+ 193 E5** ⊠ **Viale Regina Elena** ☎ **091 450 171; www.ristorantitaliani.it/charleston**
⏱ **May–Oct daily 12–2:30, 7:30–10:30; Nov–Apr Thu–Tue 12–2:30, 7:30–10:30. Closed 2–3 weeks Jan–Feb**

# Where to...
## Shop

Palermo has very definite shopping areas; you'll find a good selection of mid-range shops along the **Corso Vittorio Emanuele** and down Via Roma, while the big designer names are on and around the **Viale della Libertà**, the other side of Piazza Politeama. For serious shopping head to "new" Palermo, north of Corso Vittorio Emanuele, bearing in mind that if you're looking for artisan work, there are some good shops around the cathedral – **Sicily's Folk** (Corso Vittorio Emanuele 450, tel: 091 651 2787) sells wonderful hand-carved figures. Near here is **Pantaleone** (Corso Vittorio Emanuele 293–295, tel: 091 584 093; www.pantaleone. com), a unique store specializing in religious items. There's plenty of eccentricity at **Carnevalissimo**

(Via Volturno 30, tel: 091 585 787; www.carnevalissimo.it), a huge store that's devoted entirely to costumes.

For other gifts, be sure to take in Palermo's **street markets**. The best general markets are the **Vucciria** (▶ 60), the **Capo** (▶ 166), and the **Ballarò** (between Piazza del Carmine and Piazza Ballarò) – you could also visit the **Mercatino delle Pulci** (flea market) near the Cathedral.

If you're a cheese-lover, head a little way out of town for **Cambria** (Via Liguria 91, tel: 091 517 791), which stocks more than 100 cheeses from all over Sicily and mainland Italy, as well as cold meats, oils and pasta. Specialities include pecorino and mountain cheeses from the Madonie mountains.

# Where to...
## Be Entertained

As Sicily's capital, Palermo offers plenty to occupy your evenings. The quintessential experience would be a puppet show (▶ 59); try the **Museo delle Marionette** or check out **Figli d'Arte Cuticchio** (Via Bara all'Olivella 95, tel: 091 323 400; www.figlidartecuticchio. com) for weekend performances. Palermo's theatres, unsurprisingly, feature Italian plays, but you could take in an **opera or ballet** in the magnificent surroundings of the **Teatro Massimo** (Piazza Verdi, tel: 091 589 575; www.teatromassimo. it) or a **concert** at the **Teatro Politeama Garibaldi** (Piazza Ruggero Settimo, tel: 091 675 9511; www.orchestrasinfonicasiciliana.it). You'll find listings for performances and films at the city's cinemas in the daily *Il Giornale di Sicilia*.

June–September sees the **Kalsart Festival** (www.kalsart.it), a huge festival of dance, music, theatre and cinema in the Kalsa area. Summer, too, sees Palermo's biggest *festa*, **U Fistinu di Santa Rosalia** (mid-July), when the whole city parties non-stop in honour of its patron saint.

If you're looking for club and bar **nightlife**, you'll have to head north. In summer, the action centres round **Mondello** (▶ 63), or you could head for the current **Viale della Libertà** for the fashionable bars with a classy edge. Alternatively, head for **Via Mazzini** and **Via Principe di Belmonte**, two pedestrianized streets with plenty of outdoor bars to sample – perfect for a relaxing drink or two and some people-watching.

# Mount Etna and the Northeast Coast

# Getting Your Bearings

Northeast Sicily is dominated by the brooding mass of Mount Etna, the smouldering giant that's Europe's most active volcano. At 3,329m (10,919 feet) it covers a huge area, and you'll be aware of its presence wherever you travel in this part of Sicily. Dazzling in the sun, and trailing its signature plume of smoke, at other times, with clouds wreathing its summit, it can appear sinister and menacing, a constant reminder of the appalling powers of death and destruction it holds.

Etna's lower slopes are fertile beyond measure, planted with vines and olives and watered by rivers and streams like the Alcàntara, whose gorge provides summertime cool greenery and freshwater bathing. Near here lies picture postcard-perfect Taormina, queen of the string of villages and pretty resorts along the beautiful, rocky coastline that borders the Ionian Sea and runs north to Messina, a sprawling, largely modern city that's the jumping-off point for the Italian mainland.

North of here, the coast turns a corner westwards, and fast motorways will carry you past bustling fishing ports like Milazzo, atmospheric classical sites such as Tyndaris, looming above the sea on its steep promontory, and hard-working towns like Santo Stefano di Camastra, where artisan masters produce some of Sicily's most colourful ceramics. Inland from these coastal settlements rise the mountains of the Nebrodi and Madonie, ridge upon ridge of blue hills scattered with mountain villages and rich in flowers, birds and animals. The Madonie tumble down to the sea at Cefalù, one of the most beguiling of Sicily's coastal towns, where a Norman cathedral stands guard over the huddled streets and salty fishing port of the old town, while shining sands and clean waters entice summer visitors.

**Page 69: Mount Etna seen from Taormina**
**Right: Sheep grazing in the Madonie Natural Park**

*Map showing:*
**Cefalù** ❶
Capo Plaia
Capo Raisigerbi
**Santo Stefano di Camastra** ❺
A20
Pollina
Tusa
Mistretta
Castelbuono
A19
SS286
Nebrodi
**PALERMO**
*Parco Regionale delle Madonie*
SS117
SS120
**Petralia Soprana** ❹
Gangi
SS120
Nicosia
Cerami
Salso
A19
SS290
SS117
Leonforte
Agira
Lago Nicoletti
SS121
SS121
A19

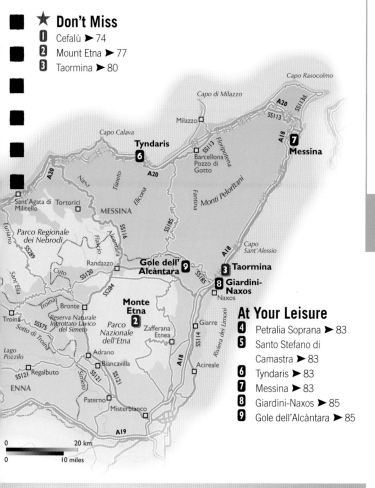

### ★ Don't Miss

Capo Rasocolmo

Capo di Milazzo

A20 · SS113d

Milazzo

SS113

Capo Calava

**Tyndaris** **6**

SS113

A20

Floripotenia

Barcellona
Pozzo di
Gotto

A18 · **7** **Messina**

Sant'Agata di
Militello · Tortorici

MESSINA

Naso · Tineto · Elicona · Fantina · Monti Peloritani

Furiano

*Parco Regionale
dei Nebrodi*

SS289 · Alcantara · Flascio · SS116

SS85

Capo
Sant'Alessio

Randazzo

**Gole dell'
Alcàntara** **9**

A18

**3** **Taormina**

Sant'Ella · Cuto · SS120 · SS284

SS185

**8** **Giardini-
Naxos**

Troina · Bronte

*Reserva Naturale
Ingrottato Lavico
del Simeto*

Naxos

**Monte
Etna** **2**

Sotto di Troina · SS75

*Parco
Nazionale
dell'Etna*

Zafferana
Etnea

Giarre

Lago
Pozzillo

Adrano · Biancavilla

SS121 · Regalbuto · Simeto · SS121 · SS121

A18

Acireale

Rivera dei Limoni

SS114

**ENNA**

Paternò

Misterbianco

A19

### At Your Leisure

0 ————— 20 km
0 ————— 10 miles

# In Four Days

If you're not quite sure where to begin your travels, this itinerary recommends four practical and enjoyable days out around Mount Etna and the northeast coast, taking in some of the best places to see using the Getting Your Bearings map on the previous page. For more information see the main entries.

# Day 1

## Morning
Start your exploration of **❶ Cefalù** (➤ 74) by heading down the **Corso Ruggero** to the **Duomo** (➤ 74), perhaps taking in the **Osteria Magno** (➤ 75) en route. From the cathedral, walk to the **Museo Mandralisca** (➤ 75), then take in the labyrinthine streets that surround the old harbour (above).

## Afternoon
From here, a stroll along the *lungomare* (promenade) is in order before an afternoon on the beach, with its limpid water, clean sands and great views back towards the town.

## Evening
If you're feeling energetic, you could climb the **Rocca** (➤ 76), or simply join the crowds along the Corso for the *passeggiata*.

# Day 2

## Morning

Head off to explore Cefalù's hinterland by taking a drive through the stunning **Madonie mountains** and villages, such as **4 Petralia Soprana** (right, ➤ 83). Alternatively, follow the coastline to browse for ceramics at **5 Santo Stefano di Camastra** (➤ 83).

## Afternoon and Evening

Have a bathe in the warm afternoon sunshine before heading back to Cefalù and enjoying a laid-back evening.

# Day 3

## Morning

An early start and the *autostrada* via **7 Messina** (➤ 84) will get you to **3 Taormina** (➤ 80) by the early afternoon.

## Afternoon

Visit the **Teatro Greco** (➤ 80), before taking your time strolling through town, being sure to take in the *passeggiata* along the **Corso Umberto I** (➤ 81), the views from **Piazza IX Aprile** and the **Villa Comunale** (below, ➤ 82).

## Evening

Time for dinner before hitting one of the bars or, if the season's right, taking in an outdoor performance at the Teatro Greco.

# Day 4

## Morning

Leave Taormina to drive through **8 Giardini-Naxos** (➤ 85) and head for a day on **2 Mount Etna**. If you're planning a trip to the crater (➤ 78), you'll need to make an early start.

## Afternoon

If you've done enough driving, you might want to see more of Etna's slopes by enjoying a trip on the **Circumetnea railway** (➤ 78); alternatively, you could head up the **9 Gole dell'Alcàntara** (➤ 85).

# 0 Cefalù

Cefalù encapsulates much of the best of Sicily – a beautiful coastal position beneath the great crag of La Rocca, a warren of medieval streets lined with fine palazzi, sandy beaches, good restaurants and tempting shops. Factor in its rich history, embodied by its superb cathedral and excellent museum, and it's easy to see how it's earned its reputation as one of Sicily's loveliest resort towns.

Cefalù is ancient indeed, first inhabited in the ninth century BC and named Kephaloidion, hence modern Cefalù, by the Greeks in the fourth century BC. The original inhabitants fled to the upper slopes under Byzantine and Arab rule, but came back down in 1131, when the Norman king Roger II erected his great cathedral and rebuilt the town by the sea. Since then it's thrived, and today, its winning combination of culture and seaside pleasures pulls in all kinds of visitors.

### The Duomo
Tight against the soaring mass of La Rocca, the twin towers of the Duomo rise above the huddled roofs of the old town, dominating the expanse of the main piazza, an elegant space shaded by palm trees. Building started in 1131, when Roger envisioned a great new cathedral as his burial place, but it was still unfinished when he died in 1154 and the church remained unconsecrated until 1267. It occupies a Roman

Old town
buildings line
the harbour
shore

site, and its interior includes 16 Roman columns, probably taken from the Temple of Diana, whose ruins still stand on the Rocca above. Climb the steps leading to the **facade** to take in the soaring towers and serene Norman-Arab arches before entering the cool, dark interior. You'll find yourself in one of Sicily's most perfect Norman churches – dignified, plain and intensely spiritual in atmosphere. At the east end glitter the mosaics of the presbytery, the earliest and best-preserved in Sicily, planned by Roger and executed by Greek craftsmen from Constantinople. The huge figure of **Christ Pantocrator**, holding an open book of biblical texts, dominates the decorative scheme, a wise and benevolent Christ radiating compassion for mankind. Below him, three tiers of figures include the Virgin, archangels, Apostles, saints, prophets and theologians, all attended by angels and seraphim. This beautiful ensemble was completed in 1148 – look for the plaque beneath the window with the date. The Duomo's 13th-century ceiling is in wonderful contrast to the modern stained-glass windows high above the nave.

## The Old Town

The streets of old Cefalù surround the Duomo, with Corso Ruggero, the main drag, running straight down towards the **old harbour**, where small boats are pulled up on the beach and fishermen still mend nets in shadowy rooms along the narrow alleys. It's worth dawdling through these ancient streets, inhabited for centuries – there's proof of this in the shape of the *lavatoio*, an Arab wash house used up until the 1980s.

One of these medieval lanes is home to the **Museo Mandralisca**, a remarkably fine museum for a town this size. The collection was bequeathed to the town by the Baron

Mandralisca (1806–64) and is housed in his old home. It includes Greek and Roman archaeological finds, coins and shells, but the chief treasure is the *Portrait of an Unkown Man* by the Sicilian master Antonello da Messina (*c.*1465–72), a superb Renaissance portrait. Mandralisca found the painting on the island of Lipari, where it was being used as a cupboard door; the sitter, with his enigmatic smile, has never been identified. Walk back up the Corso Ruggero and you'll pass some fine old buildings, including the **Osteria Magno**, a medieval palace that's now used for concerts and exhibitions.

## La Rocca

Turn left off the Corso and the Vicolo dei Saraceni steps lead you to the path that runs up to the summit of La Rocca, where the Arabs had their stronghold until 1063. It will take you an hour or so to climb the 278m (912 feet) from Piazza Garibaldi to the summit and the so-called **Temple of Diana**, actually a mix of megalithic, Greek and Roman construction. The views over Cefalù and the coast are superb – bring plenty of water and time your ascent for the early morning or evening with their cooling breezes.

The Duomo watches over the old town of Cefalù

### TAKING A BREAK

Choose one of the restaurants or cafés (€€) in the **Piazza del Duomo** for an incomparable setting and some great people-watching.

➕ 195 D3 🛈 Corso Ruggero 77; tel: 0921 421 050; www.cefalu-tour.pa.it; www.cefaluinforma.it; Mon–Sat 8–8

### Duomo

✉ Piazza del Duomo ☎ 0921 922 921 🕐 Daily 8–12, 3:30–7; cloister daily 10–1, 3–4 💷 Free

### Museo Mandralisca

✉ Via Mandralisca 13 ☎ 0921 421 547; www. museomandralisca.it 🕐 Daily 9–1, 3–7 💷 Moderate

---

## CEFALÙ: INSIDE INFO

**Top Tips** Cefalù is an increasingly popular package-holiday destination, so try to avoid July and August; book ahead for accommodation any time during the summer.

■ Cover your upper arms and shoulders and don't wear shorts if you're visiting the Duomo or you may be turned away.

■ You'll find free beach access at the east end of the sands; for comfort, toilet and freshwater showers it's worth paying for a sunbed and umbrella at one of the *lidi*.

■ Palermo is less than an hour away by train from Cefalù, making it an easy day trip.

# ② Mount Etna

The brooding presence of Mount Etna, with its telltale plume of smoke, dominates eastern Sicily. Clear weather opens up views across the whole island and into Calabria from its upper slopes; at other times, days can pass when the summit remains shrouded in cloud. Its lower slopes are fertile, its woods dense, while at higher altitudes fields of lava trace the routes of its past eruptions. It's big, potentially dangerous and awe-inspiring, and deserves a day's exploration.

## Some Facts and Figures

Mount Etna (*c.*3,329m/10,919 feet) is the **highest volcano in Europe** and among the world's **most active**. The ancients called it Aetna and believed it was the site of Vulcan's forge; the Arabs named it Mongibello, the "mountain", still its Sicilian name. Throughout the centuries its eruptions have engulfed farmland, towns and the city of Catania itself, with lava flows reaching as far as the sea. Since 1800 there have been more than 60 eruptions, and vulcanologists agree that the main crater is becoming increasingly active. In July 2001 a series of complex explosions started on the southeast side, opening up 18 temporary craters that poured out fountains of fiery lava. In 2002 an earthquake triggered activity on both the north and south flanks, threatening the towns of Nicolosi and Linguaglossa and destroying much of the ski resort of Piano Provenzano. During both these eruptions bulldozers were used to build dykes and divert the flow and the damage was contained, but further eruptions are inevitable, the latest

**The summit of Mount Etna is often obscured by cloud**

of significance occurring in August 2010 (➤ 7). The whole area is a designated **regional park**, with a unique geology, flora and fauna, and its traditional farming and way of life are protected by law.

### Tackling Etna

For a quick and easy taste of Etna, hop on the **Circumetnea**, a private railway line that loops the 114km (71 miles) around the lower slopes of the volcano, taking in a string of little villages and giving some spectacular views of the mountain and its slopes. It runs through Randazzo, built entirely of lava and the closest town to the summit, and Linguaglossa, the main tourist centre on the north side.

For a closer view, take one of the routes around the northern and southeastern flanks, which are signposted Etna Sud and Etna Nord from the main coastal roads. The southern route, known as the Strada dell'Etna, was constructed in 1934 and runs through the little town of Nicolosi, a ski resort that's home to the Museo Vulcanologico Etneo (Via Cesare Battisti 32; Tue–Sun 9:30–12:30; free), which will fill you in on Etna's history and geology. From here, the road ascends through increasingly impressive lava fields to the **Rifugio Sapienza**. You can also get here by following the **Etna Nord route** through Linguaglossa and Zafferana Etnea, a pleasant hill town that attracts hordes of weekend walkers drawn to the trails on the wooded slopes.

From **Rifugio Sapienza**, some 1,400m (4,600 feet) below the summit, a cable-car runs further up the mountain, beyond which it's a two- to three-hour walk to the highest safe point. The best bet is to take one of the four-wheel-drive minibuses that run between April and October. Accompanied by a

**Etna's craters make a vast, lunar landscape**

guide, the vehicles negotiate the lava slopes up to the **Torre del Filósofo**, built to celebrate the Roman Emperor Hadrian's climb to the summit.

Beyond here, the southeast active crater of the summit is visible, dramatically spewing smoke; explosions and molten lava are common at this height. You'll take in the extraordinary lunar landscape of the upper slopes, a desolate expanse of gritty black, grey and red lava, punctuated by pockets of snow. At this height, you'll certainly hear volcanic rumblings and get a whiff of that distinctive, unforgettable sulphurous smell. The tour includes the **Valle del Bove**, a huge chasm almost 20km (12 miles) in circumference and 900m (2,950 feet) deep, which comprises almost a sixth of the surface of the volcano. There are some spectacular walks on the lower slopes, and even near the Rifugio itself you can scramble down the hardened lava slopes to explore some extinct craters.

*If you are planning to climb up to the summit, make sure you are properly equipped*

## TAKING A BREAK

There's a choice of bars and eateries at **Rifugio Sapienza** (€–€€); you can eat (and stay) in the Rifugio itself (tel: 095 915 321).

✚ 196 C2

### Etna Tourist Information Offices
**Randazzo**
✉ Via Umberto I 197 ☎ 095 799 1611; www.prg.it/parcodelletna (Italian only) 🕐 Daily 9–1, 3–7; visitor centre daily 10–8

### Nicolosi
✉ Via Etnea 107/A ☎ 959 14588; www.prg.it/parcodelletna (Italian only) 🕐 Mon–Fri 9–2, 4–7:30

### Linguaglossa
✉ Piazza Annunziata 5 ☎ 0956 43094; www.prolocolinguaglossa.it 🕐 Apr–Sep Mon–Sat 9–1, 4–8, Sun 9–1; Oct–Mar Mon–Tue, Thu, Sat 9–1, 3–6, Wed, Fri, Sun 9–1

## MOUNT ETNA: INSIDE INFO

**Top Tips** As the wind is always strong and the temperature often below freezing, wear a warm jacket, strong shoes, a hat and glasses to protect your eyes from flying grit and debris. You can rent boots and jackets from the minibus guides.

■ Visits to the summit are always subject to volcanic activity, and visibility is often obscured by cloud and the direction of the smoke.

■ If you're based in Taormina (▶ 80) contact SAT (Corso Umberto I 73, tel: 0942 24653) about tours up Etna.

■ Jeep trips to the upper slopes are also available from Piano Provenzano – allow around three hours.

# 3 Taormina

Set above the shining blue sea, backed by Mount Etna, home to a superbly set Greek theatre and an impossibly picturesque medieval core, Taormina is Sicily's best-known resort. It may be crowded and unashamedly given over to tourism, but its streets still retain their charm, the air is still scented with orange and lemon blossom and nothing can ever detract from its superb position. Whatever your reasons for visiting Sicily, take in Taormina, an idyllic town that still – just – retains its soul under the glitz and polish.

Founded in the fourth century BC, Tauromenium flourished under the Greeks and Romans, was destroyed by the Arabs in 902, rebuilt, taken by the Normans and prospered sufficiently to become the seat of the Sicilian Parliament in 1410. By the 18th century, the first tourists were arriving, and things took off in 1864 when the first hotel was built. Royalty and high society wintered here and the town boomed, only to be bombed in 1943, when Field-Marshal Kesselring made it his headquarters. By the 1950s, things were back on track, with the beautiful people flocking to Taormina – Cecil Beaton, Jean Cocteau, Salvador Dalí, Truman Capote and John Steinbeck all spent time here.

### Teatro Greco (Greek Theatre)

It's hard to imagine a more perfect backdrop for a theatre than here, where the audience can drink in views of the sea, the coasts of Calabria and Sicily and the snow-capped slopes

Mount Etna and Taormina town provide a stunning backdrop to the Greek Theatre

of Etna, a vista that surely puts paid to the theory that the Greeks built their theatres wherever it was most convenient. They built the Teatro Greco (Greek Theatre) here in the third century BC, but the Romans almost entirely rebuilt it in the first–third centuries, adding the *scena* (the columns and niches of the stage area) and digging a trench in the orchestra to hold the animals and fighters used for gladiatorial displays. You can walk freely around, puzzling out how the audience entered through the three arched gates, tracing the *proscenium* (stage) and the *parascenia* (wings), before scrambling up the *cavea* (seating) dug out of the hillside and famous for its acoustical properties – try to catch a **summer performance** here during the arts festival (➤ 90).

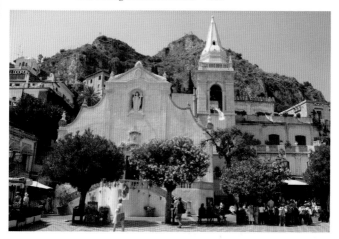

**The pretty church of San Giuseppe**

## Along and Around Corso Umberto I

From here, head through shady Piazza Vittorio Emanuele for the **Corso Umberto I**, Taormina's main street, which runs the length of the town. It's lined with 14th- and 15th-century palazzi, one of them, **Palazzo Corvaja**, home to the extremely quirky Museo d'Arte e Tradizioni Popolari (Tue–Sun 9–1, 4–8). Halfway along, the Corso widens out into Piazza IX Aprile, a beautiful open space that contains the churches of **Sant'Agostino** and **San Giuseppe** and offers superlative views and inviting cafés. Walk through the restored, 12th-century **Torre dell'Orologio** (clock tower), to continue down the oldest part of the street to the 13th-century **Duomo**, a charming building fronted by a pretty fountain. From here you can back-track through the alleys and stepped streets that surround the Corso – take your time, there's something of delight round every flower-festooned corner, including the **Naumachia**, an entire, late-Roman wall.

## Beaches and Parks

The 19th-century Brits loved Taormina, and it was a British gentlewoman, Florence Trevelyan, who, in 1899, created Taormina's lovely public gardens, signposted as the **Villa**

**Comunale**. Forced to leave Britain in a hurry after an affair with the Prince of Wales, the future Edward VII, she took solace in creating an enchanting green oasis that's packed with exotic year-round interest. There are views from the terrace down to the sea, and beach-lovers can take the **cable-car** down to Taormina's pretty coast. The nearest is Mazzarò, twin beaches where you can swim or simply admire the islet of Isola Bella.

Looking down on the tiny beach at Isola Bella

### TAKING A BREAK

If you don't have much time, head for **Terrazza Angelo** (€–€€; Corso Umberto I 38, tel: 0942 24411), a pizzeria and restaurant with two terraces right on the Corso and views down the hill.

➕ 197 E3 🏛 Palazzo Corvaja, Piazza Vittorio Emanuele; tel: 0942 23243; www.gate2taormina.com; Mon–Sat 8:30–2, 4–7

**Teatro Greco**
✉ Via Teatro Greco 📞 0942 23220
🕐 Apr–Oct daily 9–7; Nov–Mar 9–4:30
💶 Expensive

**Villa Comunale**
✉ Via Bagnoli Croce 📞 None
🕐 Summer daily 8–8; winter 8–dusk
💶 Free

**Cable-car**
✉ Via Pirandello 📞 0942 23906
🕐 Jun–Aug daily 8:30am–1am; Sep–May daily 8:30–8:15
💶 Inexpensive

### TAORMINA: INSIDE INFO

**Top Tips** If you're driving, you will be unable to take your car along the Corso Umberto I. Parking at the Parcheggio Lumbi, the main car park, is expensive (up to €20 per 24 hours), so it might be worth considering a hotel further down the hill or one with its own parking.

■ Book well ahead if you are coming in July and August, New Year or Easter.

■ Visit the Teatro Greco as early or late as possible to avoid the tour buses.

■ The best places for views of Etna and the coast are the Teatro Greco, Piazza IX Aprile and the belvedere just down the hill from Via Roma.

■ For budget travellers, Giardini-Naxos has plenty of accommodation and is linked to Taormina by half-hourly buses.

■ If you're based in Taormina, SAT (Corso Umberto I 73, tel: 0942 24653) runs bus excursions to Sicily's main sites, making it possible to visit Palermo, Monreale, Etna, Siracusa, Agrigento and Piazza Armerina.

# At Your Leisure

## ④ Petralia Soprana

Set at an altitude of 1,147m (3,670 feet) in Sicily's most densely wooded area, Petralia Soprana is the highest town in the Madonie mountains. Although attractively medieval in appearance, its origins go back to the third century BC, a thousand years before its neighbour, Petralia Sottana (➤ 178), which perches just below. It's a pretty town with spectacular views stretching as far as Mount Etna. The 14th-century church, Chiesa Madre, is ornately stuccoed, and inside you'll find one of the life-size wooden crucifixes carved by Fra Umile Pintorno (1580–1639), the village's most famous son. Too poor to work in marble, he made his name with these passionate works, found all over southern Italy.

✚ 195 D2

## ⑤ Santo Stefano di Camastra

Driving east from Cefalù, you can't miss Santo Stefano, whose streets are an unbroken line of colourful ceramic outlets. The local clay is high quality, prices are excellent and there's a huge range of styles, designs and objects to choose from, ranging from traditional to cutting-edge contemporary. This is one of Sicily's best places to buy pottery: browse in some of the dozens of showrooms that line the main street and alleys before you start to buy, and don't be afraid to haggle. If time is short, the shops on the main road through the village are a good bet; try Fratantoni Antonino, Franco Ceramiche or Fratelli Gerbino.

✚ 195 E3 ☎ www.comune. santostefanodicamastra.me.it
🍴 Restaurants and bars in town

## ⑥ Tyndaris

Founded in 396BC, the Greek settlement of Tyndaris (modern Tindari) continued to thrive under Roman rule, and much of the excavations on this beautiful site date from Roman times. Star turns include the partially restored fourth-century basilica, the vibrant mosaics in the bath complex, and two luxurious houses, one still retaining its atrium and *impluvium*, used to save water. Take these in before heading for the theatre, built in the late fourth century BC and adapted by the Romans for staging gladiatorial displays – the setting on the high promontory is dream-like, with the Aeolian islands lying to the north and views to Mount Etna on clear days. The theatre is the setting of an annual festival of classical drama, dance and music in July and August.

There are more lovely views from the Santuario di Tindari, an over-the-top shrine dedicated to the Madonna Nera (Black Madonna), a Byzantine icon of the Virgin. It's a major pilgrimage site, with all that implies – a plethora of ultra-kitsch religious souvenirs and some distinctly dodgy mosaics, frescoes and stained glass. It's especially popular on the Madonna's feast day (8 September), when there's a huge influx of pilgrims and a splendid carnival atmosphere.

✚ 196 C4

### Archaeological site

✉ Tindari ☎ 0941 369 023 🕐 Daily 9– 2 hours before dusk 💷 Inexpensive 🍴 Bar at Santuario

### Santuario di Tindari

✉ Tindari ☎ 0941 369 003; www.santuariotindari.it 🕐 Jul–Aug daily 6:45–12:30, 2:30–8; Sep–Jun 6:45–12:30, 2:30–7 💷 Free 🍴 Bar del Pellegrino

## ⑦ Messina

Ancient Messina, inhabited for nearly 3,000 years, overlooks the straits that divide Sicily from mainland Italy. It's a superb position, and the city's history owes much to its strategic importance. Greeks, Arabs and Normans all left their mark, but more

The view over the harbour from Messina's campanile

modern events are responsible for the look of the city today. Repeated earthquakes damaged the city over the years, most recently in 1908, when the coast sank by some 48cm (19in). It was largely rebuilt, only to be flattened by Allied bombers in World War II, when it became the most heavily bombed town in the whole of Italy. Modern Messina is very modern indeed.

Sicily's third largest city spreads around a sickle-shaped harbour, a stone's throw from the most important surviving medieval monument, the Duomo (cathedral). Since its construction by the Norman king Robert II in 1160, it's been heavily restored and is essentially a copy, incorporating elements of the original building. A late-Gothic portal pierces the Romanesque facade to the dim interior, complete with fine mosaics. The Treasury contains valuable reliquaries, including the Manta d'Oro (golden mantle) that covers the painting of the Madonna della Lettera, the city's patron saint. Outside, the splendid campanile (bell tower) houses one of world's largest astronomical clocks, complete with automata in the shape of a banner-waving lion that roars at noon, a cock that flaps it wings, and more besides. A good vantage point is from the

beautiful Fontana d'Orione, a fine Florentine Renaissance fountain in front of the cathedral.

From here, you could head north to Messina's suburbs, where you'll find the Museo Regionale, the province's main gallery and museum. Its chief treasures are two stunning masterpieces by Caravaggio, painted in 1609 while he was on the run from a murder charge. *The Raising of Lazarus*, emotionally dark and disturbing, is the perfect balance to the accomplished and seemingly simple *Adoration of the Shepherds*; both make a fine contrast with the museum's other treasure, the polyptych *Madonna Enthroned between Sts Benedict and Gregory*, painted in 1473 by Antonello di Messina, the city's home-grown artistic superstar.

➕ 197 F4 🛈 Via Calabria 301 (corner of Via T Capra); tel: 0906 40221; www.comune. messina.it (Italian only); Mon–Thu 9–1:30, 3–5; Fri 9–1:30

### Duomo
✉ Piazza del Duomo ☎ 0906 72179
🕐 Mon–Sat 8–6, Sun 7:30–1, 4–7:30; Treasury daily 9:30–1

### Museo Regionale
✉ Viale della Libertà 465 ☎ 0903 61292
🕐 Mon, Wed, Fri 9–1:30, Tue, Thu, Sat 9–12:30, 4–6:30, Sun 9–12:30 💶 Moderate

## 8 Giardini-Naxos

The beautiful sands and clear waters of Giardini-Naxos, Sicily's fastest-growing resort, draw thousands of visitors throughout the summer, who flock here for its modern hotels and beach life. It's the perfect place for a few days of sea and sun, with a wide choice of good accommodation and restaurants, and convenient transport links to historic Taormina (➤ 80). Giardini too, has its own fair share of history; it was the earliest Greek settlement on Sicily and got its name from the first arrivals, who came from the island of Naxos. They established their settlement on Capo Schisò in 735BC, and you can walk through the citrus groves to explore the excavations of this ancient city.

🔁 197 D3  ℹ️ Via Tysandros 54; tel: 0942 51010; www.aast-giardini.naxos.it; Mon–Fri 8:30–2, 4–7, Sat 8:30–2

## 9 Gole dell'Alcàntara

The lovely Alcàntara gorge runs inland just south of Taormina, a 19m-deep (62-foot) dramatic cleft carved by the river Alcàntara

The dramatic Alcàntara gorge

through the hardened basalt of one of Etna's ancient eruptions. It's a beautiful place, with clear water and extraordinary stone formations. You can best explore it by taking a lift down to the narrowest point, the Gola (throat), donning some protective clothing – the water's freezing – and scrambling along the river bed and in and out of the pools as far as the waterfall. Come in the summer, as in the winter the gorge is prone to flooding, and avoid Sundays, when it's heaving with locals.

🔁 197 D3  ☎️ Tours and information 0942 989 911/0942 985 010  🕐 May–Sep daily 7–7  🚠 Lift to bottom of gorge moderate  ❓ Rubber boot and salopette hire inexpensive  🍴 Bar and restaurant on upper level

---

**FOR KIDS**

The area round **Mount Etna** is a great place for kids; apart from some good **seaside towns**, there's the experience of a **trip up a genuine volcano** to enjoy. Older kids can tackle the full experience, and even younger ones will be fascinated by the lava fields. Head, too, for **Taormina**, where the Greek theatre gives an enjoyable insight to the classical past, before allowing your children let off steam in the waters of the **Gole dell'Alcàntara** or enjoy the beach at **Giardini-Naxos**. On the north coast, a good stopping place is **Santo Stefano di Camastra**, where there's plenty of pocket money-priced ceramics on offer, and more beaches nearby. Older children will enjoy **Cefalù**, where beachlife goes hand in hand with a touch of culture and the pleasures of one of Sicily's most attractive resorts.

# Where to...
# Stay

**Prices**

Expect to pay per double room, per night

€ under €130 €€ €130–€230 €€€ over €230

## CEFALU

### Baia del Capitano €€

Just 4km (2.5 miles) from Cefalù, the Baia is a great option if you want to combine the town with seaside pleasures – it's got a good pool and private access to the sea, where you can swim off the rocks or relax on a sunbed. Some of the rooms have terraces and sea views; others, in the annexe, come cheaper. The situation is beautiful, as the hotel is immersed in the green depths of an old olive grove, with large grounds and plenty of outdoor seating. The restaurant serves Sicilian specialities if you don't want to move in the evenings, and there's often live entertainment as well.

🚏 195 D3 ✉ **Contrada Mazzaforno, Cefalù**
☎ **0921 420 003; www.baiadelcapitano.it**

### Hotel Astro €

If you want to be in town, the Astro, overlooking the sea and a few minutes' walk from the station and just off the "new town's" main drag, makes a good choice, though there's no garden or pool. Rooms are large, with good-sized bathrooms; some have balconies. It's clean, fairly simple and excellent value for money; the staff are exceptionally helpful and friendly and there's the bonus of the hotel's own parking. The beach is a mere five minutes' walk downhill.

🚏 195 D3 ✉ **Via Nino Martoglio 10**
☎ **0921 421 639; www.astrohotel.it**

### Riva del Sole €€

If you want to be right at the heart of the action, the Riva is for you – a modern hotel overlooking the beach that's just a few minutes' stroll from the old town. It's bright and well-equipped, with a good choice of accommodation, including bedrooms with sea views and family rooms. The staff are friendly and obliging, and the excellent restaurant draws in non-residents and locals – an excellent recommendation. There's a terrace at the back, but no garden or swimming pool, though the position easily makes up for this. Prices drop in winter.

🚏 195 D3 ✉ **Lungomare Giardina 25**
☎ **0921 421 230; www.rivadelsole.com**

### Sea Palace €€

This modern, smart hotel has a prime position facing the beach. Rooms are bright and airy with spacious, well-equipped bathrooms. Many have balconies that look out to the sea with panoramic views of Cefalù's twin-towered Duomo. There is a pool, wellness centre and private beach for guests' use.

🚏 195 D3 ✉ **Lungomare Giardina** ☎ **0921 925 011; www.cefaluseapalace.it**

## MOUNT ETNA

### Il Nido dell'Etna €–€€

Very close to Etna and also within reach of Taormina, this welcoming, family-run hotel, built in 2006, has comfortable, well-appointed rooms adorned with modern art, and an excellent restaurant (closed at lunchtime). Excursions to Mount Etna can be booked by the helpful and knowledgeable owners.

🚏 196 C2 ✉ **Via Matteotti, Linguaglossa**
☎ **095 643404; www.ilnidodelletna.it**
🕒 **Closed Nov**

## TAORMINA

NB: When choosing a hotel here it's worth remembering that many central hotels have no vehicle access, and parking costs can add a lot to your budget.

### Grand Hotel Timeo €€€

Taormina's oldest *grand-luxe* hotel was built in *the* prime position, right next to the Teatro Greco, in 1873, and has been attracting the well-heeled ever since. The building is surrounded with beautiful gardens, overlooked by elegant terraces. All the superbly equipped rooms have a balcony or terrace. You can dine outside at the excellent restaurant gazing over the sea, and relax in the antique-strewn public rooms. The hotel has a pool and health and fitness centre, complete with Turkish bath. Service and standards are everything you'd expect in a hotel of this calibre – a real treat.

🏠 197 E3 ⊠ Via Teatro Greco 59 ☎ 0942 23801; www.grandhoteltimeo.com

### Pensione Svizzera €

You'll get a real welcome from the Vinciguerra family at this pretty, pink-washed hotel, which has been in the family since 1925. Situated just up the hill from the bus station, it's also got its own parking – a real bonus in Taormina. Nearly all the rooms have a little balcony and views to the sea – the hotel looks northwards. The gardens, where breakfast is often served, are particularly pretty, with shady palms and bright containers of flowers. The staff combine real friendliness with truly professional service, and run a shuttle service down to the private beach (May–Oct).

🏠 197 E3 ⊠ Via Pirandello 26 ☎ 0942 23790; www.pensionesvizzera.com
🕐 Closed Dec–Feb

### Villa Carlotta €€€

This smart and very welcoming boutique hotel enjoys spectacular views across the sea and out to Mount Etna. Very stylishly decorated, the rooms are individually designed using warm, earthy colours, beautiful fabrics and blending every modern comfort with antique opulence. The splendid rooftop terrace is the ideal place to enjoy the sumptuous breakfast banquet or for an *aperitivo* at sunset. The hotel runs its own private shuttle down to the beach.

🏠 197 E3 ⊠ Via Pirandello 8 ☎ 0942 626 058; www.villacarlotta.net

### Villa Ducale €€

This charming restored villa is set above Taormina in the quiet hamlet of Madonna della Rocca. The rooms are individually furnished in typical Sicilian style with antiques and ceramics crafted by local artisans. The outdoor terrace, where a splendid breakfast, home-made gourmandises and drinks are served, has breathtaking views of Mount Etna. A free shuttle bus ferries guests down and back up into Taormina and to the beach.

The villa is under the same expert ownership as the Villa Carlotta (see above), ensuring the best attention to detail.

🏠 197 E3 ⊠ Via Leonardo da Vinci 60, Madonna della Rocca ☎ 0942 28153; www.villaducale.com

### Villa Paradiso €€€–€€€

With the deep sofas, antique pieces and old prints and pictures, there's more than a touch of the country-house style about the public rooms of this lovely hotel, with its stunning views south over the coast towards Etna. You'll have to pay more for a room with a view, but all rooms have balconies and are nicely furnished; many overlook the garden. Breakfast is served on the covered terrace looking towards the mountain; it acts as the restaurant in the evenings. After dining, you can stroll into town – the hotel is situated right on the edge of the historic centre.

🏠 197 E3 ⊠ Via Roma 2 ☎ 0942 23921; www.hotelvillaparadisotaormina.com

# Where to...
# Eat and Drink

## Prices

Expect to pay per person for a meal, including wine and service

€ up to €20          €€ €20–€35          €€€ more than €35

## CEFALÙ

### Al Gabbiano €€

If you're looking for a good value local restaurant, the "Seagull" is the answer, a family-run restaurant and pizzeria right beside the sea, with a terrace and garden. Expect fresh fish and seafood and daily specials.

🚹 195 D3 🖾 Lungomare Giardina 17 🕿 0921 421 495 🕒 Daily lunch and dinner. Closed Wed in winter

### L'Antica Corte €€–€€€

Tucked off Corso Ruggero opposite the Duomo, this elegant little restaurant gets its name from its courtyard setting, where tables are set out in summer. Everything's homemade using local ingredients – try the *antipasti*. Simple grilled fish is a speciality and they also do good, reasonably priced pizzas.

🚹 195 D3 🖾 Cortile Pepe 7 🕿 0921 423 228 🕒 Fri–Wed 12–3, 7–11:30. Closed several weeks Jan–Feb

### La Brace €€

A lovely vaulted ceiling and warm wood panelling are the backdrop to the spacious tables at this welcoming restaurant in the heart of town, where diners can enjoy the excellent menu devised by

## GIARDINI-NAXOS

### Hellenia Yachting €€

Built right beside the sea in the last years of the 19th century, the Hellenia retains the style and elegance of the era, with high ceilings and some nice old furnishings. Comfort levels include a fine restaurant, a private beach and a large pool. At night you can dine overlooking the sea.

🚹 197 D3 🖾 Via Januzzo 41 🕿 0942 51737; www.hotel-hellenia.it

### Hotel Nike €

Nearly every room at this welcoming beachside hotel has its own balcony and sea view, and access to the private beach (via a lift), complete with sunbeds and umbrellas, is included in the room rate. Rooms are spacious and comfortable, the restaurant serves local specialities and the whole package is excellent value

for money. The free car park is a welcome bonus.

🚹 197 D3 🖾 Via Calcide Eubea 27 🕿 0942 51207; www.hotelnike.it

### Hotel Villa Mora €

This family-run hotel is a stone's throw from the beach in the heart of Giardini-Naxos. The clean, bright rooms are a good size and nicely furnished in Sicilian style.

🚹 197 D3 🖾 Lungomare Naxos 47 🕿 0942 51839; www.hotelvillamora.com

## MILAZZO

### Hotel Riviera Lido €

You'll need a car to reach this waterside hotel out on the Strada Panoramica. The hotel is set right on its own private beach. All the rooms have balconies and are comfortably furnished, with good-sized bathrooms. The restaurant is good and the public areas are spacious and attractive.

🚹 197 D5 🖾 Contrada Corrie 🕿 0909 283 456; www.hotelrivieralido.it

the Dutch owners, who settled in Cefalù over 25 years ago. The eclectic menu offers a change from Sicilian cooking, with dishes such as shashlik, kebabs and steaks, and the local wine list is well sourced and interesting.

🕀 195 D3 ⊠ Via XXV Novembre 10 ☎ 0921 423 570; www.ristorantelabrace.com 🕲 Wed–Sun lunch and dinner, Tue dinner

## Ostaria del Duomo €€

This pleasant hostelry enjoys a great setting in one of Sicily's loveliest piazzas, with the Duomo as the backdrop. The cuisine is traditional Sicilian, with fish as a speciality, and you can choose to sit outside or inside under the vaulted ceiling. This is one of Cefalù's most sophisticated restaurants.

🕀 195 D3 ⊠ Via Seminario 5 ☎ 0921 421 838; www.ostariadelduomo.com 🕲 Tue–Sun noon–midnight. Closed mid-Nov to Feb

## Lo Scoglio Ubriaco €€–€€€

Right at the bottom of the Corso Ruggero with a terrace hanging over the sea, the "Drunken Rock" gets its name from La Rocca. There's more than a touch of glitz in this big, bustling restaurant, its walls hung with photos of its illustrious patrons, but the food is excellent nonetheless and the long menu offers something for everyone.

🕀 195 D3 ⊠ Via Corso Bordonaro 2/4 ☎ 0921 423 370 🕲 Apr–Oct 12–2:30, 7:30–11; Nov–Mar Wed–Mon 12–2:30, 7:30–10

## A'Zammàra €€

If you're looking for an outdoor eating option, the garden of this restaurant, filled with fruit trees, fits the bill, while the interior rooms are equally attractive. The accent food-wise is on local produce and dishes, with specialities such as *pasta con le sarde* and *pasta alla Norma* preceding super-fresh fish and meat dishes such as *polpette alla foglie di limone* – delicate meat balls wrapped in lemon leaves; don't miss the home-made desserts either.

🕀 197 E3 ⊠ Via F.lli Bandiera 15 ☎ 0942 24408; www.zammara.it

## La Botte €–€€

Come here for the *cucina tipica siciliana*, served at outside tables in summer. Locals love this restaurant, and come here for the good *pizze* from the wood-fired oven, and the excellent *antipasto* buffet. There's a full restaurant menu and impressive wine list, though it has to be said the service can sometimes suffer from its own tourism.

🕀 197 E3 ⊠ Piazza San Domenico 4 ☎ 0942 24198; www.labotte1972.it 🕲 Oct daily 12–2:30, 7:30–11:30; Nov–Mar Tue–Sun 12–2:30, 7:30–10

## Casa Grugno €€€

Set in a beautiful 16th-century Gothic-Catalan former palazzo, Casa Grugno's surroundings alone ensure a memorable experience. The cooking is also excellent, presided over by Michelin-starred chef Andreas Zangerl. Expect high-quality, seasonal ingredients cooked with care and creativity in a succession of light and appetizing dishes, accompanied by a well-chosen, extensive wine list. You'll need to reserve ahead.

🕀 197 E3 ⊠ Via Santa Maria de Greci ☎ 0942 21208; www.casagrugno.it 🕲 Mon–Sat 7:30–10:30pm. Closed early Jan–early Mar

## Ristorante Taormina €€

Two big rooms down some steps off the Corso make up this jolly restaurant, where a good range of dishes from Sicily and other parts of Italy are prepared with care. While firmly catering for tourists, standards haven't slipped at this family establishment and food is vibrant and flavoursome, with meals rounded off with a complimentary *limoncello*. The terrace overlooks the sea and is perfect for alfresco dining in summer.

🕀 197 E3 ⊠ Vico Teofane Cerameo 2 (off Piazza IX Aprile) ☎ 0942 24359 🕲 Apr–Oct daily 12–2:30, 7:30–10; Nov–Mar Thu–Tue 12–2:30, 7:30–10

# Where to... Shop

In **Cefalù**, the main street is **Corso Ruggero**, though there are other possibilities in the "new" part of town, along **Via Matteotti** and **Via Roma**. Choice is limited, though you'll find a good selection of local food and wines at **Torrefazione Serio** (Corso Ruggero 120, tel: 0921 922 348); they specialize in coffee and can prepare freshly roasted blends for you. For Sicilian gourmet treats visit **Sapori di Sicilia** (Via V Emanuele 93, tel: 0921 422 871). Home decor fans could browse in **Tamburo Casarredo** (Via Roma 10, tel: 0921 421 818), which has pretty household bits and pieces, and there are numerous shops offering ceramics and souvenirs – **La Terra di Pascal** (Corso Ruggero 157) is the best bet.

Things are considerably better in **Taormina**, whose main shopping street is **Corso Umberto I**. Here are fashion outlets, antique shops, jewellers and leather stores – try **Sorelle Mazzulo** at No 35 for bags, and a full range of *alta moda* (designer labels) is on offer at **Parisi** at No 36. Farther down, **Carlo Panerello** (No 122) has antique furnishings, textiles and jewellery and **Le Colonne** (No 164) also has hand-made jewellery. You shouldn't miss the **Pasticceria Etna** (No 112), whose old-fashioned interior offers some of the best traditional cakes and sweetmeats in town. Off the Corso and up some steps you'll find **Kerameion** (Salita Santippo 16), a ceramics outlet where you can watch the craftsmen at work before you buy.

# Where to... Be Entertained

## NIGHTLIFE

The *passeggiata* (promenade) kicks off the evening in **Cefalù**, after which a late-night bar is a good option – try the **Caffè Duomo** in front of the cathedral; if you want to dance **Be Bop** (Via N Botta 4) is a good summertime bet.

In **Taormina** nightclubs such as **Bella Blu** (Via Guardiola Vecchia), glitzy and glamorous **Club Septimo** (Via San Pancrazio 50) and **La Giara** (Via La Floresta) vie for custom; or you can chill out on the sands at **Panasia Beach** (Via Nazionale, Contrada Spisone).

## FESTIVALS

**Cefalù**'s year is punctuated by feast days with processions. There's culture here from July to September when the town stages **Cefalù Incontri**, a series of music, folklore shows, cabaret and theatre, often staged outside.

Taormina's annual arts event, **Taormina Arte** (tel: 0942 21142; www.taormina-arte.com), is a far more formal affair. Running from July to September, it offers a series of concerts at various venues, including the magical Teatro Greco itself; this is also the setting for the **Teatro dei Due Mare** (tel: 0942 23243; www.teatrodeiduemari.it), when you can watch performances of classical Greek and Roman plays. Also in the summer, film buffs can attend movie screenings, some in the ancient theatre, run by the **Taormina Filmfest** (usually June; www.taorminafilmfest.it).

# The Southeast Corner – Siracusa and Inland

# Getting Your Bearings

South of Catania lies a corner packed with the best that Sicily has to offer, a wonderful mix of fine and historic cities, varied coastline and beautiful scenery that ranges from the densely cultivated to wild, hilly and untouched, its gorges cut through with rivers.

Since antiquity, the southeast corner of Sicily has been a prosperous area, and this is reflected in its gracious towns. Of these, compelling Siracusa stands out, a city whose architecture and archaeological treasures reflect its ancient role as one of the most important of all Mediterranean metropolises. Undamaged by the natural disasters that have repeatedly afflicted this corner of the island, Siracusa's sights span the centuries, providing a sharp contrast with the homogeneity of the superb baroque cities of Noto, Ragusa and Caltagirone, all built as "new towns" after the catastrophic earthquake in 1693, which wiped out the original settlements.

These cities lie to the west of Siracusa, while to the north is Catania, Sicily's dour, but vibrant, second city, a thriving commercial centre in the shadow of Etna. To the south, fast roads lead to the baroque towns, skirting the untouched coastline at Vendicari, home to one of Sicily's loveliest coastal wildlife reserves, rich in migratory and overwintering birds. Head inland from here to Noto and Ragusa, pausing perhaps to enjoy the pleasures of the smaller baroque centres of prosperous Modica and Comiso before continuing north via Grammichele to beautiful Caltagirone, a gem of a town, adorned with colourful tilework, which still produces some of Sicily's most accomplished ceramics.

**View over Ragusa Ibla from the terrace outside Santa Maria della Scala**

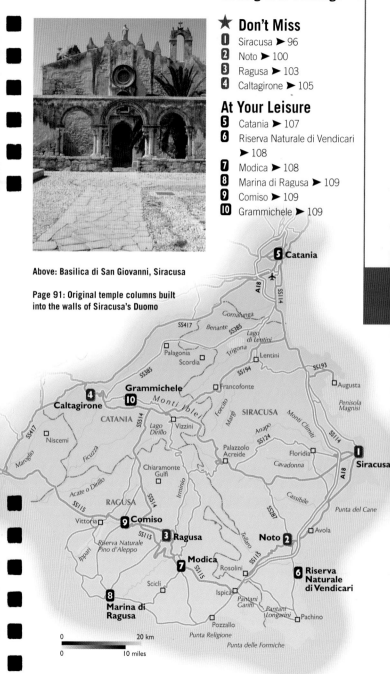

Above: Basilica di San Giovanni, Siracusa

Page 91: Original temple columns built into the walls of Siracusa's Duomo

# In Three Days

If you're not quite sure where to begin your travels, this itinerary recommends three practical and enjoyable days out in the southeast of Sicily, taking in some of the best places to see using the Getting Your Bearings map on the previous page. For more information see the main entries.

# Day 1

## Morning
In ❶ **Siracusa** (➤ 96), head straight for **Ortygia** (➤ 97) and spend the morning exploring this ancient island, perhaps starting by walking through its labyrinthine streets. Be sure to take in the **Piazza del Duomo** and its monuments (above, ➤ 97), before strolling down to the **Fonte Aretusa** (➤ 97) and heading on to enjoy the exhibits in the **Museo Regionale** (➤ 97).

## Afternoon
Head north through the modern city to the Tyche district, once outside the city, and riddled beneath ground level with **catacombs** (➤ 98). From here it's a stroll to the **Neapolis**, the archaeological zone (➤ 98), where you shouldn't miss the **Teatro Greco** (➤ 98) and the *latomie* (➤ 98).

## Evening
Round off the day with drinks and dinner on Ortygia, where there's a good choice of restaurants.

# Day 2

## Morning

If you want to visit **5 Catania** (► 107) take the N114. Otherwise, take the N115 to **2 Noto** (right, ► 100), the most beautiful of all the baroque towns in the southeast. Take your time strolling round the golden streets, rich in fine Baroque buildings.

## Afternoon and Evening

After lunch, you could either head for the coast and spend the afternoon in the **6 Vendicari reserve** (► 108), where you can swim off unspoiled beaches, or drive directly, via **7 Modica** (► 108), on the N115 to **3 Ragusa** (► 103), another baroque town packed with interest. Whatever you decide, aim to spend the night in **Ragusa**, enjoying the theatricality of floodlit **Ragusa Ibla** at night (► 103).

# Day 3

## Morning

There'll be time for another hour or so in Ragusa before you leave town and head east, taking the N514 north at the **9 Comiso** (► 109) interchange to Caltagirone, stopping off perhaps at the baroque town of **10 Grammichele** (► 109) en route.

## Afternoon

Spend the afternoon exploring **4 Caltagirone** (► 105), where there are more magnificent baroque sights to see and Sicily's best choice of ceramic shopping (below) – leave plenty of time for browsing.

# ❶ Siracusa

Nearly 3,000 years ago the Greeks founded the city of Siracusa, destined to become the most glittering of all the cities of Magna Graeca. Their light-drenched city still thrives, and nowhere else in Sicily is the sense of this glorious classical past more tangible.

Beautifully set between two sheltered harbours, the old heart of the metropolis, the island of Ortygia, encircled by water, is crammed with remnants of the past in the shape of ruins, churches and palaces. North from here lies the quietly prosperous modern city, whose streets lead north to the *latomie*, the vast quarries that provided the stone for the building of the ancient city.

## A Bit of History
Greek Siracusa, its name coined from the Phoenician *suraka*, marsh, was founded in 733BC. The position was perfect; an easily defensible island with fresh springs, a natural harbour and a fertile hinterland. By the fifth century BC Siracusa was booming, a major power, the slaves from whose foreign victories provided the labour for its building programme. The city defeated the Carthaginians in 480BC and the Athenians in 413BC, and later rulers invited luminaries such as the playwright Aeschylus and Plato the philosopher to live here. Archimedes designed the defences when Siracusa was besieged by Rome during the Second Punic War, though the city finally fell to Rome in 211BC.

**The majestic Duomo**

The Romans sacked the city, but it remained important as a trading centre, its population in due course turning to the new faith of Christianity and burying their dead in catacombs on the city's outskirts. The subsequent waves of Arab and Norman invaders left the city politically unimportant, but building on Ortygia continued nevertheless, notably after the Val di Noto earthquake of 1693, when baroque architects changed the face of the city forever.

## Ortygia

Tiny Ortygia, 1km (0.6 miles) in length and barely 500m (550 yards) across, is connected to the mainland by two bridges. Walk across the **Ponte Umbertino** and you'll be confronted with the ruins of the Doric **Tempio di Apollo** (Temple of Apollo), built in 656BC.

**Fonte Aretusa, with its papyrus plants**

From here, **Corso Matteotti** runs up to Ortygia's main square, the **Piazza Archimede**. Walk on the few dozen metres to the beautiful **Piazza del Duomo**, an elongated space surrounded by harmonious 17th- and 18th-century buildings. On one side stands the **Duomo**, built where the goddess Athena's shrine once stood and incorporating the Doric columns of the fifth-century BC pagan temple – no other building in Sicily illustrates the island's layers of civilization better. The temple, one of the richest in the ancient world, was converted into a Christian church and became the cathedral in 640. Its superbly ebullient facade was added after the 1693 earthquake, and contrasts with the muted interior, more pagan than Christian in atmosphere.

Through the piazza, another street leads down to the **Fonte Aretusa**, the freshwater spring at the sea's edge, which attracted the first settlers. Planted with papyrus and echoing with the quacks of the resident ducks, it's a charming spot; children will enjoy the **aquarium** just beside the spring. From here you can see Frederick II's **Castello Maniace**, built in 1239, to the south; walk along the tree-lined waterfront or head for the newly restored and reopened **Museo Regionale**, whose chief treasures are a serene *Annunciation* by Antonello da Messina and Caravaggio's wonderful *Burial of St Lucy*.

## The Mainland

North of Ortygia, at the far side of the commercial heart of Siracusa, the city's boundaries are marked, as they have been for over 2,000 years, by the *latomie*, a string of quarries, whose stone provided Siracusa's building materials. Beneath the area, and away from the *latomie*, early Christians, banned from inner-city burials, used the tunnels that formed part of the old Greek water supply as **catacombs**, now accessible from the ruined church of **San Giovanni**. You can take a tour of the labyrinthine underground system, complete with burial niches and traces of early Christian paintings.

Round the corner from the catacombs you'll find the **Museo Archeologico Paolo Orsi**, widely acknowledged to be among Europe's finest collections of Greek art. This is a serious and scholarly museum, which traces the history of both the pre-Greek and Greek civilizations on Sicily. Amongst the sculpture, the exquisite *Landolina Venus*, found actually in the grounds of the museum, stands out. A Roman copy of a Hellenistic piece, this knowingly sensual work depicts the goddess rising from the sea, and makes a fine contrast with the tender earthiness of the mother/goddess suckling twins. Also not to be missed are the taut, arrogant *kouroi*, fragments of statues of warriors dating back to the Greek Archaic age (500BC).

From the museum it's a short walk to the entrance to the **Neapolis,** an archaeological park that contains the Ara di Ierone II, a third-century BC altar, the spectacular Teatro Greco, the Latomia del Paradiso, largest of all the *latomie*, and the third-century Anfiteatro Romano. Star turn is the Teatro Greco, first constructed in the fifth century BC, and adapted by the Romans for gladiatorial combat. Forty-two of its 59 rows of seats remain, and are still used as seating for Siracusa's summer festival of concerts and Greek drama. From

---

### SIRACUSA: INSIDE INFO

**Top Tips** If you're driving into Siracusa for a day visit, follow the signs round the ring road to Ortygia, cross the bridge and leave the car in the supervised car park on the right.

■ If you're planning to stay in Siracusa, Ortygia is by far the nicest area; book ahead and be sure to get directions to your hotel.

■ The driving route to the archaeological zone is very badly signposted and involves negotiating a confusing maze of one-way streets. If you're based in Siracusa, it's better to take a taxi or a bus from Piazza della Posta, just over the bridge into Ortygia.

■ The archaeological zone, particularly the Teatro Greco, is very exposed; come during the cooler part of the day in summer. The catacombs are also shut for two hours over lunchtime.

■ Buses run regularly to the nearby beaches.

■ You can take a boat trip round the harbours on the Silene between April and October; details from the tourist office.

■ If you're short of time, focus on Ortygia, the Museo Archeologico Paolo Orsi and the Neapolis.

**In More Depth** The huge, modern church opposite the Museo Paolo Orsi is the Santuario della Madonna delle Lacrime (Our Lady of the Tears), built in homage to a statue of the Virgin that reportedly wept for five days in 1953.

the theatre follow the path through the arch and downhill to the Latomia, where you can wander along paths lined with trees to reach the **Orecchio di Dionisio** (Dionysius' Ear), a huge cavern whose name was the inspiration of the painter Caravaggio, impressed by its acoustic properties – even whispers are clearly audible from the top.

The cavernous Orecchio di Dionisio at Latomia del Paradiso

### TAKING A BREAK

The Piazza del Duomo in Ortygia is the nicest place to pause – try the **Caffé del Duomo** (€) opposite the cathedral, or **La Terrazza** (€€) if you want a full meal.

🚌 201 F3 🛈 Via della Maestranza 33 (Ortygia), tel: 0931 464 255; www.apt-siracusa.it; Mon–Fri 8– 2, 2:30–5:30, Sat 8–2
🛈 Via San Sebastiano 45 (near Museo Archeologico), tel: 0931 481 232; www.apt-siracusa.it; daily 8:30–1:30, 3:30–6:30

**Duomo**
✉ Piazza del Duomo ☎ 0931 65328 🕐 Daily 7:30–6 except during services 🎟 Free

**Museo Regionale d'Arte Medioevale e Moderna**
✉ Via Capodieci 16 ☎ 0931 69511 🕐 Tue–Sat 9–7, Sun 9–1 🎟 Moderate

**Aquarium**
✉ Villetta Aretusa al Foro Vittorio Emanuele II ☎ 0931 167 4461 🕐 Daily 10–7 🎟 Moderate

**Catacomba di San Giovanni**
✉ Via San Giovanni alle Catacombe ☎ 0931 67955 🕐 Daily 9:30–12:30, 2:30–4:30 🎟 Moderate

**Museo Archeologico Paolo Orsi**
✉ Viale Teocrito 66 ☎ 0931464 022 🕐 Tue–Sat 9–7, Sun 9–2 🎟 Expensive

**Parco Archeologico della Neapolis**
✉ Viale Teocrito ☎ 0931 66206 🕐 Apr–Oct daily 9–6; Nov–Mar 9–3 🎟 Expensive

**Madonna delle Lacrime**
✉ Via del Santuario 3 ☎ 0931 463118 🕐 Daily 7am–8pm

# **2 Noto**

Sublime Noto, its honey-coloured stone glowing golden in the sunlight, is the most beautiful of all Sicily's baroque towns. Its citizens call it *il giardino di pietra*, the garden of stone, and it's hard to find fault with the title. Its stately streets, harmonious squares and sweeping staircases recall some wonderful stage set, where every building has been placed to add harmony to the whole. It's perfection on a human scale, the grandeur of the design never detracting from the fact that this small town is a place for humans to live, not some cold and monumental set piece. If you see no other baroque town, see Noto.

Detail of a carving on the Palazzo Villadorata

## The Background

Noto was conceived as a replacement for the original town, some 14km (8.5 miles) distant, destroyed in the 1693 earthquake. It wasn't the inhabitants' idea to build a new city elsewhere, it was foisted upon them by the government, who moved the population, despite the fact they had started rebuilding the old town, to the new site. It was a gesture of renewal and hope for the future, and the greatest and most experienced architects of the day were commissioned – Vincenzo Sinatra, Paolo Labisi and Rosario Gagliardi. Their brief was to co-operate in the design of a city that synthesized all that was most innovative – wide streets, squares to act as focal points, vistas and stairways to lead the eye from one area to the next. They succeeded brilliantly, and that was that, and for more than 250 years this wondrous confection of a city slumbered peacefully.

The blow came in 1986, when a structural survey discovered that many of the buildings were in a state of such fragility that even the slightest tremor would destroy them all. Scaffolding went up and work began, the gravity of the situation being highlighted 10 years later when, in 1996, the cupola of the cathedral collapsed. World attention focused at last on the city, UNESCO designated Noto a World Heritage Site in 2002 and the money poured in. The covers finally came off the cathedral in 2007, and today Noto is more or less back on track, its baroque glory restored and its future safety assured.

The restored
baroque
facade of
San Nicolò
cathedral

## Seeing Noto

The main street, the majestic **Corso Vittorio Emanuele**,
runs along the flank of a hill from the Porta Reale, with
streets rising to the right and falling to the left. Just 1km
(0.6 miles) long, it's punctuated by a succession of open
spaces and sweeping stairs, and passes many of the town's
main monuments. The first of the succession of set pieces
are the churches of **Santa Chiara** and **San Francesco** and
the monastery of **San Salvatore**, each placed and decorated
to make a unified whole comprising contrasting elements, a
key element in baroque city planning. The next square along
the Corso is the Piazza Municipio, where church and state, in
the shape of two of the town's most compelling buildings, the
**cathedral of San Nicolò**, now triumphantly restored, and the
serene neo-classical Palazzo Ducezio (1746), Noto's town hall,
face each other across a piazza. A splendid staircase rises to
the doors of the cathedral; next to it is the Palazzo Vescovile
(Bishop's Palace) and the Palazzo Sant'Alfano Landolina, the
only patrician's palazzo on the main street. Beyond is the
basilica of San Salvatore.

Further on, on the left, is the church of the **Collegio**,
its audacious curved facade the perfect fanfare to its frothy
white and gilded stucco interior, the epitome of everything a
baroque church should be – you can climb the stairs of the
bell tower for a bird's-eye view over the town and towards the
sea. The next piazza, with its fountain and cool shady trees,
under which the old men gather to chat, is the Piazzale XVI
Maggio, home to the charming **Teatro Civico**; if it's open, pop

inside for a peep at its lush auditorium, surrounded by tiers of boxes. Opposite this, across the piazza, is the lovely soaring convex facade of **San Domenico** (1737–56), considered to be Gagliardi's masterpiece. Elsewhere, by turning right up Via Nicolaci, adjacent to the cathedral, you can stand open-mouthed at the **Palazzo Villadorata**, possibly Sicily's most perfect example of the mind-blowing opulence of the 18th-century nobility's taste. Its facade is adorned with wonderfully ebullient balconies supported by stonework nymphs, horses, *putti* and lions, looking for all the world like icing-sugar figures in stone.

It's worth, too, heading up the hill behind the Corso to take in some of the upper town's delights, chief of which is the vast church of the **Crocifisso**, designed by Gagliardi and finished in 1715, which contains the beautiful *Madonna delle Neve* (Our Lady of the Snow), a 15th-century marble Madonna by Laurana, brought here from old Noto.

There is something to catch the eye at every turn in Noto

### TAKING A BREAK

The **Caffè Sicilia** (€; Via Ducezio 2) has very fine-quality snacks and ice cream; but for a pause with a view, choose any of the cafés around the Piazza Municipio.

✚ 201 E2  ℹ Piazzale XVI Maggio; tel: 0931 896 654/0931 573 779; www.comune.noto.sr.it (Italian only); Mon–Fri 9–2, 3:30–6:30, Sat 9–12, 3:30–6:30. Reduced hours in winter

## NOTO: INSIDE INFO

**Top Tips** For the best first sight of Noto, walk in through the Porta Reale; you'll find several car parks at this end of town.
- The angle and clarity of the light and time of day are important, so try and see Noto at different times of day.
- The main buildings are floodlit at night.
- Most museums open 9–1:30, 3:30–7 or 8.
- The charming garden Villetta d'Ercole, behind the tourist information office, has shady palms, monkey puzzle trees and a fountain of Hercules rescued from Noto Antico.

# ③ Ragusa

Set in a rugged limestone landscape, where drystone walls delineate the fields, and olives, almonds and carobs grow, the twin towns of Ragusa and Ragusa Ibla, at first glance grey and austere, tumble down a hilly ridge. Upper Ragusa, with its rational grid of planned streets, epitomizes 18th-century town planning. Ragusa Ibla, still in parts a maze of medieval stepped streets, links post-earthquake design with an altogether more picturesque past.

**Charming Ragusa Ibla retains its medieval Arab street pattern**

## Ragusa Superiore – the Upper Town

Three dramatic bridges soar above the gorge of Santa Domenica into Ragusa Superiore (the Upper Town), constructed after the 1693 earthquake and laid out on a perfect grid pattern. Its main street is the Corso Italia, arrowing down the hill towards the old town, and scattered with some monumental palazzi. Here you'll find the **Duomo** and its campanile, which dominates the centre of town; its interior is a splendid riot of stucco and gilding. The other main draw up here is the **Museo Archeologico** (Via Natalelli, tel: 0932 622 963; open Tue–Sun 9–1:30, 4–7:30; moderate), a collection of finds from all over the province, which includes the *Warrior of Castiglione*, a seventh-century BC tomb carving.

## Ragusa Ibla

Post 1693, as forward-thinking citizens planned a new town higher up the ridge, the old guard refused to abandon the wreck of their city, and little by little, rebuilt Ibla, the lower town, retaining its medieval **Arab-inspired layout**. Fine new

**baroque buildings** went up along the ruined streets, and it's this combination of huddled alleys with the splendour of the new monuments that gives **Ragusa Ibla** its unique charm. It's approached from the upper town across an isthmus at the bottom end of the Corso Italia, where steps lead past the restored 15th-century church of **Santa Maria della Scala**.

From its terrace there's a superb view across the roofs and buildings of Ibla, with the great dome of the Duomo di San Giorgio rising ahead. You can either wend your way through the hilly lanes towards the church, or veer left along the **via del Mercato**. Either choice will eventually bring you to the heart of Ibla, the beautiful, irregular and theatrical **Piazza del Duomo**. Dedicated to San Giorgio, the Duomo was designed by Rosario Gagliardi, took 40 years to build and is one of the masterpieces of Sicilian Baroque. Its three-tiered facade, approached through huge iron gates up a flight of graceful steps, is further dramatized by its position, set at an angle to the piazza. Walk through the square to **Piazza Pola**, a further stunner, containing another Gagliardi church, **San Giuseppe**. Beyond here lies the park Giardino Ibleo, which is approached from the portal of the 15th-century **Gothic San Giorgio Vecchio**, the only remnant of a vast pre-earthquake church, and the symbol of Ragusa Ibla.

The dome of
Cattedrale di
San Giorgio

### TAKING A BREAK

Visit **Dolce Barocco** (€; Largo San Domenico tel: 0923 655 378) in Ibla for delicious *pasticceria*, snacks and ice cream – buy some of their own chocolate, *Dolce Barocco*.

✚ 200 C2  ℹ Piazza San Giovanni, Ragusa Superiore; tel: 0923 684 780; www.comune.ragusa.it; Mon–Fri 9–1, 3–7, Sat 9–1
✉ Via Capitano Bocchieri 31, Ragusa Ibla; tel: 0932 221 529; Tue–Sun 9–2, 4–6

**Duomo di San Giorgio**
✉ Piazza del Duomo  🕐 Wed–Mon 10–1:30, 4–6:30, Tue 4–6:30

### RAGUSA: INSIDE INFO

**Top Tips** There's more of interest in Ragusa Ibla, so concentrate on this part of town.
■ Ragusa's streets are steep, so wear comfortable shoes for your visit.
■ The chief pleasure of Ragusa Ibla is simply to wander; there are serendipitous delights round every corner.
■ A half-hourly bus service connects Ragusa Ibla with the upper town and will save you the climb back up the hill – buy your ticket before boarding.

# 4 Caltagirone

High in the hills behind the southeast coast stands
Caltagirone, "Queen of the Hills". It's a beautiful city, a World
Heritage Site, built of golden sandstone, its churches, palaces
and civic buildings lavishly decorated with the colourful
ceramic tiles for which the city is famed. Spick and span,
bustling and prosperous, it's a town bursting with justifiable
civic pride, an off-the-beaten-track gem that deserves to be
better known.

## The Town

Named by the Arabs for their castle, *kalat*, and the
surrounding caves, *gerum*, Caltagirone is one of the clutch of
baroque towns rebuilt after the earthquake of 1693. As you
approach through the new town at the bottom of the hill, tier
upon tier of splendid buildings, accentuated by domes and
towers, rise up, an ebullient jumble of the best of 17th- and
18th-century architecture. Close up, things get even better,
for the buildings, the towers, even the street signs and garden
benches are all adorned with glowing polychrome ceramic
tiles, giving the whole urban landscape a lightness and gaiety.

**The monumental staircase of Santa Maria del Monte, decorated with flowers**

## Seeing Caltagirone

In the valley, the pleasant public gardens are home to the
**Museo della Ceramica**, stuffed with examples of pottery
from every age, not just from Caltagirone, but from all over

Sicily. From here, you can walk along Via Roma and up into the historic centre, passing over the Ponte San Francesco, an 18th-century viaduct brilliant with majolica decoration. This leads into Piazza Umberto and the adjacent Piazza del Municipio, heart of the town. Here you'll find the **Duomo** (9–12, 4–7), set between the two squares, while Piazza Municipio frames Caltagirone's most astounding monument, the **Scala Santa Maria del Monte**. This flight of 142 steep stairs leads up to the baroque church of the same name; each step is tiled in white, yellow, blue and green, and every tile is different. Climb up to the top and you'll pass numerous tiny ceramic workshops and be rewarded with fine views over the town. The steps were built in the 17th century to link the church at the top with the Cathedral; a road had been planned, but the incline was too steep. They were originally plain, the tiles being added in 1954. The stairs look their most magical on 24 and 25 July, when they are illuminated with coloured paper lanterns in honour of San Giacomo, St James, the patron saint of Caltagirone, in a festival known as the Illuminata.

### TAKING A BREAK

Sit out in the shady bar in the **Giardino Spadaro** (€; Via San Giuseppe), close to the Scala, which serves a good selection of snacks and cool drinks.

A200 B4 ⓘ Via Volta Libertini 3; tel: 0933 53809; www.comune. caltagirone.ct.it; Mon–Fri 9–1, 4–7, Sat 9–1

### Museo della Ceramica
✉ Via Roma-Giardino Pubblico
☎ 0933 58418 ⓒ Daily 9–6:30
🎫 Moderate

### SAVING A DYING ART

The Arabs were the first to use the high-quality clay found near Caltagirone, opening potteries that introduced new techniques, colours and designs. By the 16th century, the town was famous for its ceramics and demand was high all over Italy. All went well until the 19th century, when cheaper, factory-made ware threatened the industry, which by the early 20th century had all but died out. A local priest, Luigi Sturzo, came to the rescue, gathering the surviving artisans and persuading them to pass on their skills. He founded a school of ceramics and became mayor of the town; today, there are more than 70 ceramic masters working here and his name is well known all over Sicily.

### CALTAGIRONE: INSIDE INFO

**Top Tips** Head straight for the upper, old town, where you'll find everything you'll want to see.
■ If you're looking for the **tourist office**, go through the archway into the courtyard and up the steps to the first floor.
■ The Mostra Mercato Permanente (Via Vittorio Emanuele; daily 9–8) is one of the best places for **modern ceramics**.

# At Your Leisure

Catania's Piazza del Duomo at dusk, with its symbolic stone elephant illuminated

## 5 Catania

Unashamedly commercial, Catania is Sicily's second city, an ancient settlement that thrived under the Romans. Overshadowed by the brooding presence of Mount Etna, it is a city of lava, and, at first sight, can be a dour place, with its dark, volcanic stone buildings. Look further, and you'll quickly appreciate the grandiose baroque architecture, wide boulevards, cosmopolitan amosphere and thriving entertainment scene.

Ravaged by eruption and earthquake, the city centre has been rebuilt over the centuries, most notably after the 1693 quake, when Vaccarini's architecture transformed it into a showcase baroque city. It's this you'll notice as you stand in the Piazza del Duomo, complete with its Elephant Fountain (1736), the statue carved from lava that is said to protect the city from volcanic wrath. It stands in front of the splendid Cattedrale di Sant'Agata (daily 7:30–12, 4–7), the city's patron saint. Behind the Piazza del Duomo, the labyrinthine streets come alive every morning for the colourful Pescheria fish market. From the piazza run two of the main streets, Via Garibaldi and Via Vittorio Emanuele, with the bulk of the Castello Ursino, home to the Museo Civico (Mon–Sat 9–1, 3–7), rising to the south. North of Via Vittorio Emanuele you'll find the Teatro Romano (Mon–Sat 9–1:30, 3–7) and the Museo Belliniano (Mon, Wed, Fri–Sat 9–1, Tue, Thu 9–1, 3–6, Sun 9–12:30), dedicated to Catania's home-grown opera composer. Nearby is the Teatro Massimo Bellini, inaugurated in 1890 with Vincenzo Bellini's opera Norma. This is among Europe's grandest opera houses and has splendid acoustics. From the Duomo, Via Etnea arrows north, framing a distant view of the mountain. Lined with shops, Via Etnea has Sicily's liveliest *passeggiata* – you could take it in on your way back from the Anfiteatro Romano

Bird's-eye view over the town of Modica, spread out along a steep hillside

(daily 9–1:30, 3–7), built in the second century and one of the largest amphitheatres in the Roman world.

➕ 197 D1 🏛 Via D Cimarosa 10, tel: 0957 306 211; www.apt.catania.it www.comune.catania.it; Mon–Fri 9–8; Sat 9–2

### 🄶 Riserva Naturale di Vendicari

If you're sated with the baroque and looking for sand, sea and peace, head for the Riserva di Vendicari, a nature reserve on the coast southeast of Noto. Centred round a chain of three lagoons, this flat, unspoiled stretch of coast is scattered with reminders of the fisheries that once thrived here. The beaches are wonderful – smooth stretches of sand lapped by calm seas – but bird-lovers will want to concentrate on the lagoons. These are important feeding grounds during the spring migration and attract many rare species, including a resident group of flamingos. Paths run across the marshes and through the dunes; the air is scented with eucalyptus and the aromatic herbs of the *macchia* – bring a picnic and really get away from it all.

➕ 201 E2 ✉ Main entrance: Pantano Grande (off SP19 Pachino road, 12km/ 7.5 miles south of Noto) ☎ 0931 571 457;

www.parks.it/riserva.oasi.vendicari 🕐 Always open 💶 Free; parking inexpensive

### 🄷 Modica

Modica, lying in a valley among the limestone hills, is one of the clutch of baroque towns built after the 1693 earthquake, and consists of two towns, Modica Bassa and Modica Alta, the lower and upper. It's a lovely town, its houses scrambling up the steep slopes and its main thoroughfares wide and elegant. These, Corso Umberto and Via Giarratana, cover two torrential rivers and were laid out after they were dammed following a disastrous flood in 1902. Most of the main monuments are ranged along the Corso, including the beautiful baroque church of Santa Maria delle Grazie (1624) and fine 18th-century palazzi. A flight of steps leads up to San Pietro (1698), and higher still, reached by another 250 steps, stands the superb church of San Giorgio. Its ornate facade, topped by a bell tower, is among the finest in Sicily.

➕ 200 C2 🏛 Piazza Monumento, Corso Umberto 1; tel: 0932 753 324; www.sicilyweb.com/modica; Apr–Sep daily 9–1, 4–8; Oct–Mar 9–1, 3:30–7:30

**Madre di Santa Maria delle Stelle, Comiso**

## 8 Marina di Ragusa

This former fishing village on the southeast coast swells its population dramatically in summer to become a buzzing summer resort with good watersports facilities. The beach is long and sandy, presided over by a 16th-century watchtower and fringed by plenty of good restaurants, cafés and bars. The resort is also linked with the popular television series *Il Commissario Montalbano*. Adapted from the novels by Andrea Camilleri, the series covers the adventures of the fictional Sicilian detective Montalbano at his seaside villa, and Marina di Ragusa has often been used as a location for shooting the series.

✚ 200 B1

## 9 Comiso

For more baroque pleasures, head for Comiso, a little gem of a town, rebuilt after the 1693 earthquake though still retaining the medieval castle built by its overlords, the powerful Naselli family. Pick of its churches is the Santissima Annunziata (1772–93), approached by a dramatic staircase and crowned with a blue dome, from where you can walk down to the other main church, Santa Maria delle Stelle. Nearby, the waters that feed the fountain in the Piazza Fonte Diana were used by the Romans to supply their bathhouse, and legend says they would refuse to mix with wine when poured by unchaste hands. Comiso was the birthplace of the writer Gesualdo Bufalino (1920–96), one of Italy's most important contemporary authors; the old market building houses his library.

✚ 200 B2

## 10 Grammichele

Founded by refugees after the 1693 earthquake, the baroque town of Grammichele is best seen from the air. Its ground plan is a perfect piece of geometry – a hexagon divided into six segments like an orange, each with its own piazza, that meet at a central square. The best way to appreciate the layout on the ground is to head for the heart of this imposing space, from where you'll see the *radii* stretching out all round. A stroll round town will emphasize the regularity of the design, but that's it really; today, this splendid creation is just another Sicilian backwater, heavy with southern torpor.

✚ 200 B4

---

**FOR KIDS**

The big draw for kids in the southeast is **Siracusa** – a bustling town with **beaches** nearby, ruins to explore and labyrinthine catacombs in which to give themselves the creeps. The area's other main centres have little to offer anyone younger than 12, though street life is lively and there are swings and slides to be found. **Catania** is best avoided, though you could use it as a base for Etna (▶ 77) – better to head for the **beach at Vendicari**, or let them explore **Noto**, a superbly child-friendly town. **Modica** is famous for its chocolate, made to traditional 16th-century recipes. Crunchy, grainy and delicious, you'll see it everywhere.

# Where to...
## Stay

**Prices**

Expect to pay per double room per night

€ under €130    €€ €130–€230    €€ over €230

## SIRACUSA

### Grand Hotel €€–€€€

Overlooking the Porto Grande, this old palace hotel is grand indeed, and echoes an earlier age with its art deco character. Comfort levels are high, reflected in the classically understated furnishings, large rooms and expert service. Public areas are airy and pleasant, some rooms look out to sea and all guests can enjoy the rooftop restaurant. The hotel provides a shuttle service to its own beach in summer.

➕ 201 F3 ⊠ Viale Mazzini 12 ☎ 0931 464 600; www.grandhotelsr.it

### Gutkowski €

The attractive blue-and-white facade gives a taste of what's in store at this friendly hotel, Siracusa's closest to boutique style. The cool, modern decor of the rooms is imbued with sunshine and fresh air, the style simple and elegant. There's a roof terrace where breakfast is served and the hotel has some rooms for disabled guests.

➕ 201 F3 ⊠ Lungomare Vittorini 26 ☎ 0931 465 861; www.guthotel.it

### Roma €€

Built in 1880, this mid-sized hotel in the heart of Ortygia has been extensively overhauled. Its guest rooms, some equipped for disabled travellers, are light and spacious, with parquet flooring, white drapes and cool cream and blue tones – many have wrought-iron balconies giving views over the old town. The hotel restaurant, Minosse, is among the best in Siracusa. Guests can be collected from Catania airport or leave their car in the hotel's own garage – a real bonus in Ortygia.

➕ 201 F3 ⊠ Via Roma 66 ☎ 0931 465 626; www.hotelroma.sr.it

## NOTO

### Hotel della Ferla €

Noto's most up-to-date hotel is on the edge of the historic centre. The cheery bedrooms have tiled floors; some have balconies. Downstairs all is bright and modern, and the staff, some of whom speak English, are helpful. They have a garage and a garden.

➕ 201 E2 ⊠ Via A Gramsci 5 ☎ 0931 576 007; www.hotelferla.it

## RAGUSA

### Il Barocco €€

Access to this pretty pink-washed hotel, right in the heart of Ragusa Ibla, is via a courtyard, where you can enjoy a drink or summer breakfast. The rooms, many of which have balconies, are simply and comfortably furnished with cool decor. Just a stone's throw from the central piazza and the Duomo, Il Barocco is a lovely place to stay.

➕ 200 C2 ⊠ Via S Maria la Nuova 1, Ragusa Ibla ☎ 0932 663105; www.ilbarocco.it

### Locanda Don Serafino €€€

A recent and sensitive restoration has transformed a crumbling 18th-century town house into an intimate and charming boutique hotel. Stone walls have been left exposed and furnishings are comfortable. The Rosa family look after their guests well and supervise every detail.

➕ 200 C2 ⊠ Via XI Febbraio 15, Ragusa Ibla ☎ 0932 220 065; www.locandadonserafino.it

## CALTAGIRONE

### Grand Hotel Villa San Mauro €€€

There are lovely views back to Caltagirone and over the surrounding countryside from this modern hotel, part of the Spanish chain NH Hoteles. Standards are high here; every room has a balcony, huge beds, well-chosen decor in traditional colour schemes and excellent bathrooms. The restaurant is good and you can enjoy a post-sightseeing swim in the good-sized pool before relaxing on the terrace with a drink.

**+** 200 B4 **⊠** Via Portosalvo 14 **☎** 0933 26500; www.nh-hotels.it

## CATANIA

### Villa del Bosco and VdBNext €€–€€€

A little out of the centre, north of the Via Etnea, the 19th-century mansion Villa de Bosco is comfortable, elegant and sumptuously furnished with antiques. There's a good in-house restaurant, and the frescoed breakfast room is a most attractive place to consume the ample, well-presented breakfast. The VdBNext, in the same building, is more contemporary in design and appeals more to a business clientele.

**+** 197 D1 **⊠** Via del Bosco 62 **☎** 0957 335 100; www.hotelvilladelbosco.it

# Where to...
# Eat and Drink

**Prices**
Expect to pay per person for a meal, including wine and service
€ up to €20      €€ €20–€35      €€€ more than €35

## SIRACUSA

### Il Cenacolo €€€

Come here in summer, when it's the only restaurant on Ortygia where you can eat surrounded by greenery. The food is firmly Sicilian, with dishes such as *caponata* (vegetable stew) and pasta with clams and sea urchin. The menu also offers fish couscous, normally only found in western Sicily, and many dishes have distinctly Arab and Spanish touches. The pizza oven gets going in the evening, and there are occasional musical evenings with guest singers – touristy, but fun.

**+** 201 F3 **⊠** Via del Consiglio Reginale 10 **☎** 0931 65099 **⊙** May–Sep daily 12–2.30, 7.30–10; Oct–Apr Thu–Tue 12–2.30, 7.30–10. Closed mid-Jan to mid-Feb

### Don Camillo €€€

Food is taken very seriously indeed by Giovanni Guarneri, the chef-owner of this famous restaurant, who has picked up many a prize at competitions in Italy and further afield. The great strength here is pasta, but his touch with *secondi* is equally deft, and you can expect some interesting takes on old favourites. If it's on the menu, try the seasonal *zuppa di mucco*, a

## MARINA DI NOTO

### Hotel Jonio €–€€

Just 10 minutes' drive from historic Noto, Marina di Noto is a lovely place to stay, and this family-run hotel a good find. Set just across the road from the sandy beach, the hotel has a good dining room, a big terrace and parking. All the rooms have their own balconies and good-sized bathrooms. There is a choice of reliable restaurants within a few minutes' walk.

**+** 201 E2 **⊠** Viale Lido I, Marina di Noto **☎** 0931 812 040; www.hoteljonio.eu

wonderfully fragrant seasonal broth made with tiny new-born fish. The wine list is long and interesting.

🏠 201 F3 🖾 Via Maestranza 96 ☎ 0931 67133; www.ristorantedoncamillosiracusa.it ⏰ Mon–Sat noon–2.30, 7:30–10. Closed 1 week in Jul, Feb, Christmas

### La Foglia €€

The art that adorns this Ortygia restaurant is the work of the owner and his daughter; mother's influence lies in the kitchen. Vegetarians will love this place, with its extensive choice of soups and pasta made using fresh seasonal produce, and delights such as lentils, chickpeas and tender young nettles. Main courses of carefully cooked fish and meat are available and the desserts are homemade.

🏠 201 F3 🖾 Via Capodieci 21 ☎ 0931 66233; www.lafoglia.it ⏰ Daily 12–2.30, 7:30–9:30/10

### Oinos €€€

Sicilian and Piedmontese specialities are on the menu in this attractive designer restaurant, where the white napery matches the cool, pale colours of the interior. The cuisine is creative and well presented by the young, enthusiastic staff. There is a terrace for outdoor dining in summer – the perfect spot for sampling the delicious homemade ice cream. It is also a wine bar and serves excellent snacks.

🏠 201 F3 🖾 Via della Giudecca 69/75, Ortygia ☎ 0931 464 900; www.ristorantejoinos.com ⏰ Mon–Sat lunch and dinner. Closed 2 weeks in Feb

### Trattoria Cantinaccia €€

You'll eat well at excellent prices at this down-to-earth restaurant, with its summer veranda overlooking the sea. The fish is straight off the boat and figures strongly on the big menu, which also caters for carnivores with veal, chicken and steak. The antipasto buffet makes a good start, and you could follow this with a pasta dish and one of the imaginative salads, and thus leave room for the cassata or a cannoli.

🏠 201 F3 🖾 Via XX Settembre 13 ☎ 0931 165 945 ⏰ Wed–Mon 12–2.30, 7:30–10/10.30

### NOTO

### Bar Gelateria Constanza €

Come here for one of the best ice creams you'll ever eat. The classic flavours such as coffee, vanilla, chocolate and the fruit ices such as local orange are wonderful but don't fail to sample the house specialities – carob from the local trees, prickly pear in season and a superb mulberry scented with jasmine flowers.

🏠 201 E2 🖾 Via Silvio Spaventa ☎ 0931 538 496 ⏰ Daily 7:30am–10:30pm

### Il Barocco €€

Pizza and pasta feature alongside fish and seafood in a palatial setting under vaulted ceilings. The walls are covered in playful graffiti in homage to the charismatic owner, Graziella. There is a charming courtyard for alfresco dining.

🏠 201 E2 🖾 Via Cavour 8, Noto Antico ☎ 0931 835 999 ⏰ Daily lunch and dinner

### Trattoria del Carmine €

This good example of a family-run restaurant serves food all day long, ranging from sandwiches if you're in a hurry, to excellent pasta, rabbit and grills at lunchtime. In the evening there's a full range of pizzas as well as the restaurant menu.

🏠 201 E2 🖾 Via Ducezio 1 ☎ 0931 838 705; www.trattoriadelcarmine.it ⏰ Tue–Sun 11–10

### RAGUSA

### Duomo €€€

A splendid baroque palazzo is home to Ragusa's finest restaurant, where the chef, Ciccio Sultano, has been awarded two Michelin stars, and where wonderful food is beautifully presented in surroundings to match, right in front of the Duomo. The kitchen concentrates on producing Sicilian food with a modern take, changing the menu frequently and sourcing all the ingredients locally. All pastas, breads and desserts are made on the premises and the wine list lives up to the high standard of the food. Booking ahead is essential.

➕ 200 C2 ✉ Via Capitano Bocchieri 31, Ragusa Ibla ☎ 0932 651 265; www.ristoranteduomo.it 🕐 May–Sep Mon 7:30–10pm, Tue–Sat 12–2:30, 7:30–10; Oct–Apr Tue–Sat 12–2:30, 7:30–10, Sun 12–2:30. In Aug, closed Thu lunch

### Orfeo €–€€

Eat here and enjoy the best of excellent-value Ragusan cooking at knock-down prices, with a good selection of homemade pasta dishes, straightforward grilled meat and some fish. This is a good example of a traditional eating house, well patronized by locals.

➕ 200 C2 ✉ Via Sant'Anna 117, Ragusa Superiore ☎ 0932 621 035 🕐 Mon–Sat 12–2:30, 7:30–9:30

### Ristorante Don Serafino €€€

This superbly elegant, yet intimate, restaurant in the old town offers the choice of eating in the old stables of a palazzo, beautifully converted, or outside in summer. Chef Vincenzo Candiano has been awarded one Michelin star. The food is state-of-the-art, a stunning procession of beautiful, light dishes created using old traditions and local ingredients, symphonies of colour, taste and texture on the plate. The vast wine list, featuring wines from Sicily, mainland Italy and Europe is impressive; expert guidance is at hand to help you make your choice.

➕ 200 C2 ✉ Via Orfanotrofio 39, Ragusa Ibla ☎ 0932 248 778; www.locandadonserafino.it 🕐 Wed–Mon 12–2:30, 7:30–9:30. Closed 2 weeks in Jan and 2 weeks in Nov

## CALTAGIRONE

### La Scala €€€

The setting, right at the foot of the town's famous steps, is a real draw at this well-respected restaurant, housed in two rooms of an 18th-century palazzo, with a courtyard for summer eating and a stream visible through glass panels beneath the floor. Expect Sicilian cooking, drawing on seasonal produce, and served with good local wines.

➕ 200 B4 ✉ Scalinata Santa Maria del Monte 8 ☎ 0933 57781 🕐 Thu–Tue 12–2:30, 7:30–9:30

## CATANIA

### La Siciliana €€–€€€

Long-established, justifiably popular restaurant, located in a 19th-century villa. Fish and seafood are the specialities, where traditional dishes are combined with creative flair. There are also good meat dishes, tasty pasta, including rigatoni alla Norma, as well as vegetarian options. The wine list has plenty of Sicilian labels.

➕ 197 D1 ✉ Viale Marco Polo 52a ☎ 0953 376 400; www.lasiciliana.it 🕐 Tue–Sat 12–3, 8–11, Sun 12–3. Closed 2 weeks in Aug

# Where to...
# Shop

As Sicily's second largest city, Catania has shopping for all tastes, and the stores around Via Etnea offer great variety. Just off this main shopping street is the colourful **Fera o Luni** general market (Piazza Carlo Alberto); not to be missed either is the **Pescheria** morning market (down the steps from the Duomo), where the merchandise includes cheeses, spices and wines as well as all kinds of fish.

Prosperous **Siracusa** has plenty of shopping opportunities, mainly on Ortygia. The **market** (near Tempio di Apollo, Mon–Sat mornings) is a good place to pick up food souvenirs before dropping into the **Istituto del Papiro** (Via XX Settembre, tel: 0931 483 342), which specializes in hand-made paper products, crafted using local papyrus – there's more at Galleria Bellomo (Via Capodieci 15, tel: 0931 61340). Corso Matteotti has a couple of shops worth visiting – Salmoiraghi e Viganò (No 84, tel: 0931 69581), which has an excellent range of leather bags, and the Corte degli Aranci (No 70, tel: 0931 483 400) where you'll find pretty scarves and glass and bead jewellery. Across the street Carpentieri (17/19, tel: 0931 67832) has a full range of leather goods. Elsewhere in Ortygia, Il Gusto dei Sapori Smarriti – the Flavour of Lost Tastes (Piazza C Batisti 4, tel: 0931 60069) – is more Aladdin's cave than delicatessen, full of Sicilian gourmandises. Ortigia (Via Maestranza 12, tel: 0931 461 365) is the home of potions and candles, now famous throughout the world. For something really special, visit Riccioli Salvatore (Via dei Mille 3, tel: 0931 65444), a jeweller who works in gold and silver, using the rare amber found near Siracusa.

Many shops in Noto are aimed at tourists, but the town is also noted for its beaten iron; Tomasi Fauci (Via Tafaro 8) and Francesco (Via Mascagni) both have a good selection. Ceramic fans could try Lucilla (Via dei Mille 141) or Terrecotte (Vicolo Pisacane, tel: 3290 112 365): the latter has particularly pretty pots and platters with traditional designs.

Ragusa is known for embroidery, and Modica for chocolate. Head for the oldest chocolate maker, Antico Dolceria Bonajuto (Corso Umberto 159, tel: 0932 941 2225), to see what all the fuss is about. Sweet or spicy, the chocolate is always delicious. Caltagirone is the place to buy ceramics and there are dozens of outlets, many of them either side of the Scala Santa Mara del Monte. Elsewhere, Ceramiche Lory (Via Amedeo 2, tel: 0933 57774) and Giorgio Alemanna (Via Discesa Collegio, tel: 0933 52393) specialize in reproductions of 16th- to 18th-century designs.

# Where to...
# Be Entertained

Siracusa's big arts festival, Ortygia Festival (www.ortigiafestival.it), takes place from May to July, with concerts, plays, music and exhibitions in various venues in the old town. This coincides with performances of classical Greek plays and concerts at Neapolis, where both the Teatro Greco and the Anfiteatro Romano are used for performances in the original language, which are staged in the classical fashion, with a Greek chorus. It makes for an unforgettable experience on a summer's evening; if you're interested there's information at www.indafondazione.org or call freephone 800 542 6440). The tourist office can also help with information about puppet shows, which take place at the puppet theatre at Via della Giudecca 17 on Ortygia throughout the summer months, or call 0931 465 540; www.pupari.com. The city also has plenty in the way of late-night bars with live music – pick up a copy of the listings pamphlet ZERO for full details.

Catania has the liveliest year-round nightlife in Sicily, with plenty of late-night bars in the student quarter around Via Vasta and Piazza Bellini. Piazza Bellini is also the site of Teatro Massimo Bellini, which stages concerts and operas.

There's little on offer in Noto, though a stroll through the streets past the glorious floodlit buildings is an evening must-do, and Ragusa Ibla looks stunning at night as well. Caltagirone's main festival is in July (▲ 106).

# The Heartland and the South Coast

# Getting Your Bearings

Sicily's heartland, empty and forbidding, is a world away from the bustle of the coastal cities and resorts, a vast sweep of country where the isolated, stony towns and villages are few and far between and the landscape shimmers in the great summer heat.

**Page 115 and left:
Details of mosaics,
Villa Romana del
Casale**

Beautiful in spring, when the green hills and fields are bedecked with flowers, the interior in summer is desiccated and lifeless, a silent world where few tourists venture. More should go, as here are two unforgettable sights, the mountainous city of Enna, the "navel of Sicily", visible for miles on its crag, and the fabulous mosaics of the Villa Romana del Casale, a pleasure palace built as the Roman Empire crumbled. South from here, the coast, less developed than Sicily's others, echoes the interior, its long stretches of empty shoreline home to ancient sites and huge stretches of uncrowded beaches. Head for Agrigento, perhaps the finest of all the island's classical sites, where five great temples recall the power and wealth of the Greek world.

West of here, the Greeks built a theatre on the cliff above the sands and pine woods of Eraclea Minoa, an evocative spot whose peace contrasts with the hubbub of Sciacca to the west. This thriving town combines fishing and ceramic manufacture with pampering the patrons of its spa. From here, lonely roads run inland to sleepy but distinctive villages like Corleone, Caltanissetta and Piazza Armerina. Corleone is inexorably linked with the Mafia; Caltanissetta is the interior's largest town; and Piazza Armerina is a graceful old settlement near the Roman mosaics of Casale. Strike south to the coast and you'll reach Licata, a working fishing port at the mouth of the River Salso.

## ★ Don't Miss

## At Your Leisure

Enna, perched up on
a lofty crag

Temple of Hercules, Agrigento

# In Four Days

If you're not quite sure where to begin your travels, this itinerary recommends four practical and enjoyable days out in Sicily's heartland and along the south coast, taking in some of the best places to see using the Getting Your Bearings map on the previous page. For more information see the main entries.

## Day 1

### Morning
If you've been on the south coast, take the N117 north towards **4 Piazza Armerina** (➤ 130), following the signs south of the town to the **1 Villa Romana del Casale** (➤ 120), known locally as the *mosaici* (below). Spend a couple of hours at the villa site to take in the mosaics before heading into the town of Piazza Armerina itself, where you could have lunch.

### Afternoon
Continue on the 117 for 8km (5 miles), then branch left towards **2 Enna** (➤ 123), climbing through woods of pines, deciduous trees and eucalyptus. Once in town, check in to your hotel then take a stroll round to get your bearings.

### Evening
Before dinner, join Enna's wonderfully lively *passeggiata*, finishing at the belvedere at Piazza Francesco Crispi with its superb views across the valley to the tiny village of Calascibetta and the mountains beyond.

## Day 2

### Morning
Spend the morning exploring **Enna** on foot (➤ 174), taking in the daylight views from the castle at the top of the town.

## Afternoon and Evening
Leave Enna and drive southwest to **5 Caltanissetta** (➤ 130), either stopping or simply by-passing it and heading back towards the coast on the N640, arriving in **3 Agrigento** (below, ➤ 126) in the late afternoon. You have two nights here, and you'll have time to walk up **Via Atenea** and wander the medieval streets that branch off and up to the highest point.

# Day 3

## Morning
Make an early start, arriving at the **Valle dei Templi** (➤ 128) before it gets too crowded. Spend the morning among the temples, starting in the **eastern zone** and then moving on to the **western area**.

## Afternoon
After lunch, head back up the hill to take in the **Museo Regionale Archeologico** (➤ 128), a wonderful collection from Agrigento and around that will put the site in perspective. The **temples** are beautifully floodlit at night.

# Day 4

## Morning
Head west on the N115 to **7 Eraclea Minoa** (➤ 131), where you could visit the **Greek theatre** before heading for a swim at the idyllic beach (below).

## Afternoon
Drive west to **8 Sciacca** (➤ 132), a good place for **ceramics**. You could stop here or head inland to take in **9 Corleone** (➤ 132) before returning to Sciacca for the night.

# ❶ Villa Romana del Casale

In a pretty valley 5km (3 miles) southwest of the town of Piazza Armerina lies one of the world's great treasures, the Villa Romana del Casale, a World Heritage Site that boasts the finest Roman mosaics in situ anywhere in the Roman world. Every floor surface in this huge and luxurious property is magnificently decorated – with hunting scenes, stories from classical myths and everyday life – creating a vivid picture of the interests and preoccupations of the aristocracy as the Roman Empire declined.

### The Origins

The villa was probably built towards the end of the **third century** AD, the main house of a huge estate whose owner was likely to have been a member of the **Imperial family**

– possibly Maximilian, co-emperor with Diocletian, who ruled from 286 to 305. Rather than live in Rome and try to stem the growing crisis within the Empire, the decadent members of the ruling classes fled, holing up far from trouble and frittering away the profits made at the expense of the bankrupted cities and their enslaved populations. Maximilian's summer palace was lavishly decorated with marble, frescoes and mosaics, the work of North African artists, who were noted for the realistic modelling and foreshortening used in their work, a legacy of the Hellenistic tradition. Later emperors used the villa, as did the Arabs and Normans, the waves of occupants

**Right: One of Casale's famous Bikini Girls**

**Below: Hunting scene portrayed in the Hall of the Great Hunt**

gradually destroying much of its glory. It was abandoned in the 12th century when a landslide covered it, and only came to light again when serious excavations started in the 1920s. The villa was designated a World Heritage Site in 1997.

## The Mosaics

Walkways run round the interior, from which you can examine all 40 mosaics from a raised vantage point. The route first takes you past the baths, with their depictions of the Roman bathing ritual, then in through the **vestibule** (where the mosaics show visitors being welcomed) to the **peristyle**, the open courtyard garden that was the centre of all Roman villas. The floors here show animal heads and native Sicilian birds, all decorated with laurel and ivy. From here you'll reach a series of **bedchambers** before viewing the **Hall of the Small Hunt**, a jolly scene of the villa owner enjoying the chase and the picnic after it – look for the *cirnechi* hunting dogs, a Libyan breed that's still found in villages on Mount Etna. From here steps ascend to the 60m-long (200-foot) **Hall of the Great Hunt**, the focal point of the Villa, whose extraordinary mosaics illustrate a wonderful series of hunting scenes. African and Eastern animals, destined for the circuses of Rome, are being pursued, species that would soon be hunted to extinction. In the centre, galleys travel back to Rome across an ocean packed with fish. From here you'll come to what is, perhaps, Casale's most famous mosaic, the **Bikini Girls**, ten scantily dressed maidens engaged in gymnastics – one is clearly better than the others and is being awarded a prize. Near here is the **triclinium**, the banqueting hall, whose pavements show superbly realized scenes from the Labours of Hercules. After this, there's the so-called **Erotic Chamber** – pretty mild – and two lively and charming children's rooms, one of whose floor depicts a hunt, with ducks and rabbits as the prey, the other a chariot race, with birds pulling miniature chariots driven by over-excited kids.

### TAKING A BREAK

There's a bar and restaurant (€) just outside the main entrance to the Villa.

➕ 199 F4 ✉ Villa Romana del Casale, Piazza Armerina ☎ 0935 686 667 info 333 190; www.villaromanadelcasale.it (Italian only) ⏰ Daily 9–4:30 🚍 Expensive 🚌 Linea B from Piazza Armerina Apr–Sep 9, 10, 11, 1, 4 and 5; return service on half hour from 9:30

**AT RISK**

UNESCO has designated the Villa Romana del Casale as one of the World Heritage Sites at severe risk, because an underground stream running beneath the mosaics is causing some of them to crumble. Fortunately, an even more serious danger is being averted. In the 1960s the site was covered with an ill-advised perspex structure, in theory to protect the mosaics but, in practice, causing them to fade in summer temperatures of up to 40°C (106°F) and humidity running at 80 per cent. Happily for both mosaics and tourists, the perspex is being replaced by a new shelter and the mosaics are being restored.

### VILLA ROMANA DEL CASALE: INSIDE INFO

**Top Tips** Audio guides (€€) in English are available from the STS kiosk in the row of stalls above the entrance to the Villa; they can be booked in advance on 0935 687 027.

■ You can book an English-speaking authorized guide (tel: 339 265 7640).
■ Note that because of the numerous stairways and walkways, wheelchair users are not admitted.
■ Be sure to take in the detail of the different mosaics – costume, meals, weapons, animals, birds, fruit and flowers – all identifiable.

# 2 Enna

Seemingly perched above the clouds and visible, on clear days, from all over central Sicily, ancient Enna, mountainous, stony and secretive, is the epitome of a fortress town. With its castle looming above the narrow streets, its breathtakingly wide views and its sense of isolation, it's a unique place, eons away from the soft country of the coastal plain. The very heart of the island, and known as "the navel of Sicily", it's a town to be savoured as a place apart, and to gaze out from its ramparts is an experience not be missed.

**Enna is known for its stupendous views**

Founded by the Sikels, Sicily's first people, Enna's long history is one of strife, with Greeks, Romans, Arabs and Normans besieging the city down the centuries for control of this strategic fortress. Its name has barely changed in millennia; today this mountain city, 935m (3,067 feet) above sea level, is the highest provincial capital in Italy.

## The Castello di Lombardia

The 13th-century Castello di Lombardia was built by Frederick II high on the easternmost spur of Enna's craggy ridge. It's a massive fortress, its three inner keeps ringed with thick walls and the six towers that remain of the original 20. One of them, the **Torre Pisano**, can be climbed and will reward you with views that take in vast sweeps of the countryside, with Etna's slopes prominent to the east. In 1324 the castle was the scene of a gathering of the Sicilian parliament, summoned here by Frederick III – it was his Lombard troops, stationed here to keep them out of mischief elsewhere, that gave the castle its name. Outside, there's a fine **War Memorial** by Ernesto Basile and a bronze statue commemorating Eunus, the leader of the First Slave Revolt against Rome in 135BC – a plaque draws attention to the resultant slave emancipation "2,000 years before the birth of Abraham Lincoln".

## From the Castello to Piazza Crispi

From the Castello, Via Roma runs down the ridge through a series of squares to Piazza Vittorio Emanuele, a lovely piazza that's the hub of Enna's nightly *passeggiata*. Up near the castle you'll find **Sicilia delle Miniature**, an exhibition of tiny

replicas of Sicilian architecture, while farther down, past the
now-closed Museo Alessi, you'll find the **Duomo**, built on the
site of Persephone's temple in 1307. Damaged and restored
over the years, its interior is lovely, an exuberantly decorated
space where the apricot walls and white stucco contrast with
the massively carved columns. These are decorated with
grotesques, the grey basalt surging up to the beautiful nave
ceiling, carved by Scipione di Guido. Opposite the Duomo, at
the back of Piazza Mazzini, the **Museo Archeologico** (daily
9–6:30; inexpensive) will fill you in on ancient history in the
area. Head on down to Piazza Garibaldi, dominated by some
monumental Fascist public buildings, and walk through to
Piazza Crispi, which has a wonderful belvedere, from where
you'll look across to the Arab-founded village of **Calascibetta**,
its ochre houses tumbling down the hill, and over the dreamy
landscape towards Etna.

South of Enna is the **Lago di Pergusa**, the legendary site
of Persephone's abduction by Hades. The underworld god
snatched the girl while she was gathering flowers by the
lake, causing such anguish to her mother Demeter, goddess
of agriculture, that no corn grew while she searched for
her child. Finally Zeus ruled that Persephone should be
returned to her mother, provided she had eaten no food in the
underworld; Hades tricked her into eating six pomegranate
seeds, so she had to return to the underworld for six months a
year. Demeter still grieves when her daughter is away, autumn
marking the onset of her sorrow and spring her joy at their

**View across to
Calascibetta**

## ENNA: INSIDE INFO

**Top Tips** As there are only two hotels in the centre of town, book ahead if you're planning to stay in Enna.
■ The best viewpoint in town is the belvedere behind Piazza Crispi.

**In More Depth** Southwest of Piazza Matteotti the **Torre di Frederico II** stands in the public gardens, all that's left of the king's hunting demesne. It's an octagonal structure, 24m (7 feet) high, which marks the very centre of Sicily and the crossing point of the axes that run through the three "legs" of the island, represented in Sicily's symbol, the Trinacria. Scholars posit that it may form part of an ancient geomantic network, similar to the ley lines of Britain, which links the oldest sites throughout Sicily. Whatever the theory, it's worth climbing the Torre, reputed to be linked by an underground passage to the Castello, for stupendous views across the entire island.

reunion. Today, unfortunately, the lake's beauty is wrecked by the racing circuit that runs round it.

### TAKING A BREAK

For a drink, try the **Gran Caffé Roma** (€; Via Roma 312) or the **Caffé Italia** on Piazza Garibaldi; for more restaurants ➤ 136.

🔁 199 E5 🚹 Via Roma 413, tel: 0935 528 228; www.apt-enna.com; Mon–Sat 9–1, 3:30–6.30

**Castello di Lombardia**
✉ Viale Nino Savarese ☎ 0935 500 962 🕐 Daily 9–1, 3–5

**Duomo**
✉ Via Roma ☎ None 🕐 Daily 9–12, 4–7

**La Sicilia delle Miniature**
✉ Via Roma 533 ☎ 338 502 3361 🕐 Tue–Sun 10–1, 3:30–7:30

# ❸ Agrigento

Strung, like pearls on a necklace, along a ridge beside the sea, the great Greek temples of Agrigento, ancient Akragas, are acknowledged as the finest in Italy and comparable with those in Greece itself. Set among olive and almond trees, these ancient structures evoke the genius of their designers and the glory of the Sicilian Greek city states. Overlooking this superb archaeological zone is the town of Agrigento, whose medieval heart provides all the pleasures of prosperous provincial life.

Akragas was founded in 580BC as a colony of Gela, part of the process of hellenization of the indigenous population as the Greeks spread ever farther west. It stands on a plain between the rivers Akragas (San Biagio) and Hypsas (Sant'Anna) and was laid out between the two ridges that bound this area to the north and south. The northern ridge is today the site of the modern town; the southern is the site of the majestic temples built by the Greeks. From the start the city prospered under a succession of tyrants, whose wars and trading successes funded building, making Agrigento fabulously wealthy. Its riches, though, were no guarantee of its permanence, and it was besieged by the Carthaginians, sacked by the Romans and looted by Saracens and Normans. It was only with the 18th- to 19th-century interest in archaeology that it recovered, earning its place as Sicily's top classical site.

**Agrigento's gem – the classical lines of the Temple of Concord**

## The Town

The medieval town of Agrigento, increasingly surrounded by ugly modern building, is a charming place that's centred around Via Atenea, the main artery that runs west from the central square, Piazza Aldo Moro. Along here is the 17th-century church of the Purgatorio, while from this level steps and alleys lead to the old upper town, home to **Santa Maria dei Greci**, built over a fifth-century BC temple. Further up the hill, past whitewashed houses, stands the 14th-century **Duomo**, fronted by a spacious piazza.

## Valle dei Templi

The Valley of the Temples is not really in a valley at all, but strung along a ridge, in two zones to the east and west of the road running down from Agrigento. Entering the eastern zone and walking along the Via Sacra, you'll first pass the eight standing columns of the 67m-long (220-foot) **Temple of Herakles**, built around 500BC and the oldest in the Valle. Continue past it to Agrigento's crown jewel, the stunningly serene and balanced **Temple of Concord**. Originally coated with marble stucco and brightly painted, as were all the temples on the site, it owes its superb condition to its conversion in the sixth century by the wonderfully named San Gregorio delle Rape (St Gregory of the Turnips) into a Christian church. From here, the Via Sacra continues to the far end of the ridge and the **Temple of Hera**, a half-ruined structure whose walls still show the red streaks left by the fire set by the Carthaginians when they sacked the city in 406BC. Walk back down the ridge and cross the road to the western zone, whose **Temple of Olympian Zeus**, totally destroyed by a later earthquake, is the largest Greek temple in the world. It needs imagination to make sense of the jumbled ruins, which once covered an area larger than a football field, but the sheer scale can be deduced from the huge toppled figure (*telamon*) that lies on the ground, a series of which supported the architrave. Beyond here is the remains of the earliest sacred site, the seventh-century BC Sanctuary of the Chthonic Deities, and the reconstructed Temple of Dioscuri (Castor and Pollux), in actuality a mish-mash of unrelated fragments from the site.

Surviving columns of the Temple of Hera

## Museo Regionale Archeologico

The outstanding Archaeological Museum contains finds from the temples and ancient city, as well as the surrounding area. It's a very **fine** collection, and the exhibits will help bring ancient Akragas alive. Don't miss the Greek vases in rooms 3 and 4, which date from the third to the sixth centuries BC and include a 440BC white-ground *krater* (chalice) depicting Perseus freeing Andromeda. Room 6 has models reconstructing the Temple of Zeus and a reconstructed *telamon* from its facade, while room 10 has some fine sculpture, including a Praxitelean torso. Across the road from the museum is the Hellenistic-Roman quarter, an excavated residential area of the city.

## TAKING A BREAK

**Now taking it easy, one of the massive *telamoni* that supported the Temple of Zeus**

You can get a drink and something to eat at the museum, the main entrance and at the kiosk on the Via Sacra, midway between the temples of Concord and Hera (all €).

🔲 198 B3 ℹ Piazza Vittorio Emanuele, tel: 800 236 837; www.agrigento-sicilia.it; Mon–Fri 8–2, 3–7
ℹ Via Cesare Battisti 15, tel: 0922 20 454; Mon–Sat 8:30–1:30

**Santa Maria dei Greci**
✉ Salita Santa Maria dei Greci
🕐 Daily 8:30–12:30, 4:30–7:30
💰 Free

**Duomo**
✉ Via Duomo 🕐 Sat–Thu 9:30–12:30, 4–6 💰 Free

**Valle dei Templi**
✉ Valle dei Templi ☎ 0922 621 611; www.parcovalledeitempli.it
🕐 Apr–Sep daily 9–6; Oct–Mar 9–4; subject to change if work is underway on the site 💰 Expensive

**Museo Regionale Archeologico**
✉ Via dei Templi, Contrada San Nicola ☎ 0922 401 565
🕐 Tue–Sat 9–7, Sun–Mon 9–1
💰 Expensive

## AGRIGENTO: INSIDE INFO

**Top tips** The archaeological site is big, measuring 4.5 x 3km (2.7 x 1.8 miles) and you should allow a day to see everything properly.
- If time is short, concentrate on the temples along the Via Sacra, the Temple of Zeus and the archaeological museum.
- A bus service (Nos 1, 2, 3) links Agrigento town with the Valle dei Templi. Buses run from Piazza Marconi, next to the railway station, past the archaeological museum and the Hellenistic and Roman districts to the main entrance to the site – buy your ticket at a kiosk or *tabacchi* before you get on.
- Audio guides are available from the ticket office.
- In high summer, Agrigento is both very crowded and extremely hot in the middle of the day – plan your visit to take this into account.
- There are lavatories at the museum, the main entrance and near the Temple of Hera on the Via Sacra.
- Opening times are constantly subject to change and you may find areas closed or undergoing restoration.

# At Your Leisure

## 4 Piazza Armerina

Set in the thickly wooded, gentle countryside of the southern interior, Piazza Armerina is an elegantly faded town that, until the 1950s excavations of the Roman mosaics at the nearby Villa Romana del Casale (➤ 120), saw few visitors exploring its narrow streets and crumbling palazzi. In August it's the scene of one of Sicily's major festivals, Il Palio dei Normanni, a celebration of medieval Norman jousting, complete with armoured knights, horses and winsome damsels. The event includes various parades and displays of horsemanship to celebrate Count Roger's capture of the town from the Saracens in 1087. Piazza's *centro storico* lies at the top of the hill; the best way to see it entails simply wandering – you'll be sure to stumble over a fine church or harmonious piazza. Don't miss Piazza Garibaldi, the town's hub, the 17th-century Duomo and the baroque church of Sant'Anna. Lovers of Norman architecture shouldn't miss Sant'Andrea, a serene and plain Romanesque church set amidst woods a kilometre out of town to the north.

➕ 199 F4 ℹ Piazza Santa Rosalia, tel: 0935 680 202; www.comune.piazzaarmerina.en.it; Mon–Fri 9–1, 3–7

## 5 Caltanissetta

By far the largest town in the interior, Caltanissetta lies in the rural heart of Sicily. This is poor country, where sleepy villages are locked in a timeless torpor and life is still hard. In town, things are different, and first impressions will be of a traffic-choked, bustling town. It's home to

The lofty interior of Piazza Armerina's Duomo

The blue-and-white-striped facade of San Sebastiano, Caltanissetta

17th-century churches such as San Sebastiano and Sant'Agata, and a provincial Museo Archeologico (Via Napoleone Colajanni 3; daily 9–1, 3–7), while the dilapidated ruins of the Norman Castello di Pietrarossa perch high on a crag above. In Italian minds though, Caltanissetta is associated with one thing alone – Averna, one of Italy's leading *amari* (bitters). These are drunk as *digestivi* (digestives) after meals, and are a blend of wild herbs and alcohol. Averna, containing 60 herbs, was invented by the Capuchin monks, who gave the recipe in the 1800s to Don Salvatore Averna. It's still made in the town today, so what better place to sample this Sicilian essential.

✚ 199 D4  📍 Corso Vittorio Emanuele 109, tel: 0934 530 440; www.aapit.cl.it; Mon–Fri 8–2, 2:45–6:15

## ⑥ Licata

East of Agrigento, the thriving town of Licata lies at the mouth of the River Salso, a working fishing port, raucous with boats and maritime activity, where the atmosphere makes for a town that's more than the sum of its parts. Its history stretches back to the third century BC, but Licata today is architecturally neatly split into two halves, a duo of baroque *corsi*, lined with pavement cafés, and a huddle of narrow medieval alleyways reaching back to the harbour. Mornings

see a lively market held in front of main church, or you could take in the Museo Civico (Piazza Linares Tue–Sat 9–12:30, 4–7; free), where there are displays of locally excavated prehistoric and Greek artefacts. From the main Corso Roma you can climb to the top of the town for a good view over the harbour and a stroll to the 16th-century *castello*, or simply enjoy the beach.

✚ 199 D2

## ⑦ Eraclea Minoa

By the time you've left Agrigento (► 126) the last thing on your mind may be yet more Greek ruins, but do make an exception for Eraclea Minoa, one of the most beautifully sited Greek cities in Sicily. It stands on a ridge above the sea and a smooth arc of clean sand backed by pines, with the mouth of the River Plátani on the other side. The remnants of this sixth-century BC settlement are still largely unexcavated, but the massive city walls still stand, as does the theatre, first built in the fourth century BC and restored by the Romans 700 years later. Covered to protect its soft sandstone from the weather, it's among the most stunning sites in Sicily. To get to the beach, which is one of the best on the south coast, leave the car park and follow the twisty road downhill, signed Montallegro-Bove Marina.

Out of season, you will have the beach pretty much to yourself, but come high summer the sands heave with bronzing bodies and you will need to arrive early even to get a parking space. At the western end of the beach you can lay on your very own mud bath, like the locals do. They scrape *fango* (mud) – more of a greenish slime – off the rocks and onto their bodies and bake in the sun for a few minutes. It is supposed to have great therapeutic effects and is completely free – but don't forget to wash it off.

🚩 193 E1 ⏱ 9–1 hour before dusk
💶 Inexpensive

## 8 Sciacca

It was the sulphur springs that drew the Greeks, and then the Romans, to Sciacca. You can still take the waters, with their healing properties for skin diseases and arthritis, in the grand Liberty-style Stabilimento Termale on the town's eastern edge. The Arabs were fans too, and Sciacca's name derives from the Arabic *xacca*, meaning water. The town today has additional pleasures, in the shape of a vibrant fishing port, some good beaches and the low-key Mediterranean charms of its lovely streets and piazzas. Head through the Porta San Salvatore in the walls that still encircle the upper town to walk down the Corso Vittorio Emanuele, the main drag, to Piazza Scandaliato, the place for the *passeggiata*. If you like churches, there's a cathedral to admire and a rose window on the church of the Carmine, though top prize goes to the jewel-like Renaissance Santa Margherita, just inside the gate. Behind the wider streets, tiny alleys conjure up the Moorish past, and everywhere there are signs of the ceramics for which the town is famed – Sciacca has over 30 artisan ceramicists and is one of Sicily's best places for pottery. If you're heading for the beach, best bets are San Marco and the Contrada Sobareto. In spring, Sciacca has one of the best carnivals in Sicily. It is celebrated a week before Lent with parades of floats carrying enormous papier mâché figures, which represent local characters and change year after year, thanks to diligent planning for months beforehand. Another feature of the Sciacca carnival is the remarkable consumption of the local sausage. The event ends with the burning of the mask of the Carnival King, Peppi Nappa.

🚩 193 D1  ℹ Corso Vittorio Emanuele 84;
tel: 0925 227 44; www.sciaccaonline.it;
Mon–Sat 8–2, 4–6

## 9 Corleone

Corleone, familiar to anyone who has read Mario Puzo's book *The Godfather* or seen the movie (► 26), lies amid rocky landscape overlooking a fertile valley on the main route south between Palermo and Sciacca. Its history is long and has left a legacy of a fine cathedral, palazzi, squares and fountains, but it's the town's 20th-century story and its links with one of Sicily's most notorious Mafia families that attract the visitors. From

**The busy fishing port of Sciacca**

the 1940s the town was renowned for its bloodletting, feuds and vendettas, with one of the highest murder rates in the world – 153 out of a population of 18,000 between 1944 and 1948 alone. The *capo* Salvatore Riina, the most-wanted man in Italy, was arrested in Palermo in 1993, having lived openly in Corleone, his home town, for over 20 years, and April 2006 saw the capture of Bernardo Provenzano, who had been hiding in and near the town for 40 years. You can fill in the background to all this in the **Museo Anti-Mafia**, established by the townspeople as part of the on-going attempt to face up to the problem of the *Cosa Nostra*. The locals are very proud of the museum, and very pleased to welcome visitors there. But expressing too much interest in the Mafia usually doesn't go down well in Corleone, where they are largely fed up with *Godfather* tourism. And don't go trying to find any of the locations from the film – like Bar Vitelli and the church where Michael was married. The movies were not shot here because Corleone was too developed for director Francis Ford Coppola's eye. Instead the Sicilian scenes were filmed in Sávoca and Forza d'Agro outside Taormina.

🕂 193 E3

### Museo Anti-Mafia

✉ Via Orfanotriofo 7 ☎ 0918 461 255
🕐 Mon–Fri 10:30, 11:30, 12:30, 3:30, 4:30, 5:30, Sun by appointment only 🎟 Free

### FOR KIDS

This area of Sicily is packed with some of the island's finest **archaeological sites**, which will need to be tempered with **beach days** for all but the keenest kids. They'll enjoy a quick blast of **mosaics at the Villa Romana** and a fast gallop past the Agrigento temples, but wandering around **seaside towns** like Sciacca and Licata may prove more popular. Older children will love the views and castle at **Enna**, and get a thrill from Mafia stories at **Corleone**, but, on the whole, the beaches will win hands down.

# Where to...
## Stay

**Prices**
Expect to pay per double room, per night

€ under €130   €€ €130–€230   €€€ over €230

## PIAZZA ARMERINA

### Il Gigliotto €€

10km (6 miles) south of Piazza Armerina and set in rolling agricultural countryside, this lovely old monastery, with its mellow stone and graceful arches, is now home to a family-run *agriturismo*. Bedrooms and restaurant are set around a courtyard, with a large pool and pretty gardens outside. The rooms are big, simple and comfortable, the restaurant serves organic produce from the estate and sources anything not home-produced from the local area – all in all a real find if you're looking for something peaceful and a little bit special.

🕂 199 F4 🖂 SS117 bis km 60, Piazza Armerina 🕿 0933 970 898; www.gigliotto.com

### Ostello del Borgo €

If you want to stay right in town, this budget choice wins hands down. Once a monastery and dating from the 15th century, the old cells have been converted into simple, old-fashioned rooms, some with bathrooms, some – and even less expensive – without, and there's also the option of dormitory-style accommodation. Staff are friendly and helpful and breakfast is included in the price.

🕂 199 F4 🖂 Largo San Giovanni 6 🕿 0935 687 019; www.ostellodelborgo.it

### Park Hotel Paradiso €–€€

The Park is a good modern hotel situated to the north of town. Its rooms are all well equipped and there's a more than adequate restaurant, while the grounds have tennis courts and a pool on offer – certainly the best hotel in Piazza Armerina if you want comfort and good facilities.

🕂 199 F4 🖂 Contrada da Ramaldo, Piazza Armerina 🕿 0935 680 841; www.parkhotelparadiso.it

## ENNA

### Bristol €

Opened in 2006, this modern, friendly and good-value hotel is in the heart of Enna, a stone's throw from Via Roma. The rooms are functional rather than grand luxe, but comfortable and fully equipped. Breakfast and parking are included in the price of the room.

🕂 199 E5 🖂 Piazza Ghisleri 13 🕿 0935 244 15; www.hotelbristolenna.it

### Grand Albergo Sicilia €–€€

Until 2006 the only hotel in Enna, the Grand Albergo has recently undergone a much-needed full-frontal face lift and the inside is as impressive as ever. The huge, marble reception area has access to a breakfast terrace, while upstairs the rooms are big and comfortable with pretty furnishings and gleaming bathrooms.

🕂 199 E5 🖂 Piazza Napoleone Colianni 7 🕿 0935 500 850; www.hotelsiciliaenna.it

## AGRIGENTO

### Baglio della Luna €€€

Courtyards, a 14th-century tower and rambling old buildings make up this elegant luxury hotel, set in a green oasis near the Valley of the Temples. The rich fabrics, polished floors and solid old-style furnishings of the bedrooms complement the streamlined bathrooms, while outside you can eat breakfast on the terrace, relax in the small swimming pool or enjoy a nightcap under the stars. The excellent restaurant is renowned for its exceptional wine list.

✚ 198 B3 ⊠ Via Serafino Amabile Guastella 1 ☎ 0922 511 061; www.bagliodellaluna.com

### Camere a Sud €

Tucked away off Agrigento's main street, this charming little B&B is as chic and laid back as they come. Warm colours, clean lines and good design are the order of the day, making a stay here wonderfully relaxing – and all at year-round excellent prices. Book ahead, as space is limited, and be prepared to pay in cash – although the owners are looking at accepting credit cards in the future.

✚ 198 B3 ⊠ Via Ficani 6 ☎ 349 638 4424; www.camereasud.it

### Colleverde Park €€

You can look down on the floodlit temples from the tranquil gardens of this comfortable hotel, an oasis at the end of a hot day's sightseeing. The rooms are modern, airy and well equipped and the staff very helpful, but the chief attractions have to be the beautiful outdoor dining terrace and the verdant, well-tended gardens.

✚ 198 B3 ⊠ Via Panoramica dei Templi ☎ 0922 295 55; www.colleverdehotel.it

### Hotel Costazzurra €€

If you'd like to be away from the pressure of central Agrigento, head for this family-run hotel, set right on the coast a couple of kilometres from the Valle dei Templi. All of the cool and spacious rooms have balconies and, though simple, the hotel is comfortable with good amenities. The restaurant serves local dishes, there's a private beach and plenty of shady outside areas to relax. Prices drop dramatically outside high season.

✚ 198 B3 ⊠ Via delle Viole 2, Loc San Leone ☎ 0922 411 222; www.hotelcostazzurra.it

### Hotel Villa Eos €€

Set above the sea 7km (4 miles) from Agrigento centre, the Villa Eos offers the best value in the area. A modern, family-run, 3-star hotel, it has comfortable, pretty rooms, all with balconies, a good restaurant overlooking the pool, where dinner and the buffet breakfast are served, tennis courts and a solarium. The hotel sometimes has rooms when everywhere else is booked or you could reserve ahead online for even better rates.

✚ 198 B3 ⊠ Via Giovanni Gentile ☎ 0922 597 170; www.hotelvillaeos.it

## SCIACCA

### Pensione Aliai €

Overlooking the port, this comfortable *pensione* is typical of the increasingly high standards offered by Sicilian B&Bs. The rooms, furnished in traditional style with wrought-iron bedsteads and deep mattresses, have modern bathrooms, lovely old beamed ceilings and plenty of storage space – all overlook the water and some have even got tiny terraces. You can stroll up to the town centre in the evening.

✚ 193 D1 ⊠ Via Gaie di Garaffe 60 ☎ 0925 905 388; www.aliai.com

### Rocco Forte Verdura Golf & Spa Resort €€€

Set in its own extensive grounds among olive and lemon groves, all the resort's rooms have their own private terraces and sea views. Every imaginable amenity and luxury is on site, including a state-of-the-art spa, championship golf courses and a private beach. Sciacca is 15 minutes' drive away, and the temples of Agrigento are also within easy reach (40km/ 25 miles)

✚ 193 D1 ⊠ SS115 km 131, Sciacca ☎ 0925 998 001; www.verduraresort.com

# Where to...
## Eat and Drink

### Prices

Expect to pay per person for a meal, including wine and service

€ up to €20     €€ €20–€35     €€€ more than €35

## PIAZZA ARMERINA

### Al Fogher €€€

Some 3km (2 miles) outside town, an old railway building is home to one of Sicily's most famous restaurants. This is imaginative Sicilian cooking at its best – local ingredients in exciting combinations based on traditional dishes and served with a modern twist. Fennel, artichokes, radicchio and wild salads appear in many dishes, the puddings are imaginative, while the wine list and service are everything you'd expect from a restaurant of this calibre. Booking is essential.

🚩 199 F4 ⊠ Contrada Bellia ☎ 0935 684 123; www.alfogher.net ⏰ Tue–Sat 12–2:30, 7:30–9:30, Sun 12–2:30. Closed 1 week in Jan and 1 week in Jul

### Trattoria la Ruota €€

If you're looking for a nice lunch place after visiting the Villa Romana, this pretty restaurant, housed in an old watermill, should fit the bill. Eat in or outside on the terrace or in the shade and sample good inland cooking, featuring home-made pasta, local rabbit and veal. *Contorni* are good here – try the *caponata*, a mixed vegetable dish with olives and capers.

🚩 199 F4 ⊠ Contrada Paratore Casale ☎ 0935 680 542; www.trattorialaruota.it ⏰ Daily 12–2:30

## ENNA

### Caffè Marro €

You can enjoy a *gelato* (ice cream) or a mouth-watering hazelnut pastry with your coffee at this elegant historic café, overlooking both Piazza Vittorio Emanuele and the Belvedere – the main squares in Enna. In summer the terrace is a lovely spot for enjoying alfresco refreshments while watching the world go by.

🚩 199 E5 ⊠ Piazza Vittorio Emanuele 21 ☎ 0935 591 184 ⏰ Daily 8am–10pm

### Centrale €€–€€€

Good service, a good wine list and plenty of choice are the hallmarks of this fine restaurant, run by the same family for more than 100 years. This restaurant is part of the Buon Riccordo confederation – hence the ceramic plates on the walls. Here, you can enjoy splendid inland cuisine; food is cooked to order and locally sourced. The Centrale is famed for its *antipasto* buffet – start your meal by helping yourself from a range of more than 20 succulent vegetable dishes.

🚩 199 E5 ⊠ Piazza VI Dicembre 9 ☎ 0935 500 963; www.ristorantecentrale. net ⏰ Jun–Aug daily 12–2:30, 7:30–10; Sep–May Sun–Fri 12–2:30, 6:30–10

## AGRIGENTO

### Atenea €

Among the plethora of tourist-aimed restaurants in Agrigento town, the Atenea is a good bet, serving set menus, which include wine, as well as à la carte meals. You can sit outside in the piazza and enjoy simple pasta – the *cavatelli* are good – followed by grilled meat or fish.

🚩 198 B3 ⊠ Via Ficani 32 ☎ 0922 20247 ⏰ Apr–Oct Mon–Sat 12–2:30, 7:30–10, Sun 7:30–10; Nov–Mar Mon–Sat 12–2:30, 7:30–10

## Le Caprice €€€

The theme at this stylish restaurant is fish – fresh and perfectly and simply prepared. Cooking here uses seasonal ingredients and diners would be wise to eat according to Sicilian custom, enjoying fish and seafood for *antipasto*, *primo* and *secondo*. It's a big restaurant with indoor space and a terraced area outside; both overlook green lawns and plants. The service is attentive and professional; the wines are well kept.

✚ 198 B3 ☒ Via Cavaleri Magazzeni 2 (San Leone) ☎ 0922 411 364; www.ristorantitaliani.it/lecaprice ⓦ Sat–Thu 12–2.30, 7.30–9. Nov–Mar closed Mon

## Ruga Reali €€–€€€

Right in the heart of the medieval quarter of Agrigento town, the old stables of a 15th-century palazzo is home to this rustic eating house, where you can enjoy a good range of both fish and meat dishes. The cooking is traditional so expect pasta with fish-based sauces, stuffed

calamari and home-made *fettuccine*. There is usually an excellent *cuscus di pesce* on the menu, as well as prawns, shrimp and squid.

✚ 198 B3 ☒ Cortile Scribani 8 ☎ 0922 203 70 ⓦ Thu–Fri, Sun–Mon 12–3.30, 7.30–11, Wed 7.30–11, Sat 12–3.30, 7.30–midnight

## Spizzulio €–€€

Officially an *enoteca* (wine bar), Spizzulio also has a good restaurant serving home-made dishes. As you would expect, there is an excellent wine list with around 300 labels – both local and foreign – and a professional sommelier to guide you through the tastings. The restaurant specializes in traditional Sicilian and Italian foods, and guests are sometimes entertained by the chef constructing a "food sculpture" – usually an identifiable icon. It's about 1km (0.6 miles) out of town. You will need to reserve ahead.

✚ 198 B3 ☒ Via Panoramica dei Templi 23 ☎ 0922 20712; www.spizzulio.it ⓦ Daily lunch and dinner. Closed 2 weeks in Nov

## Trattoria dei Templi €€

Terracotta floors and vaulted ceilings contribute to the charms of this restaurant, situated between the town and the Valley of the Temples. The cooking here verges on the elegant, with dishes such as *fettuccine all'aragosta* (fresh pasta ribbons with lobster) and *tagliolini con gamberoni rossi e pistachio* (with prawns and pistachio) setting the tone. As anywhere near the sea, the accent throughout is on fish, and there are some good Sicilian white wines to accompany it.

✚ 198 B3 ☒ Via Panoramica dei Templi 15 ☎ 0922 403 110; www.trattoriadeitempli.com ⓦ Jul–Sep Mon–Sat 12.30–3, 7.30–11; Oct–Jun Sat–Thu 12.30–3, 7.30–11

### SCIACCA

## Bar Scandaglia €

Sit in the main piazza and gaze over the port to sea at Sciacca's most elegant café. It's a good place for a drink, a teatime plate of *pasticceria* or a light lunch with *pizzette*, a

savoury tart, or even breakfast. Don't miss the homemade ice cream here – chocolate and pistachio are particularly good, as are the fruit ices in summer.

✚ 193 D1 ☒ Piazza Scandaliato 5 ☎ 0952 216 65 ⓦ Daily 8:30am–11pm (may close earlier)

## Hostaria del Vicolo €€–€€€

A member of the Slow Food association (as its name suggests, the antithesis of fast food), this central restaurant has well earned its reputation for its ability to meld traditional Sicilian ingredients and cooking styles with a 21st-century attitude to food. Dishes are well thought out and carefully cooked – to get an idea of what they can do, go for the tasting menu. Take the waiter's advice on the wine: everything on the list is Sicilian and it's all good so you really can't go wrong.

✚ 193 D1 ☒ Vicolo Sammaritano 10 ☎ 0925 230 71; www.trattoriadeitempli.com ⓦ Tue–Sun 12–2:30, 7:30–9.30

# Where to...
## Shop

Shops in this part of Sicily tend to cater for locals. In **Enna**, the biggest choice is along Via Roma, and ladies might like to pop into **Dibella** (Via Roma 357, tel: 0935 500 575) where there's a reasonable choice of accessories as well as clothes. The **Pasticceria Il Dolce** (Piazza Sant'Agostino 40, tel: 0935 24018) is the perfect place to sample *cannoli*. **Russo Fernando** (Via Mercato Sant'Antonio 16, tel: 0935 501 031) has the best choice of local cheese and also sells Sicilian liqueurs. Nearby at No 34, **Salumi Formaggi di Dio** (tel: 0935 525 758) specializes in Sicilian cheese, including a superb *piacentu ennese*, aged for 12 months.

In **Agrigento** star buys are the locally produced artisan wares such as baskets and rugs. The **Salumeria**

**del Buon Sapore** (Via Cappuccini 20, tel: 0925 26562) is a haven of Sicilian specialities, from salamis and cheeses to oils and fine wines. For the sweet-toothed, the **Abbazia di Santo Spirito** (Via S Spirito, next to the Museo Civico, tel: 0922 590 371) is famous for its heavenly almond confectionary, still made by the Benedictine nuns here.

**Sciacca** is famed for its pottery, much of it in the traditional colours of deep blue, turquoise and yellow. Try **Gaspare Cascio** (Via V Emanuele 115, tel: 0925 828 29), or **Montalbano** at No 54 (tel: 0925 854 330) for the huge vases, platters and dishes in traditional designs. **Carlino Antonino** (Corso V Emanuele 46, www. carlinoceramiche.it) has a superb collection of plates and figurines.

# Where to...
## Be Entertained

If you find yourself in **Piazza Armerina** in mid-August, you'll be able to experience the **Palio dei Normanni** (12–14 August), when costumed knights joust against comers from all over the interior. Competition is fierce and the processions spectacular; come early to grab a good viewing position. May sees the town bedecked in flowers when the citizens compete to decorate their courtyards and balconies, but outside these times, you'll be limited to the *passeggiata* and a late-night drink at a café.

Things aren't much livelier in **Enna**, where the best bets in the evenings are the **Caffè Italia** on Piazza Garibaldi or the **Gran Caffè Roma** (Via Roma 312).

The **Agrigento** evening scene is centred on Piazzale Aldo Moro and

Via Atenea, where you'll find plenty of outdoor cafés and a particularly lively *passeggiata*. The Viale della Vittoria is a good spot for sunset views, and it's worth heading down to the temples, all beautifully floodlit at night. Agrigento's big festival is the **Sagra del Mandorlo** (almond festival, ▶ 16–17) in February, celebrated to herald spring – there are folklore exhibits, dances, processions and music. Things are more cultured in August when the final 10 days of the month sees the **Musica Festival**, when musicians perform in the sublime setting of the Valle dei Templi.

The ancient Greek site **Eraclea Minoa** (tel: 0922 846 005) is the spectacular location for classical drama and concerts in July and August.

# Western Sicily

# Getting Your Bearings

West of Palermo, North Africa meets Italy: the hills flatten out to the south and far west, the cliffs of the northern coast give way to wind-scoured salt flats, and the landscape is dotted with white cubic houses and stately palms. The light is harsh and pure, the names of the towns and villages Arabic-based, and pasta gives way to couscous. Historically, this was Phoenician and Carthaginian territory, and the ruins of their great island city, Mozia, are among the wonders of this coast. Inland, to the northeast, lies Greek Segesta, with its magically sited temple and theatre; to the south are the ruins of the great coastal city of Selinunte; while high on a crag above the saltpans of Trapani perches picturesque Erice.

From Erice you can head for the north coast, where the low-key charms of holiday villages such as Castellammare del Golfo compete with the splendour of the cliffs and sea in the Riserva Naturale dello Zingaro. Beyond Zingaro lies San Vito lo Capo, a remote village set round one of Sicily's finest white-sand beaches and backed by dramatically lowering cliffs. From here, the road runs south towards historic Trapani, just a short sea crossing from the Egadi islands, and Marsala, inextricably connected in English minds with one of Europe's mellowest fortified wines. Head southeast from here, across the flat lands and through the vineyards, and you'll reach Mazara del Vallo, a historic town that has morphed into one of Italy's biggest fishing ports and deserves to be better known.

**Top: Greek temple at Segesta**
**Above: Facade of Erice's cathedral**

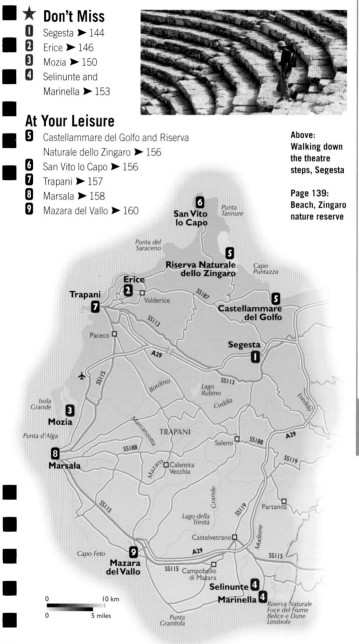

Above:
Walking down
the theatre
steps, Segesta

Page 139:
Beach, Zingaro
nature reserve

San Vito lo Capo **6**
Punta Tannure

Punta del Saraceno

Riserva Naturale dello Zingaro **5**
Capo Puntazza

Erice **2**
Valderice
SS187

Trapani **7**

Castellammare del Golfo **5**

SS113

Paceco

A29

Segesta **1**

SS115

Bordino
SS113
Lago Rubino
Cuddia

Treddio

Isola Grande

Mozia **3**

Punta d'Alga

Marcanzotta

TRAPANI

Salemi
SS188

A29

SS188

Marsala **8**

Mazaro
Calamita Vecchia

SS119

SS119

Grande

Partanna

Lago della Trinità

Castelvetrano

Modione

SS115

Capo Feto

Mazara del Vallo **9**

A29

SS115
Campobello di Mazara

Selinunte **4**
Marinella **4**

Riserva Naturale Foce del Fiume Belice e Dune Limitrofe

0          10 km
0      5 miles

Punta Granitola

# In Four Days

If you're not quite sure where to begin your travels, this itinerary recommends four practical and enjoyable days out in western Sicily, taking in some of the best places to see using the Getting Your Bearings map on the previous page. For more information see the main entries.

## Day 1

### Morning
If you're heading west from Palermo, take the A29 *autostrada*, exiting at 5 **Castellammare del Golfo** (➤ 156), where there's plenty of accommodation, if you want to visit the village (left) and explore the **Zingaro** (➤ 156). From Castellammare you can take the A187 west, then follow the minor roads to 6 **San Vito lo Capo** (➤ 156), another possible overnight stop. Alternatively, if you're planning to bypass the far northwest, continue on the motorway, taking the A29dir branch to the Segesta exit.

### Afternoon
Spend the afternoon at 1 **Segesta** (➤ 144), climbing up to the Temple (opposite, bottom) and then exploring the theatre area, before rejoining the *autostrada* and heading west.

### Evening
Plan to spend the night either at 2 **Erice** (➤ 146) or 7 **Trapani** (➤ 157).

## Day 2

### Morning
Spend the morning in **Erice**, wandering the streets of this lovely town and taking in the splendid views to both north and west coasts from the heights.

### Afternoon
Head down the hill to **Trapani** (opposite, top). You could explore the town or take the ferry to **Favignana** (➤ 171) to get a taste of the **Egadi islands**.

## Evening

Spend the evening in Trapani or, in summer, perhaps have dinner on Favignana before catching a late boat back.

# Day 3

## Morning

Head off early and take the coast road down to the ferry for **❸ Mozia** (► 150). You could take a picnic and spend the day on the island or simply a couple of hours before driving on to **❽ Marsala** (► 158).

## Afternoon

After visiting Marsala and perhaps taking a tour of one of the **wineries** (► 158), take the N115 towards **❾ Mazara del Vallo** (► 160) and then continue east towards **❹ Selinunte** (► 153). If you take the A29 *autostrada*, exit at Castelvetrano and pick up the N115d to **Selinunte**.

## Evening

Stay the night on the coast at **Marinella** (► 154).

# Day 4

## Morning

You'll need a full morning to walk round the archaeological site at **Selinunte**.

## Afternoon and Evening

Relax by spending the afternoon on the **beach at Marinella**, before enjoying a fish dinner in one of the restaurants in this laid-back resort.

# 1 Segesta

Of all Sicily's classical sites, lonely and evocative Segesta is the most compelling. High on a hill, in the midst of verdant countryside, a magnificent Doric temple and a superbly sited theatre bear witness to what was once among the most brilliant of the ancient cities. Considered to be the most magnificently sited classical monument in the world, Segesta ticks every box for visitors seeking a taste of the essence of Sicily's long past and the richness of its early culture.

Egesta, modern Segesta, was the principle city of the Elymians, legendary survivors of the Trojan war, who settled on the slopes of Monte Barbaro in the 12th century BC. By 580BC its inhabitants were thoroughly hellenized, quarrelling incessantly with neighbouring Selinunte, against whom they formed an alliance with Athens. It may have been to impress the Athenians that the great temple was built, but by 409BC, when the Athenians were defeated by Siracusa, Egesta had switched its allegiance to Carthage. It was later defeated by Siracusa and repopulated with Greeks, then went on to become the first Sicilian city to throw in its hand with the Romans, who changed its name to Segesta. It was abandoned in the late 13th century.

### The Temple
The Temple is certainly the work of a great Athenian architect and can be dated between 426 and 416BC. As you stand below, this beautiful golden masterpiece looks complete, its **36 columns, entablature and pediment** enclosing a space that lacks only a roof. Climb up though, and you'll see how unfinished the building is – the columns lack the fluting typical of the **Doric style**, the *cella* and roof were never built and the stone bosses on the stairs, used to manhandle the stone on to the site, still remain in place. It may simply

Segesta's
Greek temple
in splendid
isolation

**A visitor has the theatre and the views all to herself**

have been abandoned because it had served its purpose, a marvellous fraud, a brilliant tribute to Greek aesthetics built to impress Athens when Egesta needed its help, and left to decay once the city had no further need of the Greeks.

## The Theatre

Segesta's white theatre lies across from the temple, high on a hill with views across the slopes and plains to the sea. It was bang in the centre of the city and is surrounded by excavations that have thrown some light onto Segesta's past. It was built around or before the **third century** BC and is one of the best-preserved of all classical temples, with a diameter of 63m (207 feet) and its 20 rows of seats, facing north to the distant sea, capable of holding 3,200 spectators.

### TAKING A BREAK

There is a bar (€), serving drinks and snacks, in the shop and ticket office complex at the entrance to the site.

---

🚹 192 C4  ☎ 0924 952 356; www.trapani-sicilia.it  🕐 Summer daily 9–7; winter 9–5. Ticket office closes 1 hour before site  💷 Expensive  🚌 From Piazza Malta in Trapani Mon–Sat 8, 10, 2 and 5, returning 1:10, 4:10, 6:30

---

## SEGESTA: INSIDE INFO

**Top Tips** The theatre is a 20-minute steepish uphill walk from the ticket office. In summer, a half-hourly minibus shuttle service operates.
- Access to the Temple is up a series of shallow steps and is not recommended for disabled visitors.
- In odd-numbered years, there is a summer festival of concerts and classical Greek plays staged in the theatre; details from Trapani tourist office (► 158).

**In More Depth** The site continued to be used up until medieval times, and excavations behind the theatre have revealed traces of a mosque and Arab housing, a 13th-century Norman castle and a medieval church, which was used until the 19th century.

# 2 Erice

Perched high on a limestone spur above the sea, beautiful Erice's got the lot. Here are cobbled streets and hidden, flowery courtyards, a magnificent old cathedral, numerous churches and a historic castle, ancient city walls and tranquil gardens and, above all, views. From here, it's said you can see as far as Cape Bon in Tunisia and east to Etna itself, while steep slopes fall away towards Trapani and the sea. It may be crowded in summer and cold in winter, but it's one of Sicily's most beautiful villages and a great landmark, not only of the island, but of the whole western Mediterranean.

Erice is a holy place. Founded by the Elymians, who called it Eryx, around 1,200BC, it was the ancient world's greatest shrine to the goddess of love – Phoenician Astarte, Greek Aphrodite, Roman Venus. Her temple on this holy mountain was renowned, a landmark, mentioned by Virgil, that navigators used on their voyages from Africa. The Elymians and Greeks were eventually ousted by the Romans, but the shrine remained inviolate and it was rebuilt by Tiberius and Claudius. Later, the Arabs sensed its sanctity and called the spot Gebel-Hamed, Mohammed's mountain.

The Normans changed the name again, calling the town Monte San Giuliano, in honour of the saint who had helped their victory over the Moors, and it was only in 1934 that, thanks to Mussolini, it regained its ancient name.

## Exploring Erice

Erice is shaped like an equilateral triangle, with the main entrance, **Porta Trapani**, set at the southwest angle. From here, it's just a few metres to the cathedral church, the **Matrice**, whose wonderful fortified Gothic facade belies the 19th-century interior. To one side rises a campanile, built by Frederick III around 1315 as a lookout tower. From here, Via Vittorio Emanuele runs up towards Piazza Umberto I, the only large open space in town. As you climb, you'll get glimpses into the hidden courtyards of the stony houses, and walk past shops selling Erice's famous *pasticcerie*. The piazza is home to the **Museo Comunale Cordici**, housed in a 19th-century neo-classical building. The diverse collection includes a beautiful *Head of Aphrodite* dating from the fifth century BC, Punic and Greek coins and bronzes, and a white marble *Annunciation* by Antonello Gagini. From here, you can simply

**Above:
Doorway of
San Martino
church**

**Opposite: Erice
is spread out
below Castello
di Venere**

wander at will, exploring the myriad *vanelle*, alleys, and tiny piazzas and popping into any of the town's numerous churches that happen to be open. Eventually you should find yourself at the **Castello di Venere**, site of the classical shrine.

## The Castello di Venere

When the Normans conquered Erice, the troops were ordered to destroy all traces of the pagan temple. They did a good job, annihilating the great shrine and using its stone to build the Castello di Venere. You can still see fragments of the shrine embedded in the masonry, and a few very worn column drums still remain. The views are stupendous and you'll notice the restored 15th-century **Torre Pepoli** in the gardens below, a reconstructed Norman castle that's privately owned.

### TAKING A BREAK

Sample delicious local cakes and pastries at **Pasticceria di Maria Grammatico** (€; Via Vittorio Emanuele 14, tel: 0923 869 390).

Some of Maria Grammatico's tempting wares

➕ 192 B4 ✦ Via Tommaso Guarrisi 1, tel: 0923 869 388; www.trapani-sicilia.it; Mon–Sat 8–2

**Chiesa Matrice**
✉ Via Carvini ⏰ Daily 10–1, 3–6 🏛 Free

**Museo Comunale Cordici**
✉ Piazza Umberto I ☎ 0923 869 172 ⏰ Tue–Wed, Fri 8:30–1:30, Mon, Thu 8:30–1:30, 2:30–5 🏛 Free

**Castello di Venere**
✉ Via Conte Pepoli ☎ None ⏰ Daily 8–6

### ERICE: INSIDE INFO

**Top Tips** It's well worth planning on staying in Erice – the town comes into its own once the day visitors have left, and the sunset views are terrific.
■ In winter, Erice can be hidden in cloud. If it is, postpone your visit until the next day – once down, mist and cloud rarely lift until after dark.
■ The cobbled streets are very uneven so wear sensible shoes.
■ Even in summer, it can be cool at this height, so be prepared; average temperatures are 10°C (50°F) below those in Trapani.
■ A cable-car (Easter–Oct half-hourly 7:45am–10pm, journey time 10 minutes) runs from Via Fardella in Trapani up to Erice.

**Hidden Gems** The views form the Villa Balio, a lovely public garden just below the Castello.
■ The town walls between Porta Spada and Porta Trapani defend the only unprotected side of Erice and are made up of Elymian, Carthaginian, Roman and medieval stone work – masonry spanning 2,500 years.

## SCIENCE – THE RELIGION OF THE 21ST CENTURY

Erice may be an ancient holy place, but it's also at the cutting edge of scientific thought. In 1963, the Centro di Cultura Scientifica Ettore Majorana was established in the town, a worldwide association of scientists who support the concept of scientific freedom. Over the past 40 years 87,000 scientists from 140 nations, working at the forefront of their field, have come here to share their knowledge with younger colleagues of similar interests. The primary aim is to learn and share, and the centre is dedicated to the premise that no research or laboratories should be secret, a precept followed even at the height of the Cold War, when scientists from both East and West met here on neutral ground. You can learn more at www.ccsem.infn.it.

**The tower of Castello di Venere**

# 3 Mozia

The tiny island of San Pantaleo, set in the shallow and sheltered waters of a lagoon, is the site of the ancient city of Mozia, founded by the Phoenicians, the Mediterranean's earliest great maritime power, in the eighth century BC. It's a magical spot, a fertile, flat expanse that holds the evocative remains of what was once one of Sicily's most powerful cities. Its museum, the inspiration of the Englishman Joseph "Pip" Whitaker, who owned the island and first excavated the site, holds the finest of all Sicily's Greek statues.

### An Ancient Settlement

Mozia soon became the most important Phoenician trading post in Italy, connecting Carthage with the Elymians, their Sicilian allies, and the Etruscans, far to the north in modern Tuscany. Threatened by Greek expansion from the east, they fortified the island, moving their necropolis to the mainland, and connecting it to the island by a submerged road across the lagoon, still visible today. By 510BC, relations with the Greeks had degenerated into what was to become a long-drawn-out war, which ended in 480BC with a Greek victory at the Battle of Himera. Mozia survived, but the writing was on the wall, and in 398BC the tyrant Dionysius of Siracusa finally defeated the Carthaginians, who duly abandoned Mozia and moved their headquarters to Lilybaeum, modern Marsala (➤ 158). It was not until the 20th century, when Joseph (Pip) Whitaker, a Marsala wine merchant, began his excavations, that Mozia yielded up its history.

Mozia enjoyed an enviable, sheltered location

**Below: Pip Whitaker**
**Bottom: Villa Whitaker**

GIUSEPPE WHITAKER

## The Excavations

You'll land near the **Villa Whitaker**, now home to the museum, from where you can follow winding footpaths to discover the fascinating, if scanty, excavations. Don't miss the *cothon*, a little artificial harbour that was tucked safely within the city walls, or the walls themselves. These are particularly impressive around the **North Gate**, from where you can see the submerged road striking across to the necropolis. Near here is a *tophet*, dedicated to the goddess Tanit, where the Phoenicians sacrificed their first-born. As you wander the island, also look for the remains of the houses near the museum; the **Casa dei Mosaici** still retains its mosaic floor showing lions grappling with a bull.

## The Museum

The museum, **Museo Whitaker** is housed in the villa built by Pip Whitaker (1850–1936) to use during his visits to excavate the island,

### GETTING TO MOZIA

**By car:** Driving south from Trapani, take the N187 running between the railway and the coast. After 15km (9.5 miles), drive through San Leonardo and pick up the brown signs marked Isole Stagnone. Turn left, following the sign "Imbarco per Mozia" and drive down to the car park and ferry landing stage. The boats to the island are operated by Mozia Line (tel: 360 356 053; www.mozialine.com; Apr–Oct 9–12:45, 3–6; Nov–Mar 9–3; moderate). The museum opening times correspond with the boat times. If you are coming from Marsala, take the same road and turn off before San Leonardo. Ignore any other signs to the island; they are inaccurate.

**By public transport:** AST buses run from Piazza del Popolo in Marsala to the ferry (Mon–Sat 8–6, every 60–90 minutes, journey time 30 minutes).

and contains the collection he amassed, either on site, or by purchase from dealers. There are more than 1,000 *stelae*, grave markers, as well as huge amounts of pottery, masks and divine images, all in terracotta – look out for the smiling image mask of the god Bes. Other cases contain the jewellery and glassware so loved by the Phoenicians, pendants and collars in gold and bronze and tiny braziers used for burning aromatics as perfume. These treasures, though, are all put in the shade by the main draw, the so-called *Charioteer*. Discovered in 1979, this perfect example of the finest of Greek sculpture is thought to be the work of the master Pheidias, and dates from *c*.440BC. It shows a young man, self-confident and beautiful, the muscles of his torso rippling beneath his tunic. Sculpted in white marble, it's a stunning work, its power confirming the view of many art historians that nothing will equal the skill of the Greeks.

Statue of Giovanetto di Mozia in Villa Whitaker

### TAKING A BREAK

You can enjoy light refreshments at the bar (€) by the museum, or try the restaurant, **Mamma Caura** (€–€€), on the mainland by the car park.

➕ 192 A3

**Museo Whitaker**
✉ Mozia ☎ 0923 712 598 🕐 Apr–Oct 9–12:45, 3–6; Nov–Mar 9–3; may be subject to change 💶 Moderate

---

## MOZIA: INSIDE INFO

**Top Tips** Mozia is a lovely place to spend a whole day, but, if time is short, you should allow an hour to see the main excavations and 45 minutes for the museum, excluding the ferry time (approx 10 minutes each way).
- The island is very exposed and you should wear a hat and take water with you if you are walking round the excavations in high summer.
- Pick up a map of the island from the museum before you start; there is good signposting and information boards in English.
- There's an *enoteca*, where you can sample local island wines, next door to the museum.

# ❹ Selinunte and Marinella

Set on hills facing the sea, the ancient city of Selinus (Selinunte) was one of the most splendid of the Greek colonies, a walled city rich in magnificent temples. Never resettled or rebuilt after its fall, the site, still rich in the wild celery, *selinon*, that gave the city its name, is the epitome of everything romantic ruins should be. To the east, the little fishing village of Marinella, with its lovely beach, has developed into a laid-back, low-key summer resort, one of the more charming along this stretch of coast.

**Glorious Temple E, the most complete of the East Temples**

Selinus, the most westerly of the Greek cities, was founded around 650BC by settlers from Megara Hyblea, attracted here by the fertile plain surrounding the site. It prospered from the start, the majority of its temples and the town itself being constructed during the fifth century BC. Its wealth made it a target for the neighbouring Carthaginians and Segestans, who, in 409BC, allied against Selinus, sending 100,000 men to capture it. After a siege of nine days, the inhabitants were butchered and the city destroyed. Selinus never recovered, and earthquakes in the Middle Ages finished off the destruction of the city. The site was lost, and it wasn't until the 1820s that systematic excavations started; they have continued on and off ever since.

## The East Temples

Just north of the entrance, the **East Temples**, known only as E, F and G, stand in a group. The most complete is Temple E, a superb Doric building that was reconstructed in 1958; it was probably dedicated to Aphrodite, and is still a glorious sight. Temple F, behind it, is the oldest, dating from around 550BC, while G, save for one solitary column a vast heap of jumbled stones, was Zeus' shrine and, after the Olympieion at Agrigento (➤ 128), the largest of the Sicilian temples.

## The Acropolis and West Temples

From the hill, follow the track down, past the now buried old harbour, to the other excavated area, the **Acropolis**. This contains city streets, sections of well-preserved walls and the ruins of the five **West Temples**. Temple C was the most impressive, standing high on the hill, and probably dedicated to Apollo. Its wonderful *metopes* (panels) are now in the archaeological museum in Palermo (➤ 60), but 14 columns have been re-erected, giving an idea of its original scale. Behind here, the grid of town streets, with their houses and shops, stretch back to the North Gate; beyond which huge areas of the ancient city remain to be excavated.

Opposite: The vast acropolis sprawls across the hillside at Selinunte

## Marinella

The little village of **Marinella** sprawls down the hill to the east of Selinunte. It's a beguiling place, with a splendid beach that stretches west towards the ruins. Its main street winds down to the harbour, where the fishing boats are still pulled up, and there's a good selection of hotels overlooking the sea beyond the harbour, and more back up the hill. It's a typically relaxed Italian seaside resort, with loungers on the sands, an animated *passeggiata* every evening and a good choice of great fish restaurants.

Below: Marinella's splendid beach makes a refreshing change from ancient ruins

### TAKING A BREAK

There's a bar-restaurant (€) opposite the entrance to the archaeological site; more bars and restaurants (€–€€) in Marinella.

➕ 192 C2 ℹ️ Marinella; tel: 0924 46251; www.selinunte.net; Apr–Sep Mon–Sat 8–8, Sun 9–12, 3–6; Oct–Mar Mon–Sat 9–12, 3–5

**Selinus Archaeological Site**
✉️ Selinunte ☎️ 0924 46277/0924 462251; www.selinunte.net
🕐 Daily 9am–1 hour before sunset
💶 Expensive

### SELINUNTE AND MARINELLA: INSIDE INFO

**Top Tips** Selinunte is a big archaeological site (270ha/667 acres); if you want to explore it all, allow three to four hours and be prepared to walk.
- It's very exposed and hot in summer; wear a hat and take water if you're here in the middle of the day.
- Signposting is poor; pick up a map before your visit.
- You can buy guide books to the site at the shop in the entrance building.
- Marinella has plenty of accommodation and restaurants.
- From €3 you can hire an electric cart taxi to take you around part of the archaeological site. To cover the whole site by cart costs around €12.

# At Your Leisure

Castellammare del Golfo is a tranquil town with a busy fishing port

## 5 Castellammare del Golfo and Riserva Naturale dello Zingaro

**Castellammare del Golfo**, the ancient port for the classical city of Segesta (➤ 144), crouches beneath the hills surrounding the wide bay of the Golfo del Castellammare. It's still a busy fishing port, a beguiling town with wide quays below the remains of an Aragonese castle. Today, it's hard to believe that this tranquil town was once a hotbed of Mafia activity, with one in three men guilty of murder, a fact that reputedly inspired Mario Puzo's novel, *The Godfather*, on which the blockbusting series of movies was based. Speaking of films, the town was also the birthplace of Frank Stallone, father of the *Rambo* star Sylvester. The town has recently become a hotspot for the international glitterati, attracting long-stay celebrities like Brad Pitt and Catherine Zeta-Jones. It's a good jumping-off point for the **Riservo Naturale dello Zingaro** (www.riservazingaro.it) to the west, a 7km (4-mile) stretch of unspoiled coastline where steep slopes plunge to a succession of idyllic coves, tiny bays and clear water. Established in 1981, Zingaro was set up after local protests at a government plan to drive a road along the coast in an effort to curtail Mafia use of the hidden coves as drug-smuggling bases. There still are no roads, and entrance from the east is via the old tuna fishing village of Scopello. From here, tracks fan out at different levels, giving the chance to either head for the beaches – Capreria, Marinella and Uzzo are 1, 3 and 7km (0.6, 1.8 and 4.5 miles) along the path – or head higher to take in the incredibly varied landscape and the wealth of birds and wild flowers. Also in the reserve is the Uzzo Cave, inhabited 10,000 years ago, which has become an important archaeological site.

🚩 192 C4 🚌 Via A de Gasperi 6; tel: 0924 592 111; www.castellammaredelgolfo.com; Mon, Wed, Fri 9–2, Tue, Thu 9–2, 4–6

### Riservo Naturale dello Zingaro
✉ Park Office, Via Segesta 197, Castellammare del Golfo ☎ 0924 35108; www.riservazingaro.it

## 6 San Vito lo Capo
You can access the Zingaro from the west, coming in via San Vito lo Capo, a remote settlement at the foot of

the promontory of Monte Monaco. It's said San Vito, the patron saint of epilepsy, fled here from persecution; his church still stands at the centre of the village. Originally it was the location of a Saracen fortress, which in Christian times came to accommodate the small church dedicated to San Vito on the site where he was believed to have lived. Over time, the church grew too small for the huge number of pilgrims it attracted, and so it was enlarged until it eventually incorporated the very building that once harboured it. For centuries, coral and tuna fishing brought in the money, but the 20th century saw the start of the tourist boom, as Italians discovered the San Vito's stunning beaches, vast stretches of glistening sands whose colour changes as the light fades. In high summer, they come in droves, to stroll the neat 18th-century streets and browse the exhibits in the **Museo del Mare** (May–Sep 10–1, 6–9), but outside high season, you'll have the town virtually to yourself. It's a charming place, its cuboid white houses hung with vivid bougainvillea and geraniums, where your main worry will be which fish restaurant to patronize. There are good walks too; climb up for wide views, stroll out across the flatlands to Capo San Vito itself or head along the coast to the coves of the Zingaro.

**192 B5 In the Museo del Mare, Via Savoia 57/Via Venza 12; tel: 0923 974 300; www.sanvitoweb.com; summer daily 9–1, 5–11; winter 9–1**

## 7 Trapani

Trapani's name derives from the Greek *drepanon* (sickle) – apt indeed, for the curving, narrow spit of land occupied by the old town. Legend says it was formed by the sickle that was dropped by the goddess of agriculture, Demeter (Ceres), while she desperately searched for her daughter Persephone, who had been carried off by the god of the underworld. To the south stretch miles of saltpans, dotted with windmills, a dream-like landscape shifting in the summer heat haze. Trapani has traditionally made its money from tuna, salt and carved coral – canned tuna was invented here – but today only the salt industry remains, though its port is still busy, its ferries serving the Egadi islands (► 171) and Tunisia.

**The beautiful beach at San Vito lo Capo seems to change colour as the light fades**

Once through the bland suburbs, you'll find yourself in one of western Sicily's most handsome towns, with fine buildings, stately churches, a wide waterfront and a general air of discreet prosperity. The "sickle" is little more than 200m (218 yards) wide, and dissected by Corso Vittorio Emanuele, first laid out in the 13th century. At one end stands the splendid Baroque Palazzo Cavaretta (1701); behind it a little piazza holds the Fontana di Saturno (1342). Down the Corso you'll find the Collegio del Gesuiti (1636), a Jesuit church whose harmonious facade is spiced up with Baroque accents, and the cathedral of San Lorenzo (1635), fronted by a portico designed by Giovanni Biagio Amico in 1683. He was also responsible for the Purgatorio to the south, a church housing the *Misteri*, 21 life-size wooden figures of Christ's Passion, which are carried in procession each Good Friday. The town's other main sight, the Santuario dell'Annunziata (Sanctuary of the Annunciation), is out in the new town (bus 25 from Piazza Umberto). It houses a beautiful 14th-century marble statue of the Madonna, made by the great Pisan school of sculptors. Legend tells of a Pisan knight crusader fleeing the Holy Land with his precious statue, only to be stranded after a storm in Trapani, where the locals promptly stole his Virgin and made her their own. The shrine complex also contains the **Museo Regionale Pepoli**, an eclectic and once private collection that ranges from archaeological finds to silver and paintings; don't miss the extraordinary carved coral, fished from the reefs off Trapani and once a speciality of the area.

➕ 192 A4 ❘ Piazza Garibaldi, tel: 0923 29000; www.apt.trapani.it; Jul–Aug Mon–Sat 8–2, 2:30–8, Sun 9–1; Sep–Jun Mon–Sat 8:30–1:30, 2:30–7:30, Sun 9–12

### Museo Regionale Pepolo
✉ Via Conte Agostino Pepoli ☎ 0923 553 269 🕐 Mon–Sat 9–1:30, Sun 9–12:30 💰 Moderate

## ❽ Marsala

Standing at the westernmost point of Sicily, ancient Marsala was home to Greeks, Carthaginians and Romans, an important and rich city, trading with Africa. From here, Scipio Africanus finally conquered Carthage, and later, the Arabs named the town Marsah-al-Allah, the "port of God". Its original name was Lilybaeum ("lily" for water and "baeum" referring to the Eubei, who were the town's pre-Phoenician inhabitants). Although the Arab name for Marsala stuck, Lilybaeum is still the name of the headland on which the town is sited. Still prosperous in the Middle Ages, it really came into its own in 1773, when the Englishman John

### SALT IN THE AIR
All along the coast between Trapani and Marsala are the shallow waters that form Sicily's salt flats, the enclosed pans glistening, mirror-like, in the sun. Over the course of 80–100 days the water evaporates, leaving some of Europe's tastiest salt. It is then carted in barrows to be piled in huge heaps, ready for cleaning and packing. You can learn more at the **Museo Salina** (Salina Calcasi, tel: 0923 867 442, Apr–Sep Mon–Sat 9–12:30), housed in a 16th-century windmill complex in the depths of the salt flats.

## MARSALA WINE

English sailors had traditionally enjoyed a tipple at sea, and wine had, for many years, been fortified with spirits to preserve it during voyages, port being the staple choice. By the 1770s, the English fleets were increasingly operating in the Mediterranean and a local supply made sense. John Woodhouse, an English merchant, added alcohol to the local wine and shipped it to Liverpool in 1773. It was an immediate success, endorsed, in 1798, by Admiral Nelson himself, who placed a large order. Other wine businesses were established, and Marsala was soon shipped all over the world. Today, the wine houses retain their English company names, but are mainly Italian owned, the *baglios* still prominent buildings in the town. Marsala is sweet and strong – a great dessert wine or pick-me-up. www.consorziovinomarsala.it

### Stabilimento Florio
✉ Lungomare Mediterraneao ☎ 0923 723 846 ⏰ Hour-long guided visits Mon–Fri 10, 3:30, Sat 9:30, 11

### Pellegrino
✉ Via del Fante 39 ☎ 0923 719 911; www.carlopellegrino.it ⏰ Mon–Fri 9–12, 2:30–5:30; Sat 9–12

### Donnafugata
✉ Via Lipari 18 ☎ 0923 724 245; www.donnafugata.it ⏰ Mon–Fri 9–1, 2:30–6:30; book online via website or call Wiebke Petersen (tel: 0923 724 245)

Woodhouse started the wine trade, and in 1860 Garibaldi and his thousand landed here, making it the first city of a united Italy.

It's a fine town, its historic core approached through gates in the surrounding walls and sprinkled with trees and greenery. To the west, a broad expanse of wasteland, once the heart of the Roman city, stretches to the sea. Here are a scattering of archaeological excavations, including an *insula*, a block of flats, while on the seafront you'll find the **Museo Archeologico**. It's housed in an old *baglio*, wine-making complex, and displays finds from Marsala's past, including the remains of a Phoenician galley, found in the 1980s on the seabed off the island of Mozia (► 150). It's far from complete but nevertheless impressive, a 31.5m-long (103-foot) hull once manned by 68 oarsmen – cannabis leaves were found nearby, probably used

as a stimulant by the rowers. Heading east, walk through the Porta Garibaldi to Piazza della Repubblica, the main square that's home to the cathedral dedicated to St Thomas of Canterbury. Behind here the **Museo degli Arazzi** displays a set of eight fine 16th-century Flemish tapestries, a gift to the city. Sightseeing over, head for one of the Marsala companies, to learn more about the wine trade and taste some of the wines.

🔢 192 A3 ℹ Via XI Maggio 100, tel: 0923 714 097/993 270; www.lagunablu.org; Mon–Sat 8–8, Sun 9–12

### Museo Archeologico Baglio Anselmi
✉ Lumgomare Boéo ☎ 0923 952 535 ⏰ Mon–Tue, Thu–Fri 9–1, Sat, Wed 9–1, 4–7 💶 Moderate

### Museo degli Arazzi
✉ Via Giuseppe Garraffa ☎ 0923 711 327 ⏰ Tue–Sun 9–1, 4–6 💶 Inexpensive

Arabic-Norman architecture makes Mazara del Vallo distinctive

## 9 Mazara del Vallo

Historically the most important of Sicily's Moorish towns, Mazara del Vallo makes the most of its seafront position, with a shady *lungomare* and gardens stretching along the waterfront to the fishing port, home to one of Italy's biggest fishing fleets. It's this combination of hard-working, earthy port and the splendid baroque churches and civic buildings of the old centre that gives the town its charm, and there's nowhere in western Sicily with a stronger North African atmosphere. Head for the Tunisian quarter, or Casbah, home to many of the North Africans that work the boats, and wander the maze of souk-like streets – mainstream Sicily seems far away. Southeast of here, the beautiful Piazza della Repubblica is home to the Duomo, flanked by a harmonious mix of Baroque buildings, complete with porticoes and arcades. Near here, the **Museo del Satiro** displays a bronze *Dancing Satyr*, more than 2.4m (8 feet) high, fished from the waters near the island of Pantelleria in 1998.

🔢 192 B2   ℹ️ Piazza San Veneranda 2; tel: 0923 941 727; www.apt.trapani.it; Mon–Sat 8–2:15, Sun 9–12

**Museo del Satiro**
✉️ Sant'Egidio, Piazza Plebiscito   ☎ 0923 933 917   🕐 Tue–Sat 9–7, Sun 9–1   💶 Moderate

### FOR KIDS
If you're travelling with kids, there's enough variety in the west to keep them happy – **beach days** at **Castellammare** and **San Vito** and a good day out by sea to visit the **Egadi islands** (► 171). From **Trapani**, the **funicular** up to Erice would be a hit and most children will enjoy exploring this hilltop town, complete with castle. **Segesta** is unlikely to appeal except to older kids, though if you want to visit **Selinunte**, you could offer a beach outing to **Marinella** as a bribe. All children will enjoy the boat across the lagoon to **Mozia**, and the island itself is good for a day out – take a picnic.

# Where to...
## Stay

**Prices**
Expect to pay per double room, per night

| € under €130 | €€ €130–€230 | €€€ over €230 |
| --- | --- | --- |

## ERICE

### Elimo €–€€

This lovely hotel, right on Erice's picturesque main street, has wonderful views down to Trapani, and pretty rooms, all with beamed ceilings, old tiles and marble bathrooms. You can relax in the cosy bar, or sit out on the terrace or in the courtyard. There's an excellent breakfast buffet and the restaurant, with more lovely views, has a good range of delicious options, all tastefully presented. Use the private parking, or leave the car just outside the town gates.

🕂 192 B4 ⊠ Via Vittorio Emanuele 75 ☎ 0923 869 377; www.hotelelimo.it

### Moderno €€

At the mid-sized Moderno you can choose between rooms with modern, light styling and the more traditional, furnished with antiques and rugs. There's a good bar and a terrace with astounding views, but it's the roof-terrace restaurant that's the main draw. Belonging to the Buon Ricordo confederation, it serves seasonal local dishes – the fish couscous is its speciality.

🕂 192 B4 ⊠ Via Vittorio Emanuele 63 ☎ 0923 869 300; www.hotelmodernoerice.it

## MARINELLA DI SELINUNTE

### Miramare €

Right opposite its own private stretch of beach, the Miramare's a great choice and very good value. Front-facing bedrooms have balconies with sea views, bedrooms are furnished with pretty cane chairs and tables and the bathrooms have high-pressure showers. The long-established restaurant serves fish straight off the boats. One caveat – some of the rooms can be noisy late in the evenings in high summer.

🕂 192 C2 ⊠ Via Pigafetta 2 ☎ 0924 46045; www.hotelmiramareselinunte.com

## MARSALA

### Villa Favorita €

About 2km (1 mile) outside Marsala, the Villa is indeed what it says, a 19th-century, beautifully converted villa, set in a lovely park with views to sea and the Egadi and Stagnone islands. Rooms are nicely decorated with easy chairs and good bathrooms; the public areas have beautiful vaulted ceilings and lovely old tile work. There's an outdoor pool and tennis court, and the restaurant is one of the better ones in the area.

🕂 192 A3 ⊠ Via Favorita 27 ☎ 0923 989 100; www.villafavorita.com

## MAZARA DEL VALLO

### Kempinski Hotel €€€

Set on the outskirts of Mazara del Vallo amid olive groves, vineyards, palms and flower-filled gardens sprinkled with fountains, this was the first 5-star hotel to open in this corner of the island. Rooms are beautifully decorated with ample bathrooms and every attention to detail. In the grounds are swimming pools, tennis courts and a spa, and guests also have access to a private beach.

🕂 192 B2 ⊠ Via Salemi, Giardino do Constanza ☎ 0923 675 000; www.kempinski-sicily.com

# Where to...
# Eat and Drink

## Prices

Expect to pay per person for a meal, including wine and service

€ up to €20    €€ €20–€35    €€€ over €35

## SAN VITO LO CAPO

### Miraspiaggia €€

Miraspiaggia means "beach view", and this low-built, whitewashed hotel is indeed just across from the beach, its fish-speciality restaurant spilling out on to the terrace. Superior rooms all have sea-view balconies, while the interior rooms are spacious and comfortable. The hotel has its own beach, complete with sun beds and umbrellas; waiter service is also available here. The hotel also has a number of self-catering apartments and offers an airport pick-up service.

**➕ 192 B5 ✉ Via Lungomare 6 ☎ 0923 972 355; www.miraspiaggia.it 🕖 Closed Dec–Feb**

## TRAPANI

### Ai Lumi €

Walk off the main street and through a plant-hung courtyard to find Ai Lumi, a classy and friendly bed and breakfast with style. Rooms are simple and elegant, with distinctive touches such as antique tables, old tiles and pretty pottery pieces. The restaurant is one of the best in town, and as a bonus bed-and-breakfast guests will get a 15 per cent discount if they eat here. There are also self-catering, fully equipped apartments.

**➕ 192 A4 ✉ Corso Vittorio Emanuele 75 ☎ 0923 540 922; www.ailumi.it**

### Nuovo Albergo Russo €–€€

Sicily's good, traditional hotels are gradually disappearing but this wonderful survivor will give you a chance to still experience the real thing. Family-run, it's in an 18th-century palazzo opposite the cathedral. Its lofty rooms may be old-fashioned, but they come with everything you need in the way of modern comforts and the public areas are a taste of old Sicily. Breakfast is not included in the room price.

**➕ 192 A4 ✉ Via Tintori 4 ☎ 0923 22163; www.chshotels.com**

## ERICE

### Maria Grammatico €

Erice is famous for its speciality *pasticcerie*, and this is the best place to sample these – browse at the counter before you choose from the feather-light cakes, the mouthwatering *cannoli* (pastry tubes filled with ricotta and candied fruit), the *cassata* and the myriad almond sweetmeats. They'll happily make up attractive selection boxes to take away.

**➕ 192 B4 ✉ Via Vittorio Emanuele 14 ☎ 0923 869 390; www.mariagrammatico.it 🕖 Daily 10–8 (later in summer)**

### Monte San Giuliano €€–€€€

You can eat in or outside in the courtyard at this fine restaurant, which prides itself on its use of local produce and adherence to traditional recipes using Mediterranean ingredients – with a modern twist. The smoked fish platter, seafood heaped high, pasta with sardines, and couscous are all here, but leave room for the *cassata*. They're used to vegetarians here, and the dishes are both imaginative and good.

**➕ 192 B4 ✉ Vicolo San Rocco 7 ☎ 0923 869 595; www.montesangiuliano.it 🕖 Tue–Sun 12–2:30, 7:30–9:30**

## La Pineta €€

Set among pine trees with panoramic views, this excellent restaurant specializes in typical dishes of the area such as fish couscous, tuna and *pasta alla Norma* (as well as a sprinkling of meat dishes). There is an attractive outdoor terrace, while the main dining room can seat up to 100 guests. It is part of the Hotel Villaggio, also a good accommodation choice.

➕ 192 B4 ✉ Viale Nunzio Nasi ☎ 0923 860 127; www.lapinetadierice.com 🕐 Daily 1–2.30, 8–10.30

## MARSALA

### Trattoria Garibaldi €€

A long-established restaurant in the heart of town, where the accent's on fresh, local produce – expect fresh pasta with lobster or sardines, fish couscous, light and crisp *fritto misto* (mixed fried fish) or bream simmered in fish broth. If you can't quite decide what to order, then opt for the antipasti to sample as much as possible of the kitchen's range, and then finish your meal with a glass of Marsala.

➕ 192 A3 ✉ Piazza dell'Addolorata 35 ☎ 0923 953 006 🕐 Apr–Oct daily 12–2.30, 7.30–10; Nov–Mar Mon–Fri 12–2.30, 7.30–9.30, Sat 7.30–9.30, Sun 12–2.30

## MARINELLA DI SELINUNTE

### Pierrot €€

Grab a table near one of the big picture windows overlooking the beach in this light and airy restaurant and enjoy super-fresh seafood and fish. If you've never tried *ricci* (sea urchin) this is the place to come; other specialities include pasta with swordfish and capers and a good couscous. The set lunch menu represents excellent value, though avoid Sundays, when it's packed with locals.

➕ 192 C2 ✉ Via Marco Polo 108 ☎ 0924 46205 🕐 May–Oct daily 12–2.30, 7.30–10; Nov–Apr Wed–Mon 12–2.30, 7.30–9.30

## MAZARA DEL VALLO

### La Bettola dal 1972 €€

Very popular with the locals, this restaurant specializes in excellent fish and seafood dishes. The chef/patron Pietro Sardo personally discusses your Sicilian feast before preparing it. Everything is home-cooked, including the delectable puddings – try to leave room for the heavenly *cassata siciliana*. The extensive wine list includes more than 200 Sicilian labels.

➕ 192 B2 ✉ Via F Maccagnone 32 ☎ 0932 946 422; www.ristorantebettola.it 🕐 Thu–Tue 12:30–2.30, 8–10.30

## SAN VITO LO CAPO

### Da Alfredo €€

Alfredo's pretty terrace overlooks the sea and it's sea produce you'll eat here, including San Vito's speciality *primo*, *busiati alla sanvitese*, home-made pasta with tuna roe. You can try *bottarga*, dried tuna roe, too, on *bruschetta* (toasted country bread), before moving on to fresh fish, simply grilled, and a salad.

➕ 192 B5 ✉ Contrada Valanga, 1km (0.6 miles) south of San Vito ☎ 0923 972 366 🕐 Tue–Sun 12–2.30, 7.30–10. Closed 4 weeks end Oct–end Nov and lunch in Jul

## TRAPANI

### Cantina Siciliana €€

The decor may be a bit busy but the food is spot on at this family restaurant run by Pino Maggiore. A native of Trapani, he's keen to showcase local produce and it's the fish and produce of the *terra* that inspire him. Home-made *busiate* (Trapanese pasta) are served with *pesto all trapanese* (tomato, basil, garlic and almond pesto) and fresh swordfish accompanied by tiny tomatoes and capers from the island of Pantelleria. They also sell local wines and food products in the *cantina*, and run a cookery school.

➕ 192 A4 ✉ Via Giudecca 36 ☎ 0923 28673; www.cantinasiciliana.it 🕐 Daily 12–2:30, 7:30–9:30

# Where to...
## Shop

As a big tourist draw, **Erice** has some specialist shops that are well worth browsing. On Viale Pepoli, at No 55, you'll find traditional rugs at **Pina Parisi Tappetti** (tel: 0923 869 049); some are woven in geometric patterns, others depict charming scenes of country life. Elsewhere in town, **Altieri 1882** (*Via Cordici 14,* tel: 0923 869 237) makes unique pieces in gold and coral, as well as vibrant pottery, while two doors down at No 16 the **Bazar del Miele** (tel: 0923 869 181) is a treasure house for honey lovers, with a huge selection of local honey plus cheeses, olive oil and preserved goods. If you're looking for ceramics, try **Antonino Catalano** (*Via Guarnotta 15,* tel: 0923 869 126) or the **Ceramica Ericina** at Fontanarossa (tel: 0923 869 040);

both have a good selection. Both **Marinella** and **Castellammare** have the usual range of seaside shops. For something more special, **Trapani** is the place to buy boxes of the richly flavoured, strong salt produced locally, and you'll also find charming ceramic figurines at **Perrone Ceramiche** (*Corso Vittorio Emanuele 106,* tel: 0923 29609). Traditional coral jewellery is still made here and the best outlets are **Platimiro Fiorenza** (*Via Osorio 36*), and **Saverio D'Angelo** (*Via Cuba 19*), which carries antique coral jewellery. The winning buy in **Marsala** is wine; it's available direct from the producers at any of the *baglios* (▶ 159), or try **Alimentari Gerardi** (Piazza Mameli 11–14, tel: 0923 29874), which sells a range from different producers.

# Where to...
## Be Entertained

For most of the year **Erice** goes early to bed, with little entertainment on offer, but in summer it's a different story, with the streets crowded with tourists until late. Summer also sees Erice's big artfest, when July brings the week-long **Festival of Medieval and Renaissance Music** (www.prolocovalderice.it), with performances in the Duomo and elsewhere – the tourist office has details. If you're in **Selinunte** between mid-July and the end of August, check at the archaeological site for details of the performances staged among the ruins, which range from dance and music to re-enactments of the classical myths. July, too, is the time for opera, when the **Estate Musicale Trapanese** (www.lugliomusicaletrapanese.it)

hosts outdoor performances at Villa Margherita. Both **Castellammare** and **San Vito** offer the usual seaside pleasures – the *passeggiata*, lively local bars and weekend discos, though if you're in San Vito in September you can experience the **Couscous Fest** (www.couscousfest.it), when every aspect of couscous goes on display (▶ 17). Prosperous **Marsala** has a couple of popular late-night bars that draw the crowds, including the **E&N Café** (*Via XI Maggio 130,* tel: 0923 951 969) in the heart of town, **Di Vino Rosso** (Largo di Girolamo 13/V, tel: 0923 711 770) and the **Irish Pub O'Mahenrans's** (Via Francesco Crispi 98, tel: 0923 952 275). The city also hosts the **Marsala Doc Jazz Festival** in late July, which attracts international performers.

# Walks and Tours

# Palermo

*Walk*

**This walk gives you a varied look at the main streets and side alleys of central Palermo, with a couple of the city's best markets to browse in, some over-the-top baroque churches, the city's opera house and plenty of shopping en route.**

**DISTANCE** 3km (1.8 miles) **TIME** Allow 2 hours with visits **START/END POINT** Piazza G Cesare **WHEN TO GO** Mornings are when the markets are at their liveliest 🗺 202 off C1

## 1–2

With your back to the main entrance to the **Stazione Centrale**, cross Piazza G Cesare and walk straight ahead down **Via Roma**. This busy, mid-range shopping street was driven through the historic Kalsa district of Palermo in 1922 to connect the old city with the broad streets of the area on either side of 19th-century Via della Libertà. Continue over the crossroads with **Via Vittorio Emanuele** and take the steps down to the right into the **Vucciria market** (➤ 60).

## 2–3

Follow the market street of Via Maccheronai along to your left to emerge on to **Piazza San Domenico**. Turn left, cross via Roma and walk up **Via Bandiera** to Via Maqueda. Cross via Maqueda and walk up **Via Sant'Agostino**, home to the **Capo market**.

The **Colonna dell'Immacolata**, a prominent city landmark, towers over the theatrical facade of the **San Domenico**, an 18th-century church with a lovely 14th-century cloister.

Sant'Agostino, almost hidden by the market stalls, has a 14th-century foundation with an elegant rose window and lava mosaics round its main door; it stands at the heart of the **Capo quarter**, a warren of souk-like alleys that makes this vibrant, noisy, colourful market one of the most compelling in Palermo.

## 3–4

At the top of Sant'Agostino, turn right and walk along, past the Madonna della Mercé, to **Via Volturno**. Turn right and walk towards the monstrously big **Teatro Massimo**, the prime opera and ballet venue in Palermo.

The **Teatro Massimo** in Piazza Verdi (1875–97; open Tue–Sun 10–3:30,

### TAKING A BREAK

Enjoy one of the best *pizze* in town, baked in a stone oven, at Antica Trattoria del Monsù (€–€€; Via Volturno 41, tel: 091 327 774).

---

Piazza Vittorio Emanuele Orlando

Via Carini

Via Tripoli

Via Tunisi

Via Mura S Vito

VIA VOLTURNO

Via San Gregorio

Piazza Stigmate

Via Favara

Via Sant'Agostino

**Mercado del Capo**

Via Antonio Amico

Via Donizetti

Via Rossini

Piazza Giuseppe Verdi

**Teatro Massimo**

VIA P ARAGONA

MAQUEDA

Via Bara Olivella

Via dell'Orologio

Via Giacalone

Via Trabia

Via S Basilio

VIA CAVOUR

Via Monteleone

VIA ROMA

Piazza San Domenico

**San Domenico**

④

③

Sant' Agostino

0    100 m
0    100 yds

www.teatromassimo.it), designed by Giovanni Battista Basile, was inaugurated with a performance of Verdi's *Falstaff* – the composer gave his name to the surrounding piazza, where you'll find a pair of Liberty-style kiosks, once the ticket offices, designed by Basile's son, Ernesto, who was responsible for many of Palermo's finest Liberty buildings.

## 4–5

In front of the Teatro, turn right onto **Via Maqueda**, one of the city's most historic streets. Continue to the **Quattro Canti** (▶ 61), the iconic crossroads of the four old city quarters.

## 5–6

Cross the road to visit the baroque church of **San Giuseppe dei Teatini** and then continue along Via Maqueda. You'll notice the **Piazza Pretoria** across the road on your left (▶ 61) as you walk past the entrance to the Law Faculty of the **University**. Via Maqueda will lead you back to Piazza G Cesare and the station.

The southwest screen of the Quattro Canti virtually hides the huge church of **San Giuseppe dei Teatini** (Mon–Sat 8:30–11, 6–8, Sun 8:30–12:30, 6–8), whose 17th- to 18th-century interior is a blast of over-the-top baroque decoration at its most ebullient, a riot of gilt and stucco. It makes a fine pair with **Santa Caterina**, an exuberant late 16th-century Dominican baroque church, all polychrome marble and trompe l'oeil frescoes, across the street on the north side of Piazza Pretoria. The courtyard of the Università, with its clean lines and scholarly tranquillity, makes a fine contrast to all the excitement and provides a haven from the chaos of the traffic roaring past outside.

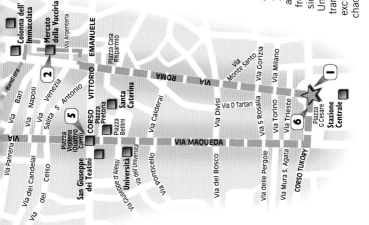

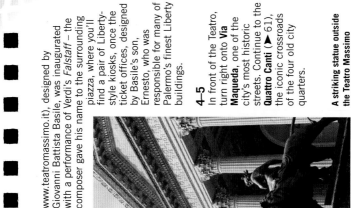

**A striking statue outside the Teatro Massimo**

# 2 Ortygia, Siracusa
*Walk*

Follow this route to enjoy the wonderful variety of Siracusa's island centre, where local life ticks over in the shadow of classical monuments, medieval palazzi and baroque churches.

**DISTANCE** 3.5km (2.2 miles) **TIME** 1.5–2 hours **START POINT** Ponte Umbertino
**END POINT** Piazza del Duomo **WHEN TO GO** Morning, when the streets are lively, is a good time ⊞ 201 F3

## 1–2
Walk across the **Ponte Umbertino** and walk up through Piazza Pancali to the **Tempio di Apollo** (▶ 97). Take **Via Savoia** to the right in front of the temple and walk along to the **Porta Marina**.

The **Porta Marina**, built in the 15th century, was conceived as the gateway to the **Porto Grande**, the Great Harbour, and formed part of the city's medieval walls. In front spreads the vast natural harbour, dotted with fishing boats, tankers, liners and pleasure boats. Just inside, look to your left and you'll see the little church of **Santa Maria dei Miracoli**, its doorway resting on the back of two little lions.

## 2–3
Walk through the gateway and along Via Ruggero Settimo until you see trees below

you on the right. Turn left up **Via Collegio.** At the intersection turn right and continue along Via Landolina to the **Piazza del Duomo** (▶ 97).

As you walk up Via Collegio, the church of the Collegio, built between 1635 and 1687, is on your left. The **Piazza del Duomo** occupies a space first inhabited by the original Sicilians, the Sikels, whose tombs were found below when the piazza was being repaved. The Greeks built a major temple, now the Duomo, and later generations added to the square's monuments. The **Town Hall** (1628) stands on the site of another Greek temple, while next to the Duomo, you'll see the beautiful façade of the 18th-century Palazzo Arcivescovile (Archbishop's Palace). The curved, pink building is the **Palazzo Gaetani,** and the church at the end of the piazza is dedicated to **Santa Lucia.**

## 3–4
At the far end of the Piazza from the **Duomo,** head straight on down Via Picharale and bear right to emerge at the Fonte Aretusa.

**The 15th-century gateway of Porta Marina is the only surviving city gate**

The spring of the **Fonte Aretusa** was one of the most venerated spots in the classical world. Legend tells of the nymph Arethusa bathing in the River Alpheus, near Mount Olympia, when she was surprised by a river god. Fleeing in terror, she plunged into the Ionian Sea, only to re-emerge here. The goddess Artemis transformed her into a spring, and the Greeks believed that the river god mingled his water with that of the spring, and

that this Sicilian water source was connected with the river in the Pelopponese. In actuality, it was probably the abundance of the water here that had much to do with colonization of Ortygia; 2,000 years later Admiral Nelson used the spring to fill his water barrels before the Battle of the Nile.

### 4–5

From the Fonte Aretusa, detour along the **Foro Vittorio Emanuele**, known locally as the Marina, a good place for a pause. Backtrack to the Fonte Aretusa and continue on to the **Castello Maniace**, at the end of Ortygia.

The so-called **Marina**, shaded with magnificent ficus trees, is a lovely place to walk beside the harbour, and there are plenty of bars for a drink if you want to sit and enjoy the views. As you approach the **Castello Maniace**, today a barracks, you'll get a better idea of the huge bulk of this medieval fortress, built around 1239 and named after the Byzantine admiral George Maniakes, who fought the Arabs here in 1038.

**Left: Fonte Aretusa, the freshwater spring that attracted Ortygia's first settlers**
**Right: The Duomo's exuberant facade**

## 5–6

With your back to the Castello, head down **Via Salomone**, cross the road at the junction and continue along Via San Martino. At the junction with **Via Capodieci** (➤ 97). Turn right, then almost immediately left down Via Roma and continue all the down the street to **Piazza Archimede**.

**Piazza Archimede** is the principal square on Ortygia and is linked to the bridges by **Corso Matteoti**, a wide modern street with plenty of shopping opportunites. The central fountain (1910) shows the nymph Arethusa as she was transformed into the spring, and some of the surrounding buildings still show traces of their medieval origins. For the real thing, pop round the corner into **Via Montalto**, where the **Palazzo Montalto** (1397) is a fine example of Siracusan Gothic.

## 6–7

Turn right along **Via Maestranza** and continue to a crossroads and the church of the **Immacolata**. Turn right here down **Via Giudecca**, then take the second right on to Via del Crocifisso. At the junction, turn left, then right to follow **Via Minerva**, which will lead you back to **Piazza del Duomo**.

**Via Maestranza** was once the home of the wealthy guilds; it's a lovely and varied street, with some great buildings and tempting shops. As you turn into **Via Minerva**, you'll walk along the side of the Duomo, giving you a splendid view of how the columns of the ancient Greek temple were incorporated into the cathedral.

**The walk passes through the grand sweep of Piazza del Duomo**

### TAKING A BREAK

Finish up by sampling the very best of Sicilian pastries at Corsino, Le Antiche Siracusa (€; Via Maestranza 2, tel: 0931 622 048).

## 3 A Taste of the Egadi Islands

*Excursion to Favignana*

Hop on a boat in Trapani for a trip to the Egadi, the most accessible of Sicily's offshore islands, where, on Favignana, you can explore, walk, swim and sample the island-life atmosphere.

**DISTANCE** Favignana is 17km (10.5 miles) from Trapani **TIME** Allow a full day if you want to swim and explore, or just half a day for the trip and brief visit to Favignana town **START/END POINT** Stazione Marittima, Trapani **WHEN TO GO** Any time (weather permitting), but best between May and September ✚ 192 A4

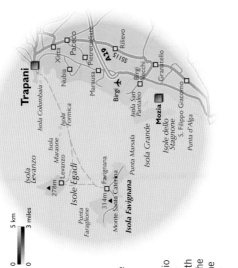

### 1–2

You can get to **Favignana** either by *traghetto* (ferry) or *aliscafo* (hydrofoil) operated by Siremar (tel: 0923 545 455; www.siremar.it) and Ustica (tel: 0923 22200; www.usticalines.it) lines out of Trapani; there are also services from Marsala. Both have **numerous daily departures** throughout the year, with services more frequent in the summer months. *Traghetti* leave from the Stazione Marittima and *aliscafi* from the piers on Via Ammiraglio Staiti, around 200m (218 yards) to the east. You can buy tickets for both from the office opposite the waterfront on Via Ammiraglio Staiti; buy just a one-way ticket to give you the freedom to decide when, and with which operator, you travel back. Board the *traghetto* by walking through the Stazione building, or access the hydrofoil directly from the quay.

**Fishing boats bob in Porta dei Pescatori, Favignana**

The old tuna canneries around Favignana's harbour

## 2–3

The crossing from Trapani to Favignana takes about 20 minutes on the hydrofoil and an hour by ferry. Boats may stop at **Levanzo**, another of the islands, either on the way out or coming back.

During the crossing, you'll pass the islets known as the **Formiche** (Ants), one of which has the remains of an old tuna cannery. On the starboard side, the island of **Levanzo** lies to the north, while straight ahead is Marettimo, the most isolated of the group. **Favignana** itself is often compared to a butterfly, the narrow "waist" between the two wings containing Favignana town, where most of the population of the island lives. To the west the land is hilly, rising to 300m (984 feet) at the lofty summit of **Monte Santa Caterina**, which is crowned with a ruined castle.

To the east, the island flattens out into an agricultural tufa landscape, peppered with the holes made when the islanders quarried tufa for export.

## 3–4

Once disembarked, walk up into **Favignana town** for a look round. As you arrive, you will notice the desolate buildings of the old

tuna canneries by the harbour; the tuna canning process was invented in Trapani, and Favignana is still renowned for its *mattanza*, the tuna slaughter. The grand old building on the way up from the harbour is the **Stabilimento Florio**, the mansion built by the entrepreneur who ran the islands in the 1870s and established the canneries. Once in town, a 10-minute stroll, walk through the **Piazza Europa** to the other square, the elongated **Piazza Madrice**. The island's main church is at one end of the square, and opposite is the bulk of **Forte San Giacomo**, founded in 1120 and rebuilt in 1498. It was converted to a jail in 1837 and today is one of Italy's maximum-security prisons. Stroll round the town, perhaps picking up some *bottarga*, dried tuna roe, delicious grated on pasta.

the legendary landing place of Odysseus before his encounter with the Cyclops. This part of the island is dotted with trees and the tiny, tufa-enclosed fields the islanders keep for their cattle in winter, and everywhere you'll notice the square white houses, all constructed from tufa. In spring, this area is particularly rich in wild flowers, with carpets of colour spreading across the fields and down to the sea. Nearer town, on the north coast,

**Cala Rossa** nestles at the edge of towering tufa cliffs – perfect for rock bathing. If you don't want to venture far from town, the **town beach** is perfectly adequate, though it can be crowded in summer.

**5–6**

Once you've decided which way to return to Trapani, buy your ticket from the kiosks at Favignana port to return to mainland Sicily.

**Favignana island is small enough to make exploring by bicycle a tempting prospect**

**TAKING A BREAK**

La Tavernetta (€€; Piazza Madrice 61, Favignana town, tel: 0923 921 639) is excellent for fish, seafood and pasta.

**4–5**

If you want to see more of the island, buses leave the stop near the harbour regularly and trundle on three different routes round most of the asphalted roads on the island, each route taking around half an hour. For sightseeing, you could stay on for two consecutive routes, or get the driver to let you off at one of the beaches en route if you want to swim. If you plan to spend the day on the beach, pick up a picnic before you leave town, though there are summer beach snack bars at Cala Azzurra, near the lighthouse to the east, and Burrone, on the south of the island. You can also rent bicycles and scooters in town.

You can swim off the rocks and beaches at numerous points round the island; **Lido Burrone** is a favourite, as is **Cala Azzurra**, to the east, with its intense blue sea and white rocks. To the west, the best spot is **Miramare**, though it's worth going further to **Cala Rotonda**,

## 4 A Circular Walk in Enna
*Walk*

**DISTANCE** 3km (1.8 miles) **TIME** Allow 1.5–2 hours **START POINT** Piazza San Cataldo **END POINT** Piazza Vittorio Emanuele **WHEN TO GO** Morning to enjoy the town going about its business, or late afternoon when the light is best for the views ╋ 199 E5

Follow this route through Enna to take in the heart of the old town and its monuments and enjoy some of Sicily's finest panoramas. It can be chilly here, so a sweater or jacket is useful.

### 1–2

With your back to the church of **San Cataldo**, walk to the main road and **Piazza Matteotti** and cross diagonally right to head up **Via Roma** and into **Piazza Vittorio Emanuele** (➤ 123).

**San Cataldo** (rebuilt in the 18th century) has a beautiful carved font (1473), the work of Domenico Gagini, a Lombard sculptor who trained under Brunelleschi in Florence, came south and founded a whole dynasty of carvers and sculptors on the island.

Piazza Vittorio Emanuele is home to the church of **San Francesco d'Assisi** – its fine 16th-century tower was one of Enna's series

A fine view of neighbouring Calascibetta can be glimpsed from this walk around Enna

of watchtowers, designed to link the town's churches with the Castello. The fountain is later – its bronze statue recalls Enna's mythical past (➤ 124) and is a copy of Bernini's *Rape of Persephone* in the Galleria Borghese in Rome.

### 2–3

Continue up Via Roma, passing **San Marco** on the left and Piazza Umberto I, another of the string of squares that punctuate Via Roma's uphill course, on your right. Look left to take in the Moorish-style **campanile of San Giovanni Battista**, one of the only surviving structures from the Arab occupation. Walk on up, passing San Giuseppe, until you see Piazza Colaianni on your right. The massive old building with the courtyard on your left is the **Palazzo Pollicarini**, a medieval Catalan-Gothic palace that retains its typically Catalan exterior staircase. A statue of Napoleone Colaianni, a 19th-century Sicilian politican, overlooks the

piazza and the facade of **Santa Chiara** – if it's open it's worth slipping inside to admire the majolica pictures on the tiled floor.

## 3–4

Via Roma now leads up past the **Duomo** and **Piazza Mazzini** and its museum (▶ 124). Once the street narrows, you're in Via Lombardia, where you'll find **Sicilia delle Miniature** (▶ 123); the road ends in a spacious piazza in front of the **Castello** (▶ 123).

## 4–5

Take the left-hand road around the castle and past the entrance steps and continue straight on until you see the rocky mass of the **Rocca di Cerere** ahead. The Rocca di Cerere, named for Ceres, the Latin name for the goddess Demeter, is one of Sicily's most ancient holy sites, where first the Great Goddess and, later, Demeter, were worshipped. Gelon built a sumptuous temple here in the fourth century BC, and this evocative outcrop has one of the town's finest views.

## 5–6

Walk back to the front of the Castello and take the right-hand street, **Viale Caterina Savoca**, with more views to be glimpsed through the trees, downhill. Follow this down, pass the post office on your right, until you reach **Piazza Garibaldi** (▶ 124).

## 6–7

Leave the square in the northwest corner and walk down **Viale Marconi**, to the gardens of the belvedere in Piazza Crispi, perhaps Enna's paramount viewpoint, before cutting through and back to Piazza Vittorio Emanuele.

**The interior of Enna's Duomo is all baroque, including lovely paintings by Guglielmo Borremans and Filippo Paladini**

View over the Castello ruins

## TAKING A BREAK

The Bar Azimut (€), between the Castello and the Rocca di Cerere, has lovely views from its terrace.

# 5 A Drive through the Madonie Mountains

*Drive*

**Take this wonderfully varied, circular route into the heart of one of Sicily's most beautiful mountain areas to discover untouched hill towns and villages set in superb scenery in an area that stretches south from the north coast towards the interior.**

**DISTANCE** 135km (84 miles) **TIME** 7 hours (includes stops) **START/END POINT** Cefalù
**WHEN TO GO** Best in spring and autumn, though lovely at any time of year; avoid mid-winter when inland roads can be icy and snow-covered ✦ 195 D3

## 1–2

Start outside the station in **Cefalù** (➤ 74) and follow the signs right to the *centro*, picking up the green signs to the *autostrada*. Drive uphill, away from the sea, then swing left to descend to the sea and drive along the coast towards Messina on the SS113. After 8km (5 miles) turn right following the brown sign to **Parco Naturale Regionale delle Madonie** and the blue sign to Castelbuono, a distance of 13km (8 miles).

**Castelbuono**, billing itself as the capital of the Madonie, is a handsome town that

spreads itself across the lower slopes of the mountains. The 14th-century seat of the powerful Ventimiglia clan, it's dominated by their **castle** (tel: 0921 671 211; Tue–Sun 8:30–2, 2:30–8; moderate), built in 1438, a sober fortress enlivened by the graceful stucco work of Giacomo Serpotta in its little baroque chapel. Elsewhere, you'll find the 14th-century **Matrice Vecchia**, a lovely old church with some good frescoes. The town hit the international

The colourful houses of Castelbuono

## 2–3

Leave town on the SS286, following the signs to **Geraci Siculo** along the road known as the Strada dei Castelli. Geraci too, has its castle, a Saracen stronghold that's a steep climb from the town with a reward of huge views at the top.

## 3–4

Continue deeper and higher into the mountains on the same road for 5.5km (3.4 miles) to the *bivio* (junction) Geraci. At the junction turn right on the SS120, signposted **Petralia**, and continue for 4.7km (3 miles) to the outskirts of **Petralia Soprana** (▶ 83). Leave the main road and head uphill to explore the village, parking your car on the outskirts to avoid the steep and narrow streets of the town.

## 4–5

Rejoin the main road and continue to **Petralia Sottana**, leaving your car in the car park on the left as you enter the village if you're planning to explore the Ventimiglias of Castelbuono extended as far as this stony mountain village, with its steep streets and tall houses. Founded in the 13th century as

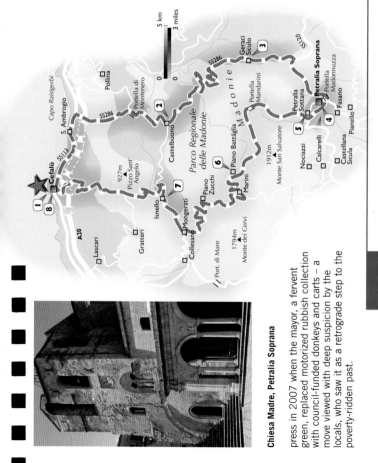

**Chiesa Madre, Petralia Soprana**

press in 2007 when the mayor, a fervent green, replaced motorized rubbish collection with council-funded donkeys and carts – a move viewed with deep suspicion by the locals, who saw it as a retrograde step to the poverty-ridden past.

a defensive outpost for Soprana, it's well-endowed with churches – a fine **Chiesa Madre** near the top of the town and two older ones, facing each other. If you want to know more about the **Madonie Natural Park**, created in 1989, this is the place to come – the park's headquarters are on the main street, at Corso Paolo Agliata 16 (tel: 0921 684 011; www.parcodellemadonie.it). They'll fill you in on the park's background, including the conservation programme to preserve the seriously threatened *Abies nebrodensis*, the Sicilian high-altitude conifer. This beautiful high-altitude conifer is the subject of a huge regeneration programme, and the park office will tell you where to find specimens. Elsewhere in the park, peasant farmers still harvest the crystallized, sugary sap of the manna ash (*Fraxinus ornus*), a natural sweetener, used for centuries in these mountains, that's packed with goodness and is now attracting increasing interest from the medical profession.

### 5–6

Leave **Petralia Sottana** and fork right, following the signs to Collesano, Piano Battáglia and Piano Zucchi. This 15km (9.5-mile) stretch of road climbs higher and higher through

**Mountain scenery in the Madonie Natural Park**

increasingly mountainous country, with wooded hills planted with mixed deciduous and coniferous trees and spreads of heather on either side of the road. **Piano Battáglia** is one of the highest settlements in the Madonie at 1,865m (6,119 feet) and the centre of a tiny ski area, complete with Swiss-chalet style houses. The ski facilities here are pretty low key, but nevertheless attract thousands of Palermitani during winter weekends.

You're more likely to be here in spring and summer, when the altitude brings a welcome freshness to the air. These limestone hills are particularly rich in wild flowers and up until June, you'll have to walk only a few metres from the car to come across myriad colourful species – look out for orchids, gentians and spreads of heavenly blue myosotis and globularia in particular.

### TAKING A BREAK
The Trattoria da Salvatore (€€; Piazza San Michele 3; tel: 0921 680 169; closed Tue) in Petralia Soprana is an excellent little restaurant serving local specialities. It's best to reserve ahead in summer.

## 6–7

Follow the road round to the right at Piano Battáglia, following the brown signs to Piano Zucchi and the blue signs to Isnello. At Piano Zucchi continue straight on towards Isnello. After 7km (4.3 miles) turn right to Isnello, a very typical inland village. If you want to explore it's a short detour off the main road – follow the signs to the *centro*. **Piano Zucchi** (1,105m/3,625 feet) is another winter sports centre, though, due to its lower altitude, its season is much shorter. It's a beguiling place, with scattered houses and a couple of hotels; the walking from here is superb.

From here you lose altitude rapidly as the road snakes its way north down the wooded slopes. Keep your eyes open, as this is a good place to spy wild boar, who sometimes cross the road followed by a procession of tiny striped piglets. **Isnello**, a short detour off the road, is a quintessentially Sicilian mountain village, in some ways barely touched by the 21st century. There's not much to see, but if you want a taste of traditional life, stroll through town – you'll see even young women in the black they'll wear for the rest of their lives, old men in conversation round the fountain and few signs of modern trappings.

## 7–8

Some 3km (1.8 miles) after Isnello turn left and follow the steeply descending road northwards for another 22km (13.6 miles)

**Isnello is a typical inland Sicilian village, surrounded by stunning mountain landscapes**

through more dramatic scenery and past the spectacularly sited Santuario di Gibilmanna back to **Cefalù**. This road rejoins the main coastal road on the upper outskirts of Cefalù.

# 6 A Drive through Valle d'Anapo

*Drive*

A drive west from Siracusa to the valley of the River Anapo, visiting the lovely baroque town of Palazzolo Acreide en route, with views of gorges, upland country, Mount Etna and the sea.

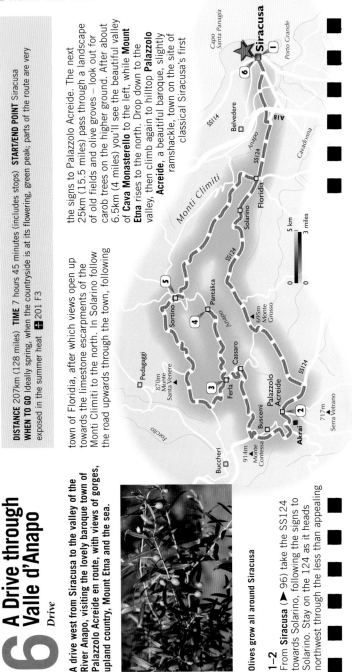

Olives grow all around Siracusa

**DISTANCE** 207km (128 miles) **TIME** 7 hours 45 minutes (includes stops) **START/END POINT** Siracusa
**WHEN TO GO** Ideally spring, when the countryside is at its flowering, green peak; parts of the route are very exposed in the summer heat ✚ 201 F3

## 1–2

From **Siracusa** (▶ 96) take the SS124 towards Solarino, following the signs to Solarino. Stay on the 124 as it heads northwest through the less than appealing town of Floridia, after which views open up towards the limestone escarpments of the Monti Climiti to the north. In Solarino follow the road upwards through the town, following

the signs to Palazzolo Acreide. The next 25km (15.5 miles) pass through a landscape of old fields and olive groves – look out for carob trees on the higher ground. After about 6.5km (4 miles) you'll see the beautiful valley of **Cava Monasterello** to the left, while **Mount Etna** rises to the north. Drop down to the valley, then climb again to hilltop **Palazzolo Acreide**, a beautiful baroque, slightly ramshackle, town on the site of classical Siracusa's first inland colony. Stop in town to take in the **Casa-Museo Antonino Uccello** (Via Machiavelli 19, tel: 0931 881 499; daily 9–1, 3:30–7; free), eastern Sicily's finest collection of rural artefacts, room reconstructions and folk art, its 5,000 objects collected over 30 years by the museum's founder. From here, it's a 20-minute stroll out to the **Akrai** (daily 9am–1 hour before sunset; moderate), the archaeological remains of the Siracusan city founded in the seventh century BC. Most complete is the **Teatro Greco** (c.300BC), whose perfect semicircle held 600 people; it's still used sometimes for performances.

### 2–3

Leave town on the SS124 (signposted Caltagirone), crossing the upper reaches of the River Anapo and bypassing the village of Buscemi. At the junction (8km/5 miles) leave the 124, turning right to follow the signs to **Ferla**. The road runs through limestone slopes to olive groves around the village of Cassaro (6.5km/4 miles). Drive through here and follow the SP10 to Ferla, roughly halfway along the route and a good lunch stop.

**The Teatro Greco at the ancient site of Akrai**

### TAKING A BREAK

Dell'Arco (€–€€: Via Arco Lantieri 5, Ferla, tel: 0931 870035) is a family-run trattoria with a terrace at the rear of the building.

### 3–4

Drive uphill through Ferla and follow the brown tourist signs to **Pantálica**, a great Bronze Age necropolis (tel: 0931 954 805; free) first used between the 13th and 10th centuries BC and later the site of classical Hybla. Park at the Casello del Principe entrance (9.5km/6 miles from Ferla) and follow the path to explore the gorge of the Anapo and the tombs of Sicily's largest necropolis. Two rivers, the Anapo and the Calcinara, cut through gorges eroded in the limestone plateau of Monti Iblei; you can walk down to the riverbed or simply view the tombs from above, all that remain of the settlement of the Sikel people, who flourished from around 1250BC until the eighth-century BC Greek domination. These limestone caves were dug out of the cliff walls and many contained the skeletons of this ancient people. It's a beautiful place, rich in superb flora, willow and holm oak – in spring

look out for spreads of wild orchids – while the river is edged with iris, watermint and cress. From the higher slopes there are wonderful views, tempting you to continue your walk.

## 4–5

From the gorge there is no through route for cars on to Sortino, so retrace the route to Ferla by car by first heading southwest on the SP13. Then follow the twisting, panoramic back road northeast past Monte Santa Venere towards Sortino, which gives glimpses of the gorges of the Anapo Valley and deep clefts sculpted by water erosion. Drive into **Sortino**, known as La Città del Miele (City of Honey) and famous for its annual festival, Sagra del Miele, on the first weekend of October. The town is also home to the **Museo Civico**

dell'**Opera dei Pupi** (Piazza San Francesco 9, tel: 0931 952 079; Mon–Sat 9:30–12:30; free), which traces the history of Sicily's traditional puppet theatre. The museum is famous for its collection of large puppets – some are as tall as 1.5m (5 feet) and weigh more than 35kg (77 lb). You may be lucky enough to catch a performance of one of the plays, whose themes are based on the struggles of the Christian King Charlemagne and his knights against the Saracens, with plenty of humour, romance and folklore thrown in. Sortino is liberally endowed with fine churches; the 16th-century **Chiesa Madre** is the pick of the bunch.

## 5–6

Follow the signs to Siracusa out of Sortino, looking out for the right turn on to the SP28, which then follows the course of the Anapo, crossing and recrossing the river several times. After about 18km (11 miles) the road converges with the SP114 to Siracusa. Stay on this to the SS124 exit, which will bring you back into the city to the Parco Archeologico della Neapolis (➤ 98).

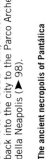

**The ancient necropolis of Pantálica**

# Practicalities

## BEFORE YOU GO

### WHAT YOU NEED

| | | | UK | Germany | USA | Canada | Australia | Ireland | Netherlands | Spain |
|---|---|---|---|---|---|---|---|---|---|---|
| ● | Required | Your passport should be valid for | | | | | | | | |
| ○ | Suggested | six months beyond the date of entry | | | | | | | | |
| ▲ | Not required | into Sicily. | | | | | | | | |
| △ | Not applicable | | | | | | | | | |
| Passport | | | ● | ● | ● | ● | ● | ● | ● | ● |
| Visa (regulations can change – check before booking your trip) | | | ▲ | ▲ | ▲ | ▲ | ▲ | ▲ | ▲ | ▲ |
| Onward or Return Ticket | | | ● | ● | ● | ● | ● | ● | ● | ● |
| Health Documentation | | | ● | ● | ▲ | ▲ | ▲ | ● | ● | ● |
| Travel Insurance | | | ● | ● | ● | ● | ● | ● | ● | ● |
| Driving Licence (national) | | | ● | ● | ● | ● | ● | ● | ● | ● |
| Car Insurance Certificate | | | ● | ● | ● | ● | ● | ● | ● | ● |
| Car Registration Document | | | ● | ● | ● | ● | ● | ● | ● | ● |

### WHEN TO GO

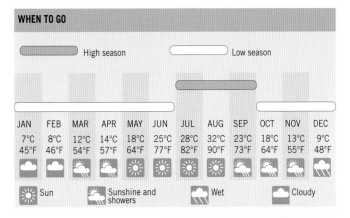

| | High season | | Low season |
|---|---|---|---|

| JAN | FEB | MAR | APR | MAY | JUN | JUL | AUG | SEP | OCT | NOV | DEC |
|---|---|---|---|---|---|---|---|---|---|---|---|
| 7°C | 8°C | 12°C | 14°C | 18°C | 25°C | 28°C | 32°C | 23°C | 18°C | 13°C | 9°C |
| 45°F | 46°F | 54°F | 57°F | 64°F | 77°F | 82°F | 90°F | 73°F | 64°F | 55°F | 48°F |

Sun    Sunshine and showers    Wet    Cloudy

Sicily's climate is predominantly Mediterranean, with wet winters and hot summers. Spring (March–April) is the best time to visit, when the countryside is green and the wildflowers are at their best, although it can also be wet at this time. By May and June temperatures are soaring and the sea is warm enough to swim, though the island is still uncrowded. July–September is peak tourist season with crowds everywhere and very high temperatures. The landscape is parched and brown and the *scirocco*, the suffocating wind from North Africa, can blast the island for days on end. By October, things are pleasanter after the first autumn rains, and the sea is still warm. November and December bring the winter rains everywhere. The coast remains mild, but inland, fog can descend for weeks and there is snow in the Madonie and Nebrodi mountains and on Mount Etna – a skiing holiday in Sicily is perfectly feasible.

**GETTING ADVANCE INFORMATION**

**Italian State Tourist Board**
www.enit.it

**Italian National Parks**
www.parks.it

**Sicilian Regional Tourist Board**
www.regione.sicilia.it/turismo

**In the UK**
Italian National Tourist Office
1 Princes Street
London W1B 2AY
☎ 020 7408 1254

## GETTING THERE

**By Air** Palermo, Catania and Trapani have international airports. From the UK direct flights to Catania are operated by British Airways (tel: 0870 850 9850; www.ba.com) and Air Malta (tel: 0845 607 3710; www.airmalta.com) and to Palermo by Ryanair (tel: 0871 246 0000; www.ryanair.com) and Easyjet (tel: 0905 821 0905; www.easyjet.com) with a flight time of around 3 hours. Ryanair also flies to Trapani. Most seats on charter flights are sold by tour operators as part of a package holiday, but it is usually possible to buy a flight-only deal. A charter flight can restrict your trip to a period of 7 or 14 days.

**From the US** There are no direct flights to Sicily. Travellers can either fly to Rome or Milan and connect with an internal flight, or route via London to fly with a low-cost carrier.

**By Car** To save on the long drive south through Italy, drivers could take a ferry from Genoa or Livorno (Grandi Navi Veloce; www.gnv.it) or Naples (Tirrenia, www.tirrenia.it); book well in advance. If you drive all the way south, you can cross the Straits of Messina via car ferry or hydrofoil from Villa San Giovanni (crossing time 25 minutes) or Réggio di Calabria (crossing time 15 minutes). Buy your ticket from the kiosks on the way to the ferry.

**By Rail** It's possible to travel by rail from London to Sicily, via Paris, Milan, Rome and Naples. It's a distance of over 2,600km (1,615 miles) to Messina with a journey time of around 40 hours (Eurostar, www.eurostar.co.uk; Italian State Railways, www.fs-on-line. com; Rail Europe, www.raileurope.co.uk).

## TIME

Sicily is one hour ahead of Greenwich Mean Time (GMT) in winter, and 1 hour ahead of BST in summer, 6 hours ahead of New York and 9 hours ahead of Los Angeles. Clocks are advanced 1 hour in March and turned back in October.

## CURRENCY AND FOREIGN EXCHANGE

**Currency** The euro (€) is the official currency of Italy. Euro coins are issued in denominations of 1, 2, 5, 10, 20 and 50 euro cents and €1 and €2. Notes are issued in denominations of €5, €10, €20, €50, €100, €200 and €500.

**Exchange** Foreign currency and traveller's cheques can be changed at banks and exchange bureaux (*cambio*), as well as in some resort hotels. Exchange bureaux generally offer the best deal, but it pays to shop around and compare commission charges. You will need to show your passport when cashing traveller's cheques. You can also withdraw cash from ATMs using your credit or debit card and a PIN. Your own bank will usually make a charge for this service.

**Credit cards** Major credit cards (*carta di credito*) are accepted in larger hotels, restaurants and shops, though cash is preferred in remoter places and smaller establishments. In the countryside it is advisable to have small-denomination notes to hand.

**In the USA**
Italian National Tourist
Office, 630 Fifth Avenue,
Suite 1565
New York NY 10111
☎ 212/245-5168

**In Australia**
Italian National Tourist
Board, Level 4
46 Market Street
Sydney 2000 NSW
☎ (02) 9262 1666

**In Canada**
Italian National Tourist
Office, 175 Bloor Street
East, Suite 907, South
Tower, Toronto, Ontario
☎ (416) 925 4882

## WHEN YOU ARE THERE

### NATIONAL HOLIDAYS

| | |
|---|---|
| 1 Jan | New Year's Day |
| 6 Jan | Epiphany |
| Mar/Apr | Easter Monday |
| 25 Apr | Liberation Day |
| 1 May | Labour Day |
| 2 Jun | Republic Day |
| 15 Aug | Ferragosto (feast of the Assumption) |
| 1 Nov | All Saints' Day |
| 8 Dec | Feast of the Immaculate Conception |
| 25 Dec | Christmas Day |
| 26 Dec | St Stephen's Day |

### ELECTRICITY

 The power supply is 220 volts AC. Sockets take two-pronged round continental plugs. Visitors from the UK will need an adaptor, and visitors from the US will need a transformer for 100–120 volt devices.

### OPENING HOURS

○ Shops ● Post Offices
● Offices ◐ Museums/Monuments
◐ Banks ○ Pharmacies

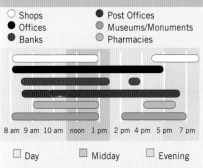

8 am  9 am  10 am  noon  1 pm  2 pm  4 pm  5 pm  7 pm

☐ Day   ■ Midday   ☐ Evening

**Shops** In general Tue–Sat 8–1, 4:30–8, though food shops are also open on Mondays as are shops in holiday resorts. Shops in larger towns and cities may be open all day (*orario continuato*).

**Banks** Generally banks are open 8:30–1:20 and 3–4.
**Post offices** Mon–Sat 8:30–6:30 at main branches, shorter hours and Saturday closing in provincial areas.
**Museums and churches** Generally 9–1 and 4–6, but this can vary and many are closed on Monday. Archaeological sites are open from 9 until an hour before sunset.
**Pharmacies** Usually open Mon–Sat 9–1, 4–8, but duty chemists will be open 24 hours on a rota system.

### TIPS/GRATUITIES

Tipping is not expected for all services and rates are low. Restaurants, bars and cafés include a service charge so a tip is not expected, although many people leave a few coins. As a general guide:

| | |
|---|---|
| Taxis | round up to nearest €0.50 |
| Tour Guides | discretion |
| Porters | €1 per bag |
| Chambermaid | €1 per night |
| Lavatory attendants | small change |

### USEFUL WEBSITES

**www.addiopizzo.org** The Goodbye Protection Money organization supports Mafia-free commerce, and guides you towards those businesses that refuse to pay the *pizzo*.
**www.bestofsicily.com** Informative site covering culture, sights, history and food and wine.

### TIME DIFFERENCES

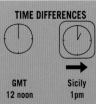

| GMT | Sicily | Australia (Sydney) | Germany | Spain | USA (New York) |
|---|---|---|---|---|---|
| 12 noon | 1pm | 10pm | 1pm | 1pm | 7am |

## STAYING IN TOUCH

Stamps (*francobolli*) can be bought at tobacconists, post offices and some gift shops. Mail to EU countries should arrive within 5–7 days, and to the US within 10 days. Send urgent mail by *posta prioritaria* and ensure that you use a blue post box. Other boxes are red.

There are numerous Telecom Italia public telephones on the street and in Telecom Italia offices. They take coins, credit cards and phonecards (*schede telefóniche*); these are on sale at newsstands and *tabacchi* (tobacconists). Tear the corner off the card before use. You can also send a text from a public telephone. International calls are cheaper between 10pm and 8am Mon–Fri and all day Sunday. Calls from hotel rooms will invariably attract a heavy premium.

**International Dialling Codes**
**Dial 00 followed by**

| | |
|---|---|
| UK: | 44 |
| USA / Canada: | 1 |
| Irish Republic: | 353 |
| Australia: | 61 |

**Mobile providers and services** Italy has three main operators: Vodafone (www.vodafone.it), TIM (www.tim.it) and Wind (www.wind.it). All sell pre-paid SIM cards costing from €10 to €15, which you can use in an unlocked GSM phone to make calls at local rates and avoid high roaming charges. You will need proof of ID to open an account. Incoming texts and calls are generally free, while the cost of outgoing calls and texts varies.

**WiFi and Internet** There are plenty of internet places on the island, mostly in the bigger towns and cities. Many local municipal offices have internet rooms alongside their libraries and there are public internet points as well as cyber cafés. You will normally be asked to show your ID at public internet points. Prices vary, but expect to pay about €5 an hour, although free WiFi access is increasingly available in bars and better hotels.

## PERSONAL SAFETY

Violence against tourists is unusual in Sicily, but petty crime such as pickpocketing and bag snatching and theft from cars is common.

- Do not wear or display expensive equipment or jewellery.
- Always lock valuables in hotel safety deposit boxes.
- Try never to leave anything inside your car. If you have to, lock it out of sight in the boot.
- Beware of pickpockets in crowded markets and busy streets.
- Use common sense and stick to well-lit streets at night.
- Carry shoulder bags slung across your body.
- Report any theft straight away to get a reference number if you need to make an insurance claim.
- If going walking in remote areas, make sure you take emergency food, drink, clothing and, ideally, a mobile phone.

**Police assistance:**
☎ 112 from any phone

| EMERGENCY 113 |
|---|
| POLICE 112 |
| FIRE 115 |
| AMBULANCE 118 |

## HEALTH

 **Insurance** Citizens of EU countries receive reduced-cost emergency health care with relevant documentation (European Health Insurance Card), which you must obtain before travelling. Comprehensive travel and private medical insurance are always advised for everybody. Ask at your hotel for details of English-speaking doctors.

 **Dental Services** Dental treatment is not covered by the health service and you will have to pay for treatment, but your insurance should cover the costs.

 **Weather** The sun can be intense at all times of year, and it is possible to burn very quickly. Cover up with high-factor sunscreen, wear a hat and drink plenty of water, especially if walking in the hills or along the coast. If you sleep with the windows open, insect repellent and an electrical mosquito zapper may be useful.

 **Drugs** Pharmacists (*farmacie*) are open Mon–Sat 9–1 and 4–8. Some open through lunch and the late-night duty chemist is posted in pharmacy windows. Pharmacists are highly trained and can sell some drugs that require prescriptions in other countries. However, take adequate supplies of any drugs you take regularly as they may not be available.

 **Safe Water** Tap water is safe but most people drink mineral water. Ask for sparkling (*gassata* or *frizzante*) or still (*naturale* or *liscia*) bottled water.

## CONCESSIONS

**Young People/Senior Citizens** There are no reductions for students or young adults in Sicily and the ISIC card is not valid. Under-18s and over 65s have free entrance into all museums and archaeological sites.

## TRAVELLING WITH A DISABILITY

Facilities for disabled travellers in Sicily are poor, with many older hotels and public buildings still inaccessible. It's best to discuss your needs with your tour operator or hotel before booking a holiday. In the UK Holiday Care (tel: 0845 124 9971; www.holidaycare.org. uk) publishes information on accessibility. In the US, the Society for the Advancement of Travellers with Handicaps (SATH, tel: 212/447-7284; www.sath.org) has plenty of tips for disabled travellers.

## CHILDREN

Hotels and restaurants are generally child-friendly, and some hotels by the coast have playgrounds and children's pools. Facilities such as baby-changing rooms are rare.

## TOILETS

There are public toilets in museums, and bars will let you use theirs for the cost of a coffee. Ask for *il bagno* or *il gabinetto*.

## CUSTOMS

Visitors arriving in Italy from non-EU countries may import, duty free, 1 litre of spirits or 2 litres of wine; 50g perfume; 250ml eau de toilette; 200 cigarettes.

## EMBASSIES AND HIGH COMMISSIONS

**UK**
☎ 091 326 412
www.british
embassy.gov.uk

**USA**
☎ 091 305 857
www.usis.it

**Ireland**
☎ 06 697 9121
www.ambasciata-
irlanda.it

**Australia**
☎ 06 852 721
www.italy.
embassy.gov.au

**Canada**
☎ 06 854 441
www.dfait-
maeci.gc.ca

## SURVIVAL PHRASES

yes/no **sì/non**
please **per favore**
Thank you **grazie**
You're welcome **di niente/prego**
I'm sorry **mi dispiace**
goodbye **arrivederci**
good morning **buongiorno**
goodnight **buona sera**
how are you? **come sta?**
how much? **quanto costa?**
I would like... **vorrei...**
open **aperto**
closed **chiuso**
today **oggi**
tomorrow **domani**
Monday **lunedì**
Tuesday **martedì**
Wednesday **mercoledì**
Thursday **giovedì**
Friday **venerdì**
Saturday **sabato**
Sunday **domenica**

## DIRECTIONS

I'm lost **mi sono perso/a**
Where is...? **dove si trova...?**
the station **la stazione**
the telephone **il telefono**
the bank **la banca**
the toilet **il bagno**
Turn left **volti a sinistra**
Turn right **volti a destra**
Go straight on **Vada dritto**
At the corner **all'angolo**
the street **la strada**
the building **il palazzo**
the traffic light **il semaforo**
the crossroads **l'incrocio**
the signs for... **le indicazione per...**

## IF YOU NEED HELP

Help! **Aiuto!**
Could you help me, please?
**Mi potrebbe aiutare?**
do you speak English? **Parla inglese?**
I don't understand **Non capisco**
Please could you call a doctor quickly?
**Mi chiami presto un medico, per favore**

## RESTAURANT

I'd like to book a table
**Vorrei prenotare un tavolo**
A table for two please
**Un tavolo per due, per favore**
Could we see the menu, please?
**Ci porta la lista, per favore?**
What's this? **Cosa è questo?**
A bottle of/a glass of...
**Un bottiglia di/un bicchiere di...**
Could I have the bill? **Ci porta il conto?**

## ACCOMMODATION

Do you have a single/double room?
**Ha una camera singola/doppia?**
with/without bath/toilet/shower
**con/senza vasca/gabinetto/doccia**
Does that include breakfast?
**E'inclusa la prima colazione?**
Does that include dinner?
**E'inclusa la cena?**
Do you have room service?
**C'è il servizio in camera?**
Could I see the room?
**E' possibile vedere la camera?**
I'll take this room **Prendo questa**
Thanks for your hospitality
**Grazie per l'ospitalità**

## NUMBERS

| | | | | | | | |
|---|---|---|---|---|---|---|---|
| 0 | zero | 12 | dodici | 40 | quaranta | 400 | quattrocento |
| 1 | uno | 13 | tredici | 50 | cinquanta | 500 | cinquecento |
| 2 | due | 14 | quattordici | 60 | sessanta | 600 | seicento |
| 3 | tre | 15 | quindici | 70 | settanta | 700 | settecento |
| 4 | quattro | 16 | sedici | 80 | ottanta | 800 | ottocento |
| 5 | cinque | 17 | diciassette | 90 | novanta | 900 | novecento |
| 6 | sei | 18 | diciotto | 100 | cento | 1,000 | mille |
| 7 | sette | 19 | diciannove | 101 | cento uno | 2,000 | duemila |
| 8 | otto | 20 | venti | 110 | centodieci | 10,000 | diecimila |
| 9 | nove | 21 | ventuno | 120 | centoventi | | |
| 10 | dieci | 22 | ventidue | 200 | duecento | | |
| 11 | undici | 30 | trenta | 300 | trecento | | |

## MENU READER

**acciuga** anchovy
**acqua** water
**affettati** sliced cured meats
**affumicato** smoked
**aglio** garlic
**agnello** lamb
**anatra** duck
**antipasti** hors d'oeuvres
**arista** roast pork
**arrosto** roast
**asparagi** asparagus
**birra** beer
**bistecca** steak
**bollito** boiled meat
**braciola** minute steak
**brasato** braised
**brodo** broth
**bruschetta** toasted bread
with garlic or tomato topping
**budino** pudding
**burro** butter
**cacciagione** game
**cacciatore, alla** rich
tomato sauce with
mushrooms
**caffè corretto/ macchiato**
coffee with liqueur/spirit, or
with a drop of milk
**caffè freddo** iced coffee
**caffè latte** milky coffee
**caffè lungo** weak coffee
**caffè ristretto** strong
coffee
**calamaro** squid
**cappero** caper
**carciofo** artichoke
**carota** carrot
**carne** meat
**carpa** carp
**casalingo** homemade
**cassata** Sicilian fruit ice
cream
**cavolfiore** cauliflower
**cavolo** cabbage
**ceci** chickpeas
**cervello** brains
**cervo** venison
**cetriolino** gherkin
**cetriolo** cucumber
**cicoria** chicory
**cinghiale** boar
**cioccolata** chocolate
**cipolla** onion
**coda di bue** oxtail
**coniglio** rabbit

**contorni** vegetables
**coperto** cover charge
**coscia** leg of meat
**cotolette** cutlets
**cozze** mussels
**crema** custard
**crostini** canape with
savoury toppings or croutons
**crudo** raw
**digestivo** after-dinner
liqueur
**dolci** cakes/ desserts
**erbe aromatiche** herbs
**facito** stuffed
**fagioli** beans
**fagiolini** green beans
**faraona** guinea fowl
**fegato** liver
**finocchio** fennel
**formaggio** cheese
**forno, al** baked
**frittata** omelette
**fritto** fried
**frizzante** fizzy
**frulatto** whisked
**frutta** fruit
**frutti di mare** seafood
**funghi** mushrooms
**gamberetto** shrimp
**gelato** ice cream
**ghiaccio** ice
**gnocchi** potato dumplings
**granchio** crab
**gran(o)turco** corn
**griglia, alla** grilled
**imbottito** stuffed
**insalata** salad
**IVA** VAT
**latte** milk
**lepre** hare
**lumache** snails
**manzo** beef
**merluzzo** cod
**miele** honey
**minestra** soup
**molluschi** shellfish
**olio** oil
**oliva** olive
**ostrica** oyster
**pancetta** bacon
**pane** bread
**panino** roll
**panna** cream
**parmigiano** Parmesan
**passata** sieved or creamed

**pastasciutta** dried pasta
cooked, with sauce
**pasta sfoglia** puff pastry
**patate fritte** chips
**pecora** mutton
**pecorino** sheep's milk
cheese
**peperoncino** chilli
**peperone** red/ green pepper
**pesce** fish
**petto** breast
**piccione** pigeon
**piselli** peas
**pollame** fowl
**pollo** chicken
**polpetto** meatball
**porto** port wine
**prezzemolo** parsley
**primo piatto** first course
**prosciutto** cured ham
**ragù** meat sauce
**ripieno** stuffed
**riso** rice
**salsa** sauce
**salsiccia** sausage
**saltimbocca** veal with
prosciutto and sage
**secco** dry
**secondo piatto** main course
**senape** mustard
**servizio compreso** service
charge included
**sogliola** sole
**spuntini** snacks
**succa di frutta** fruit juice
**sugo** sauce
**tonno** tuna
**uovo affrogato/in carnica**
poached egg
**uovo al tegamo/fritto** fried
egg
**uovo alla coque** soft boiled
egg
**uovo alla sodo** hard boiled
egg
**uova strapazzate** scambled
egg
**verdure** vegetables
**vino bianco** white wine
**vino rosato** rosé wine
**vino rosso** red wine
**vitello** veal
**zucchero** sugar
**zucchino** courgette
**zuppa** soup

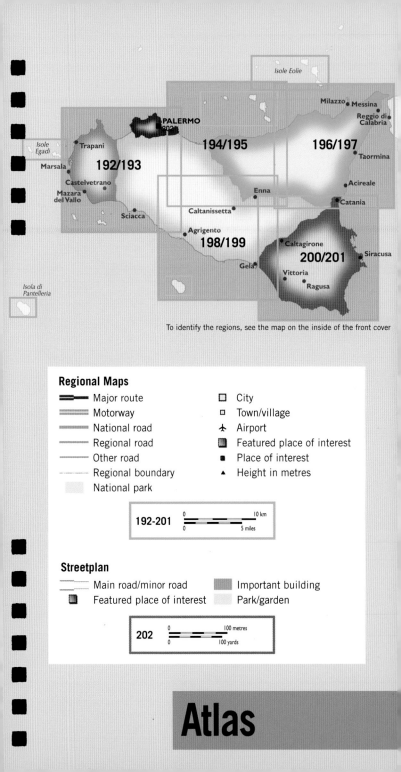

To identify the regions, see the map on the inside of the front cover

## Regional Maps

| | | | |
|---|---|---|---|
| Major route | | □ | City |
| Motorway | | ▫ | Town/village |
| National road | | ✈ | Airport |
| Regional road | | ▣ | Featured place of interest |
| Other road | | ▪ | Place of interest |
| Regional boundary | | ▲ | Height in metres |
| National park | | | |

**192-201**  0 — 10 km
0 — 5 miles

## Streetplan

Main road/minor road     Important building

Featured place of interest     Park/garden

**202**  0 — 100 metres
0 — 100 yards

# Atlas

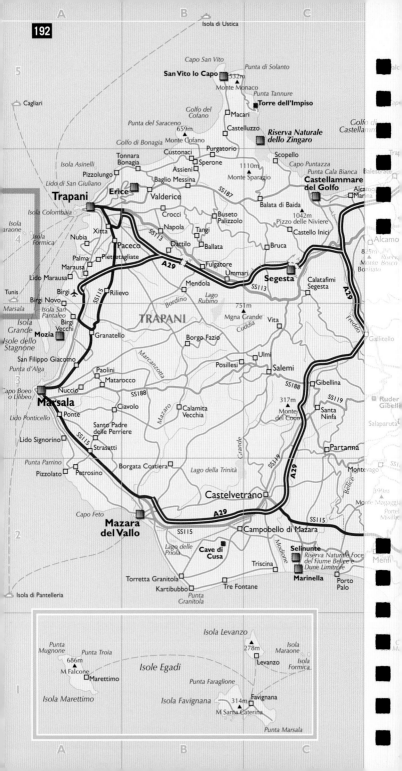

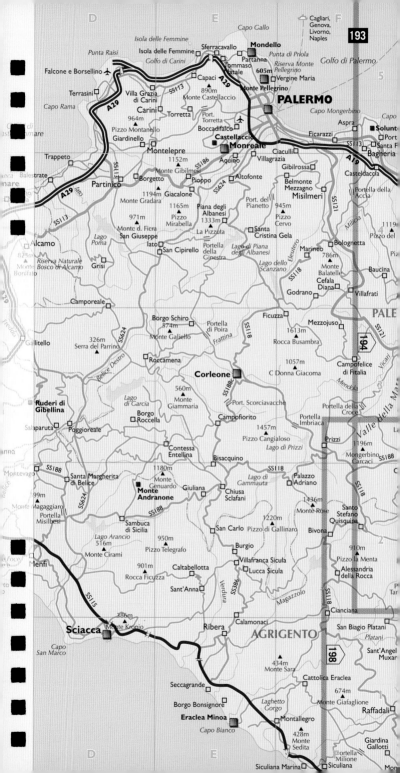

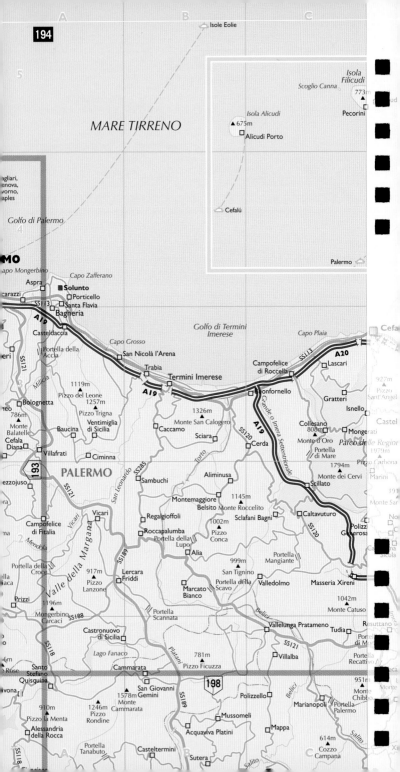

**Isola Salina**
Malfa
*Capo Faro*
Pollara
962m ▲ ☐ Santa Marina Salina
Rinella ☐ Lingua
*Punta Grottazza*
*Canale della Salina*
Acquacalda
Quattropani
**Isola Lipari** 594m ☐ Canneto
▲
Mte S. Angelo
Pianoconte
Termo di S. Calogero ☐ Lipari
369m ☐
**Isole Eolie**
*Bocche di Vulcano*
Porto di Ponente ☐ Porto di Levante
391m ☐
**Gran Cratere** ■ 500m ☐
M. Aria ▲ *Punta Bandiera*
**Isola Vulcano** Gelso ☐

Cefalù        Palermo        Cefalú

Isole Eolie

Sant'Agata Militel
Acquedolci

**Cefalù** Sant' Marina di Caronia SS113 **Grotta di San Teode**
Ambrogio *Capo Raisigerbi*
Finale Milianni Castel Torremuzza Canneto San Fratello
di Tusa **SS196**
SS113 Caronia 833m ▲
**Santo Stefano** Pizzo Filio
**di Camastra**
SS286 Tusa Motta 1260m ▲
Pollina d'Affermo Reitano Pizzo Luminaria
27m ▲ Pollina 1027m ▲ Pettineo 1167m ▲ 1287m ▲
Pizzo Borrello Pizzo Taverna Monte Trefinaidi Pizzo
Sant'Angelo Portella di **Mistretta** 1686m ▲ Lippo
Montenero 1223m ▲ Pizzo Fau Fe
nello Pizzo Voturo **Nebrodi** 1544m ▲
Pizzo
Castelbuono San Mauro Castelverde Monte Porriere
Mongerati
co delle **Regionale Madonie** 1346m ▲ Castel di Lucio Capizzi Lago Ancipa
1919m ▲ Timpa del Grillo 1567m ▲ Pizz
Pizzo SS286 Monte Castelli
Carbonara **Madonie** Colle del Contrasto SS120
Cervi Marini Geraci 1558m ▲ Cerami
1912m ▲ Portella Siculo Monte Tr
Monte San Salvatore Mandarini 901m Sambughetti
Pizzo Cosimo
Nociazzi Petralia
Calcarelli Sottana SS120 1013m ▲
ellana **Petralia Soprana** Gangi Monte Schino Gagliano
Sicula Portella SS120 della Croce Castelferrato
Fasano Madonnuzza Sperlinga
Pianello 1332m ▲ **Nicosia**
Blufi Monte Zimmara
Bompietro Casalgiordana 1025m ▲ 764m ▲ Lago Pozzi
Alimena Monte la Guardia Serra del Bosco
Villadoro Portella Creta SS117 Nissoria Agira SS121
Resuttano Cacchiamo Leonforte San Giorgio
Portella SS290 Lago **ENNA**
recattivo Nicoletti Assoro
Recattivo Villapriolo SS290 SS121
825m ▲ **SS199** Calascibetta Lago Pozzillo
Monte Matarazzo Villarosa Lago
Santa Caterina Villarosa Dittaino A19
Villamosa SS121
Portella A19 **Enna** Calderari SS192
del Vento
Xirbi SS122 Pergusa 487m ▲ Libertinia
Lago di **SS200** Cozzo Arginemele
Pergusa Mulinello

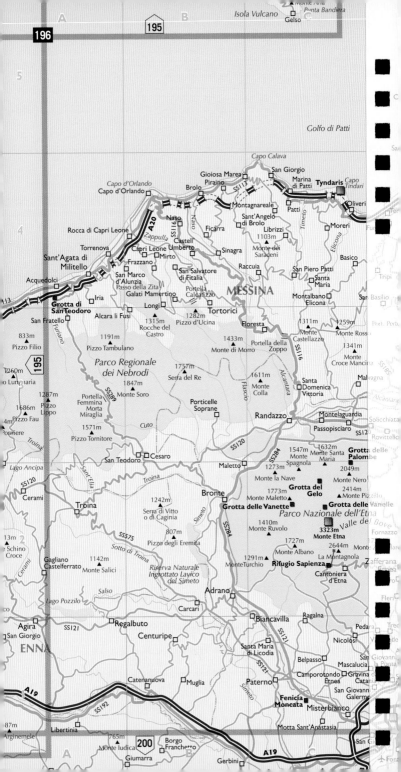

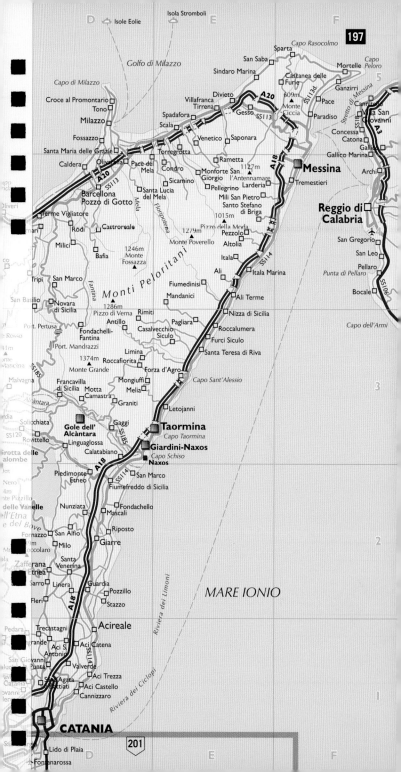

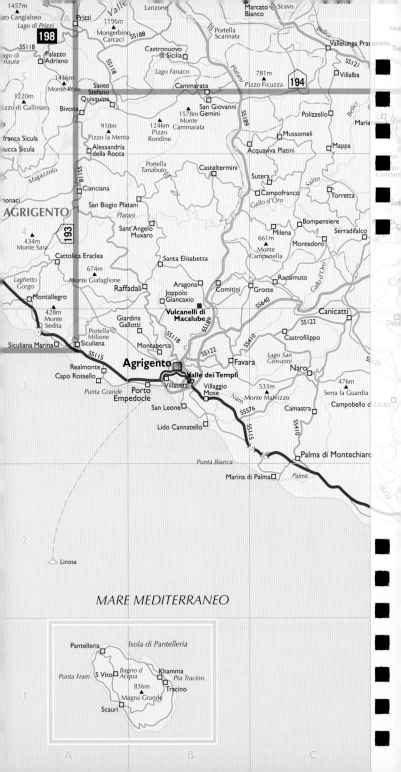

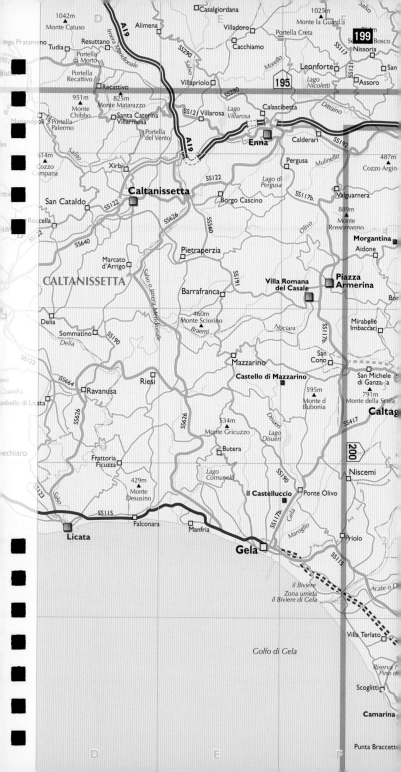

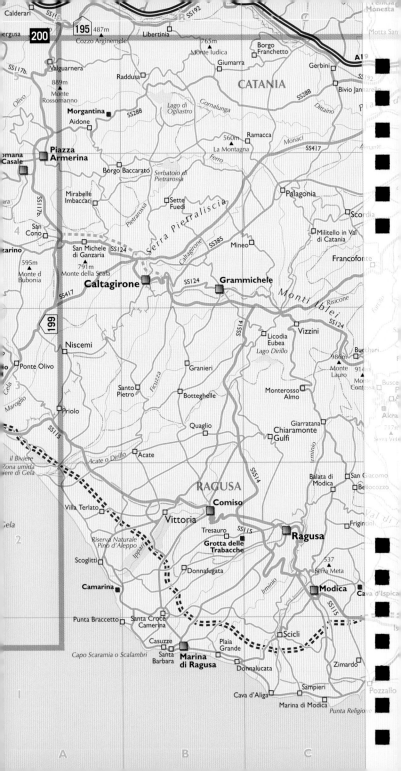

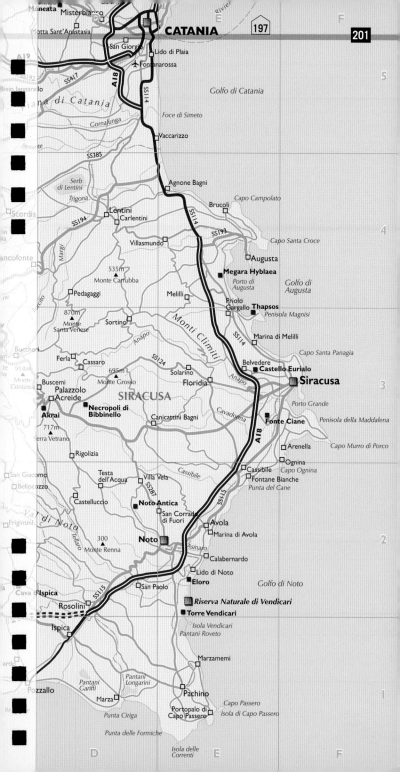

Moncada
Misterbianco
Motta Sant'Anastasia
San Giorgio
**CATANIA**
197
A19
192
SS417
A18
SS114
Piana di Catania
Gornalunga
Foce di Simeto
Fontanarossa
Lido di Plaia
*Golfo di Catania*
Vaccarizzo
Benante
Trigona
Serb di Lentini
SS385
SS114
Agnone Bagni
Brucoli
*Capo Campolato*
Lentini
Carlentini
Villasmundo
SS194
SS193
Margi
Scordia
ncofonte
535m
Monte Carrubba
Pedagaggi
870m
Monte Santa Venere
Sortino
Ferla
Cassaro
695m
Monte Grosso
SS124
Solarino
Buscemi
Palazzolo Acreide
914m
Monte Contessa
Akrai
717m
Serra Vetrano
**Necropoli di Bibbinello**
Canicattini Bagni
Rigolizia
San Giacomo
Bellocozzo
Testa dell'Acqua
Villa Vela
SS287
Castelluccio
**Noto Antica**
San Corrado di Fuori
Frigintini
300
Monte Renna
**Noto**
Asinaro
Ispica
Rosolini
SS115
San Paolo
Ispica
Cava d'Ispica
ardo
Pozzallo
Pantani Gariffi
Marza
*Val di Noto*
Tellaro
Villasmundo
Augusta
**Megara Hyblaea**
*Porto di Augusta*
*Golfo di Augusta*
Melilli
Priolo Gargallo
**Thapsos**
*Penisola Magnisi*
Monti Climiti
SS114
Marina di Melilli
*Capo Santa Panagia*
Belvedere
**Castello Eurialo**
Floridia
Anapo
Anapo
**SIRACUSA**
Siracusa
201
F
*Golfo di Catania*
*Capo Santa Croce*
Augusta
Cavadonna
Cassibile
*Porto Grande*
A18
**Fonte Ciane**
*Penisola della Maddalena*
Arenella
*Capo Murro di Porco*
Ognina
SS115
Cassibile
*Capo Ognina*
Fontane Bianche
*Punta del Cane*
Avola
Marina di Avola
Calabernardo
Lido di Noto
**Eloro**
*Golfo di Noto*
**Riserva Naturale di Vendicari**
**Torre Vendicari**
*Isola Vendicari*
*Pantani Roveto*
Marzamemi
**Pachino**
*Capo Passero*
Portopalo di Capo Passero
*Isola di Capo Passero*
*Punta Ciriga*
*Punta delle Formiche*
*Isola delle Correnti*

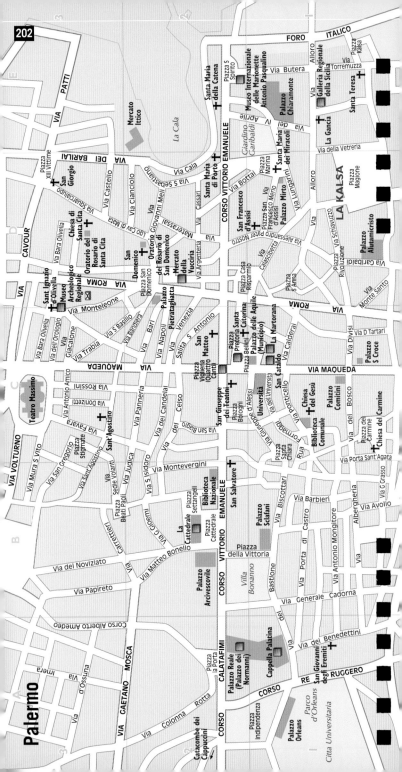

## Picture Credits

The Automobile Association wishes to thank the following photographers and organizations for their assistance in the preparation of this book.

Abbreviations for the picture credits are: – (t) top; (b) bottom; (l) left; (r) right; (c) centre; (AA) AA World Travel Library

2(i) AA/C Sawyer; 2(ii) AA/N Setchfield; 2(iii) AA/N Setchfield; 2(iv) AA/C Sawyer; 2(v) AA/N Setchfield; 3(i) AA/N Setchfield; 3(ii) AA/N Setchfield; 3(iii) AA/N Setchfield; 5l AA/C Sawyer; 5c AA/N Setchfield; 5r AA/C Sawyer; 6/7 AA/C Sawyer; 8 AA/N Setchfield; 9tl AA/C Sawyer; 9tr AA/N Setchfield; 10 AA/C Sawyer; 11 AA/N Setchfield; 12 AA/N Setchfield; 13t AA/N Setchfield; 13c AA/N Setchfield; 13b AA/N Setchfield; 14t AA/C Sawyer; 14c AA/N Setchfield; 14b AA/N Setchfield; 15 AA/N Setchfield; 16 Gianni Muratore/Alamy; 16/17 side, Marshall Ikonography/Alamy; 17 Marshall Ikonography/Alamy; 18c Neil Setchfield/Alamy; 18b Hemis/Alamy; 19 Lonely Planet Images/Alamy; 20 The Art Gallery Collection/Alamy; 21 Mary Evans Picture Library/Alamy; 23tl Gianni Muratore/Alamy; 23tr Osservatore Romano/AFP/Getty Images; 24 Fototeca ENIT/Vito Arcomano; 25cl Cubolmages srl/Alamy; 25ct Look Die Bildagentur der Fotografen GmbH/Alamy; 26 AF archive/Alamy; 27 Pictorial Press Ltd/Alamy; 28/29 AA/N Setchfield; 30 Fototeca ENIT/Sandro Bedessi; 31l AA/N Setchfield; 31c AA/N Setchfield; 31r AA/N Setchfield; 43l AA/N Setchfield; 43c AA/N Setchfield; 43r AA/N Setchfield; 44 AA/N Setchfield; 45 AA/N Setchfield; 46t AA/N Setchfield; 46b AA/N Setchfield; 47c AA/N Setchfield; 47b AA/N Setchfield; 48 AA/N Setchfield; 49 AA/N Setchfield; 50 Assessorato al Turismo Regione Siciliana; 52 AA/N Setchfield; 53 AA/N Setchfield; 54 Fototeca ENIT/Vito Arcomano; 55 AA/N Setchfield; 56 AA/N Setchfield; 57 AA/N Setchfield; 58 AA/N Setchfield; 59 Mark Bassett/Alamy; 60 AA/N Setchfield; 61 AA/N Setchfield; 62 Progallery/Alamy; 62/63 Assessorato al Turismo Regione Siciliana; 69l AA/C Sawyer; 69c AA/C Sawyer; 69r AA/N Setchfield; 70/71 Fototeca ENIT/Sandro Bedessi; 72 AA/C Sawyer; 73t AA/N Setchfield; 73b Fototeca ENIT/Sandro Bedessi; 74/75 AA/N Setchfield; 76 AA/N Setchfield; 77 AA/N Setchfield; 78 AA/C Sawyer; 79 AA/N Setchfield; 80 AA/C Sawyer; 81 AA/N Setchfield; 82 AA/N Setchfield; 84 Look Die Bildagentur der Fotografen GmbH/Alamy; 85 AA/N Setchfield; 91l AA/N Setchfield; 91c Fototeca ENIT/Vito Arcomano; 91r AA/N Setchfield; 92 AA/N Setchfield; 93 AA/N Setchfield; 94 AA/C Sawyer; 95t AA/C Sawyer; 95b AA/N Setchfield; 96/97 Fototeca ENIT/Sandro Bedessi; 97 AA/N Setchfield; 99 AA/N Setchfield; 100 AA/N Setchfield; 101 AA/N Setchfield; 102 AA/C Sawyer; 103 AA/N Setchfield; 104 AA/N Setchfield; 105 AA/N Setchfield; 106 Fototeca ENIT/Vito Arcomano; 107 EmmePi Europe/Alamy; 108 AA/N Setchfield; 109 AA/N Setchfield; 115l AA/N Setchfield; 115c AA/N Setchfield; 115r AA/N Setchfield; 116 AA/N Setchfield; 117t Assessorato al Turismo Regione Siciliana; 117b AA/N Setchfield; 118 AA/N Setchfield; 119t AA/N Setchfield; 119b AA/N Setchfield; 120/121 AA/C Sawyer; 121 AA/N Setchfield; 122 AA/N Setchfield; 123 Assessorato al Turismo Regione Siciliana; 124/125 AA/N Setchfield; 126/127 AA/N Setchfield; 128 AA/N Setchfield; 129 AA/N Setchfield; 130 AA/N Setchfield; 131 Cubolmages srl/Alamy; 132/133 AA/N Setchfield; 139l AA/N Setchfield; 139c AA/N Setchfield; 139r AA/C Sawyer; 140c AA/C Sawyer; 140b Fototeca ENIT/Sandro Bedessi; 141t AA/C Sawyer; 142 AA/N Setchfield; 143t AA/N Setchfield; 143b AA/C Sawyer; 144 Witold Skrypczak/Alamy; 145 AA/C Sawyer; 146 Fototeca ENIT/Sandro Bedessi; 147 AA/C Sawyer; 148 AA/N Setchfield; 149 AA/N Setchfield; 150 Fototeca ENIT/Sandro Bedessi; 151t AA/N Setchfield; 151b AA/N Setchfield; 152 AA/N Setchfield; 153 AA/N Setchfield; 154 AA/N Setchfield; 155 Assessorato al Turismo Regione Siciliana; 156 AA/N Setchfield; 157 AA/N Setchfield; 158 Assessorato al Turismo Regione Siciliana; 159 Fototeca ENIT/Sandro Bedessi; 160 Sandro Messina/Alamy; 165l AA/N Setchfield; 165c AA/N Setchfield; 165r AA/C Sawyer; 167 AA/N Setchfield; 168 Francesco Gavazzeni/Alamy; 169l AA/N Setchfield; 169r AA/N Setchfield; 170 Ian Dagnall/Alamy; 171 Cubolmages srl/Alamy; 172 Cubolmages srl/Alamy; 173 Cubolmages srl/Alamy; 174 AA/N Setchfield; 175l Cubolmages srl/Alamy; 175r AA/N Setchfield; 176 Cubolmages srl/Alamy; 177 AA/N Setchfield; 178 Look Die Bildagentur der Fotografen GmbH/Alamy; 179 Cubolmages srl/Alamy; 180 AA/K Paterson; 181 AA/N Setchfield; 182 AA/N Setchfield; 183l AA/N Setchfield; 183c AA/N Setchfield; 183r AA/N Setchfield; 187t AA/A Mockford & N Bonetti; 187c AA/A Mockford & N Bonetti; 187b AA/M Jourdan

Every effort has been made to trace the copyright holders, and we apologize in advance for any unintentional omissions or errors. We would be pleased to apply any corrections in a following edition of this publication.

# SPIRALGUIDE
# Questionnaire

## Dear Traveller

Your comments, opinions and recommendations are very important to us. Please help us to improve our travel guides by taking a few minutes to complete this simple questionnaire.

You do not need a stamp (unless posted outside the UK). If you do not want to remove this page from your guide, then photocopy it or write your answers on a plain sheet of paper.

Send to: The Editor, Spiral Guides, AA World Travel Guides, FREEPOST SCE 4598, Basingstoke RG21 4GY.

## Your recommendations...

We always encourage readers' recommendations for restaurants, night-life or shopping – if your recommendation is used in the next edition of the guide, we will send you a FREE AA Spiral Guide of your choice. Please state below the establishment name, location and your reasons for recommending it.

_____

_____

_____

_____

**Please send me AA Spiral** _____
(see list of titles inside the back cover)

## About this guide...

Which title did you buy?

_____ **AA Spiral**

Where did you buy it?_____

When? m m / y y

Why did you choose an AA Spiral Guide? _____

_____

_____

_____

Did this guide meet your expectations?

Exceeded ☐   Met all ☐   Met most ☐   Fell below ☐

Please give your reasons_____

_____

_____

_____

continued on next page...

**Were there any aspects of this guide that you particularly liked?**

_____

_____

_____

_____

**Is there anything we could have done better?**

_____

_____

_____

_____

## About you...

Name (Mr/Mrs/Ms) _____

Address _____

_____ Postcode _____

Daytime tel no _____ email _____

Please *only* give us your email address and mobile phone number if you wish to hear from us about other products and services from the AA and partners by email or text or mms.

**Which age group are you in?**

Under 25 ☐   25–34 ☐   35–44 ☐   45–54 ☐   55–64 ☐   65+ ☐

**How many trips do you make a year?**

Less than one ☐   One ☐   Two ☐   Three or more ☐

Are you an AA member? Yes ☐   No ☐

---

About your trip...

**When did you book?** m m / y y      **When did you travel?** m m / y y

**How long did you stay?** _____

**Was it for business or leisure?** _____

**Did you buy any other travel guides for your trip?** ☐ Yes ☐ No

**If yes, which ones?** _____

**Thank you for taking the time to complete this questionnaire. Please send it to us as soon as possible, and remember, you do not need a stamp (unless posted outside the UK).**

The information we hold about you will be used to provide the products and services requested and for identification, account administration, analysis, and fraud/loss prevention purposes. More details about how that information is used is in our privacy statement, which you'll find under the heading "Personal Information" in our terms and conditions and on our website: www.theAA.com. Copies are also available from us by post, by contacting the Data Protection Manager at AA, Fanum House, Basing View, Basingstoke, RG21 4EA. We may want to contact you about other products and services provided by us, or our partners (by mail, telephone) but please tick the box if you DO NOT wish to hear about such products and services from us by mail or telephone.

☐